CONTENTS

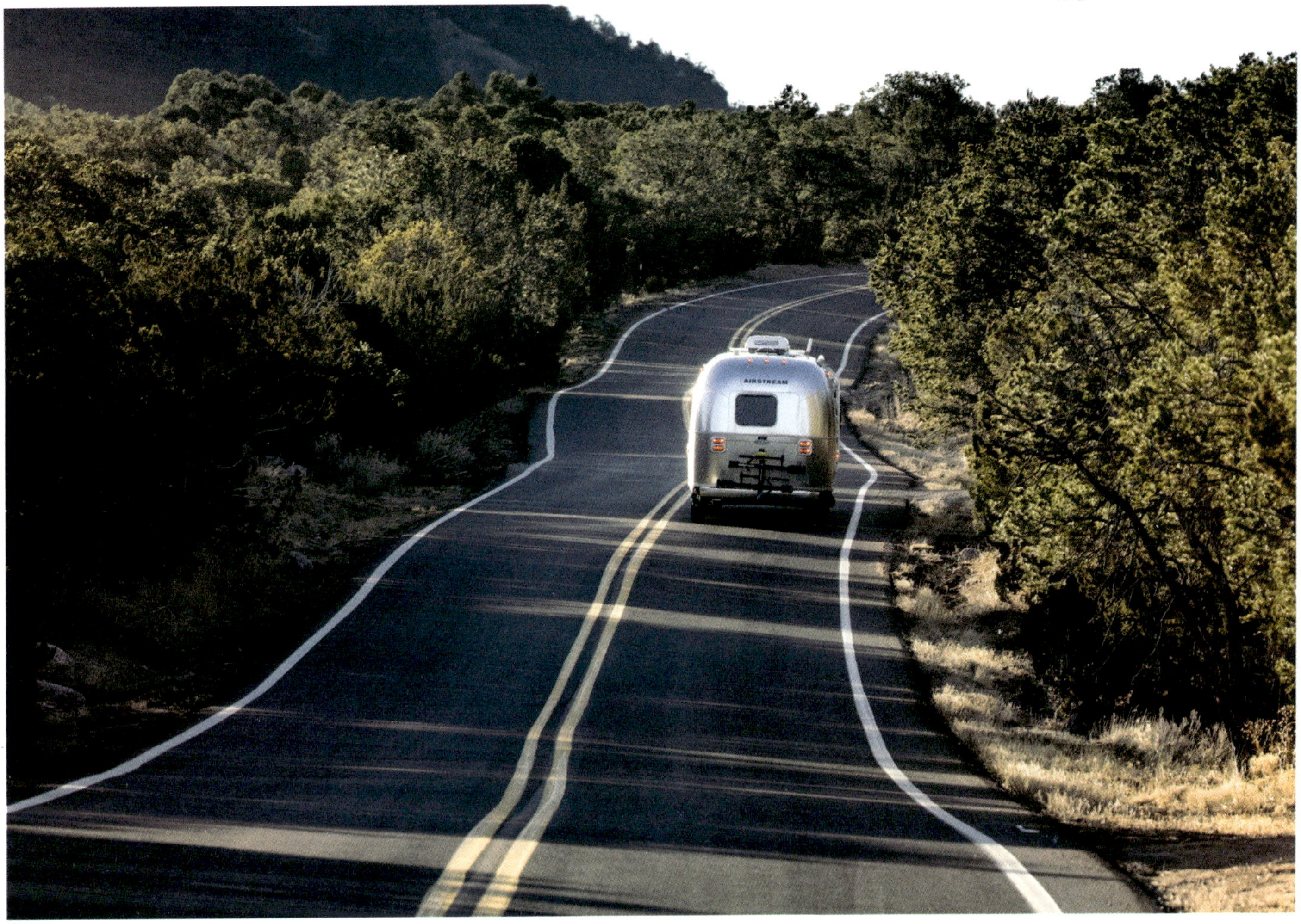

Whether with a camper in tow or in a classic car, the slower-paced drive along the original alignment of Route 66 from Santa Fe toward Pecos is an enchanting ride.

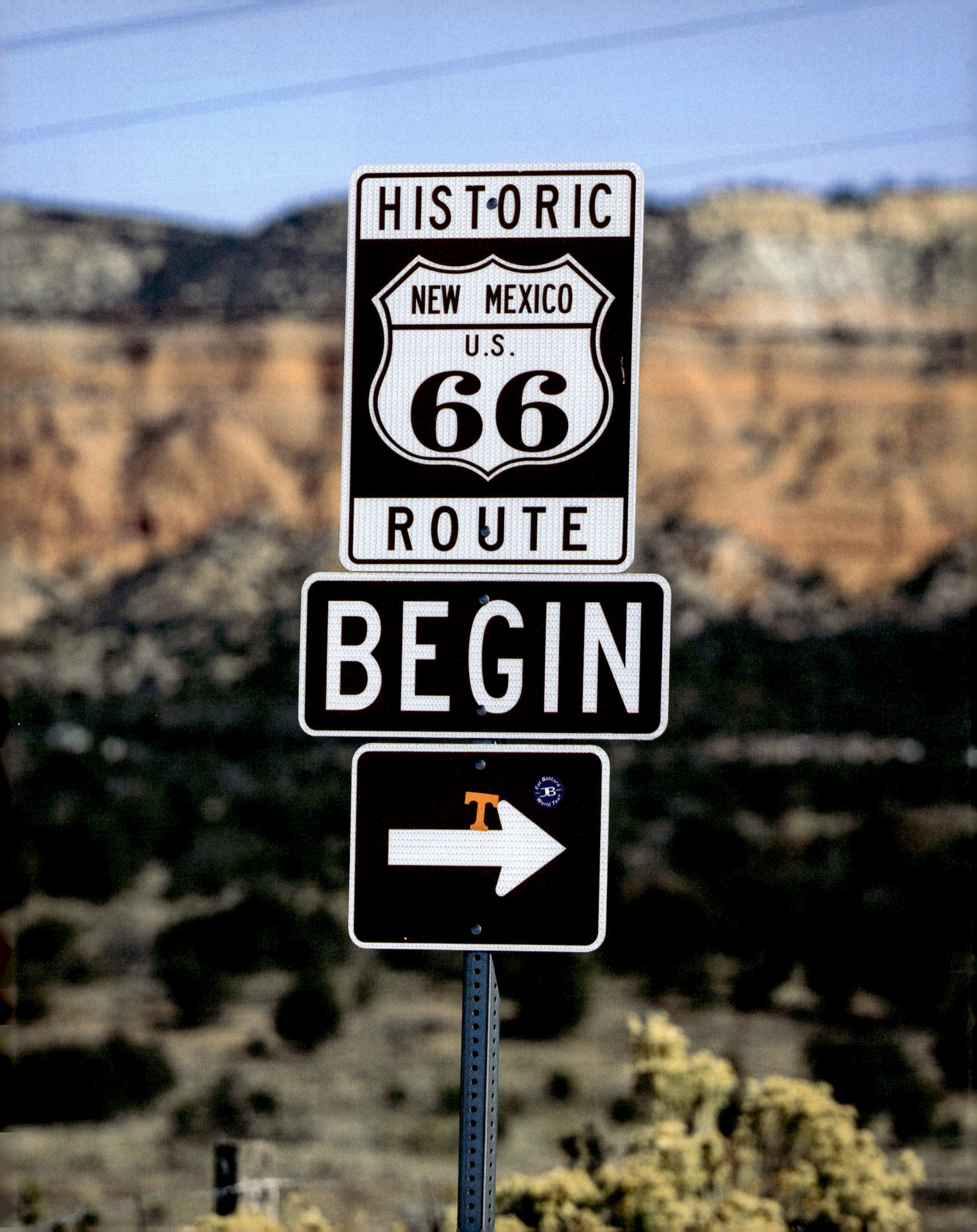
HISTORIC
NEW MEXICO
U.S.
66
ROUTE
BEGIN

GOING STRONG

Fueled by nostalgia and fresh energy, the heartbeat of historic Route 66 continues— one momentous road trip at a time.

By Lynn Cline

L
Follow the Route 66 signs—like this one near the Continental Divide—where you can.

Cruising into Tucumcari at dusk on historic Route 66, I'm greeted by a kaleidoscope of neon, glittering like jewels. The flickering signs light up mom-and-pop diners, curio shops, and retro motels, tempting me to stop for the night.

After fueling up on New Mexican chiles rellenos at Del's Restaurant, open since 1956, I check into the Blue Swallow Motel. Built in 1939, the roadside icon boasts a glowing arched sign with a blue bird in flight. It's one of the most famous neon beacons on all 2,448 miles of the Mother Road.

This former railroad town was a major stop during Route 66's heyday, when billboards touting "Tucumcari Tonite" lined the highway in both directions for miles. Today, it's a don't-miss stop for motorists on the Great American Road Trip, whether they're retracing a childhood family adventure or discovering the freedom and fun of driving Route 66 for the first time.

Towns like Tucumcari exist all across Route 66 in New Mexico. In its golden age (from the 1930s to roughly the early 1960s), the highway stretched 535 miles from Glenrio to Gallup. Today, an estimated 265 miles are drivable. The road leads straight into yesteryear, where nostalgia and kitschy Americana thrive. In cities and towns along the route, people have worked passionately, with a lot of elbow grease, to keep the highway's heartbeat strong.

Commissioned in 1926 by the federal government, the route was pieced together from a patchwork of mostly unpaved roads as a lifeline connecting rural towns to a national highway. Stretching through eight

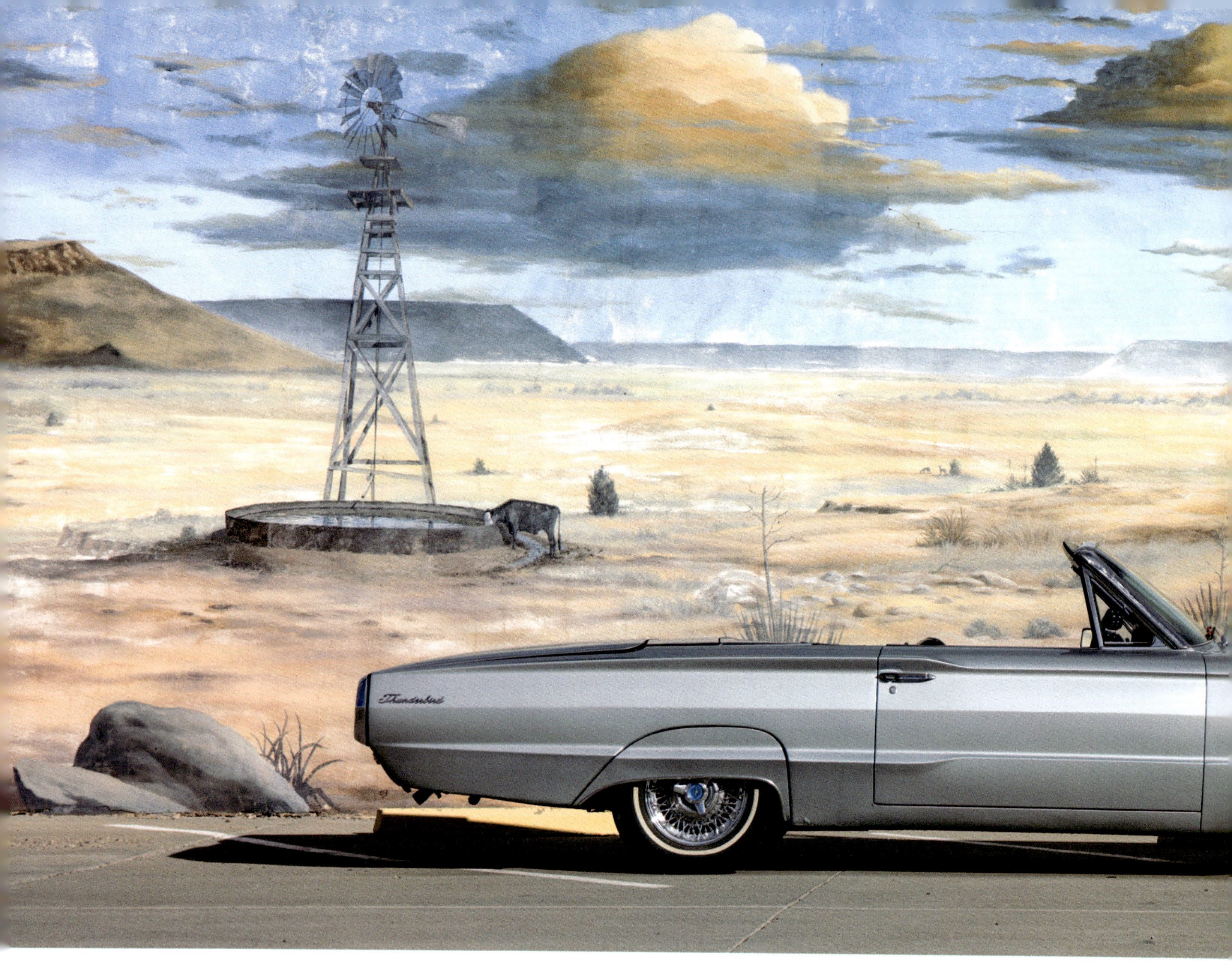

states, the highway connected Chicago and Santa Monica. In 1926, New Mexico had the longest stretch of any state, with 507 miles. In the 1930s, migrants fleeing the Dust Bowl traveled the highway to California in search of a better life. Their exodus prompted novelist John Steinbeck to dub the highway the Mother Road in *The Grapes of Wrath*.

During World War II, troops and supplies were transported along the highway. Travel on Route 66 accelerated in the postwar years, when GIs and their families hit the road to discover America in all its dazzling neon-lit glory. "After World War II, people started purchasing modern, affordable cars, and once you purchased a brand new car, you wanted to go cruising," says Johnnie Meier, a historic preservationist who restores neon signs throughout New Mexico. "People started building motels, gas stations, and restaurants to provide services for these travelers."

The boom would not last. The 1956 creation of the U.S. interstate highway system steered the Mother Road into slow decline, overlaying Route 66 with multilane interstates that bypassed small roadside towns like Tucumcari. In 1985, US 66 was officially decommissioned.

Yet the highway lived on thanks to ardent preservationists and Route 66 enthusiasts around the world. "When the road was decertified in 1985, immediately fans started clawing it back," says Jerry McClanahan, whose *EZ66 Guide for Travelers* has helped countless motorists navigate a route that is now chopped into segments. "It's an ongoing, breathing thing. We keep reinventing it, adding to it. There are people dedicated to this dream."

Leaving Tucumcari, I think of the millions of motorists who have passed this way over a century, driving the fabled Mother Road to discover New Mexico's distinct cultures, stunning landscapes, tasty cuisine, and quirky roadside attractions. Long stretches of Route 66 are tricky to drive—bumpy and narrow, with no protective shoulders. Where

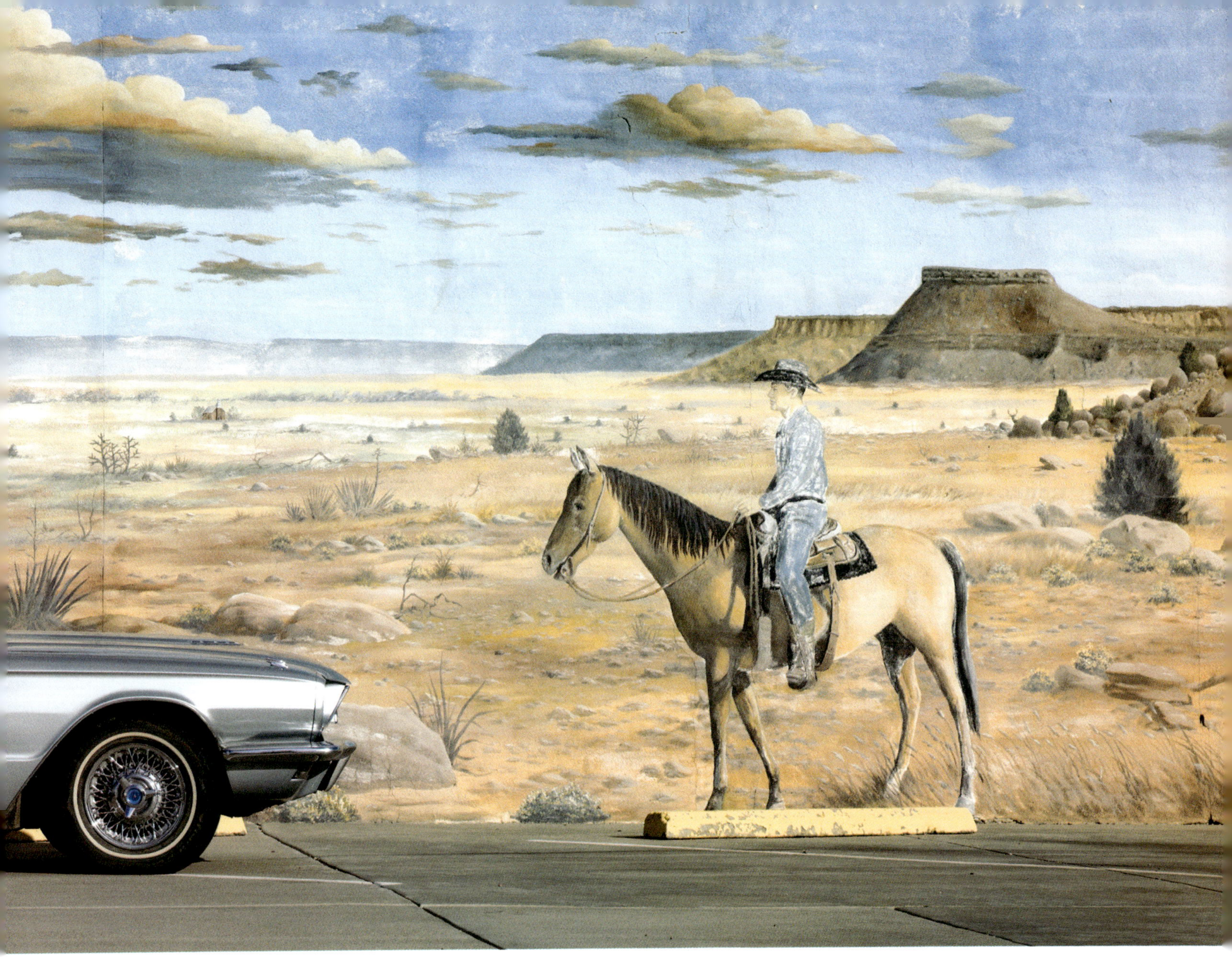

A 1966 Thunderbird parks in front of the *Ranch Scene* mural on Second Street in Tucumcari. The town has more than 100 colorful murals, in addition to its brilliant neon.

the road parallels I-40 and semis race past my car, I embrace the slow rhythm of the road less traveled. Along the way, remnants of the past stand like sentinels—crumbling trading posts, vestiges of Whiting Bros. gas stations, and ghost towns with abandoned buildings.

It's also a joy to see Route 66 roar back to life as I make my way from Santa Rosa to the Santa Fe Loop, which ran through the capital city from 1926 until 1937, when a realignment steered it in another direction. In Moriarty, Albuquerque, Grants, and Gallup, downtown streets are still lined with vintage auto courts, retro motels, family-run diners, curio shops, trading posts, and Route 66 museums packed with shiny cars and memorabilia. Contemporary businesses are part of the mix, from trendy cafes and restaurants to a speakeasy scene, boutiques, colorful murals, and art installations.

Route 66 continues to cast its spell on travelers of every kind. Although my road trip ends in Gallup, it won't be the end of the line. With so many layers to the Route 66 experience in New Mexico, I can't wait to be on the road again. ✴

LYNN CLINE is the author of three books, including *The Maverick Cookbook*. She also co-edited *The New Mexico Magazine Centennial Cookbook: A Century of Flavors* with Molly Boyle.

CHAPTER

1

RUST & RELICS

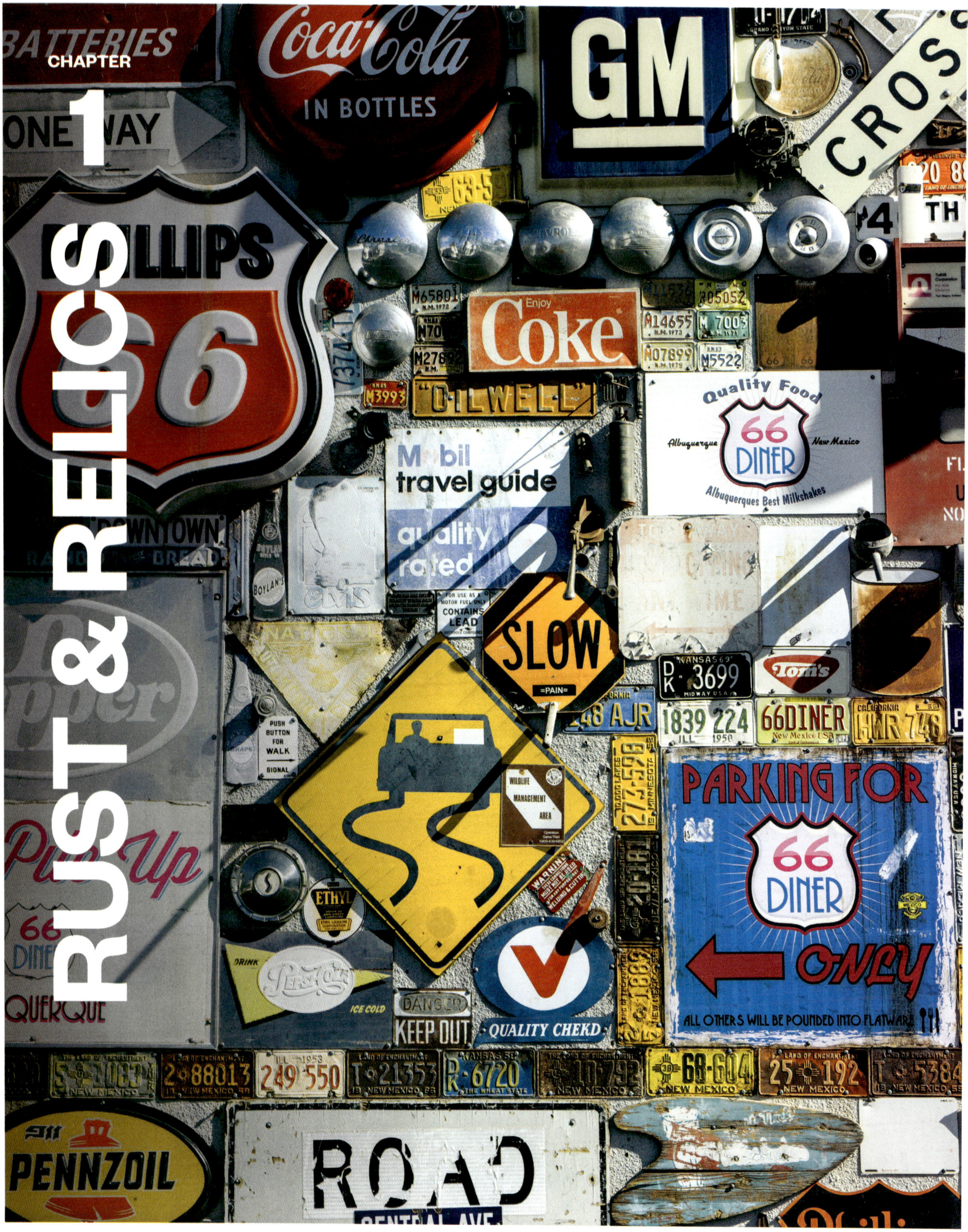

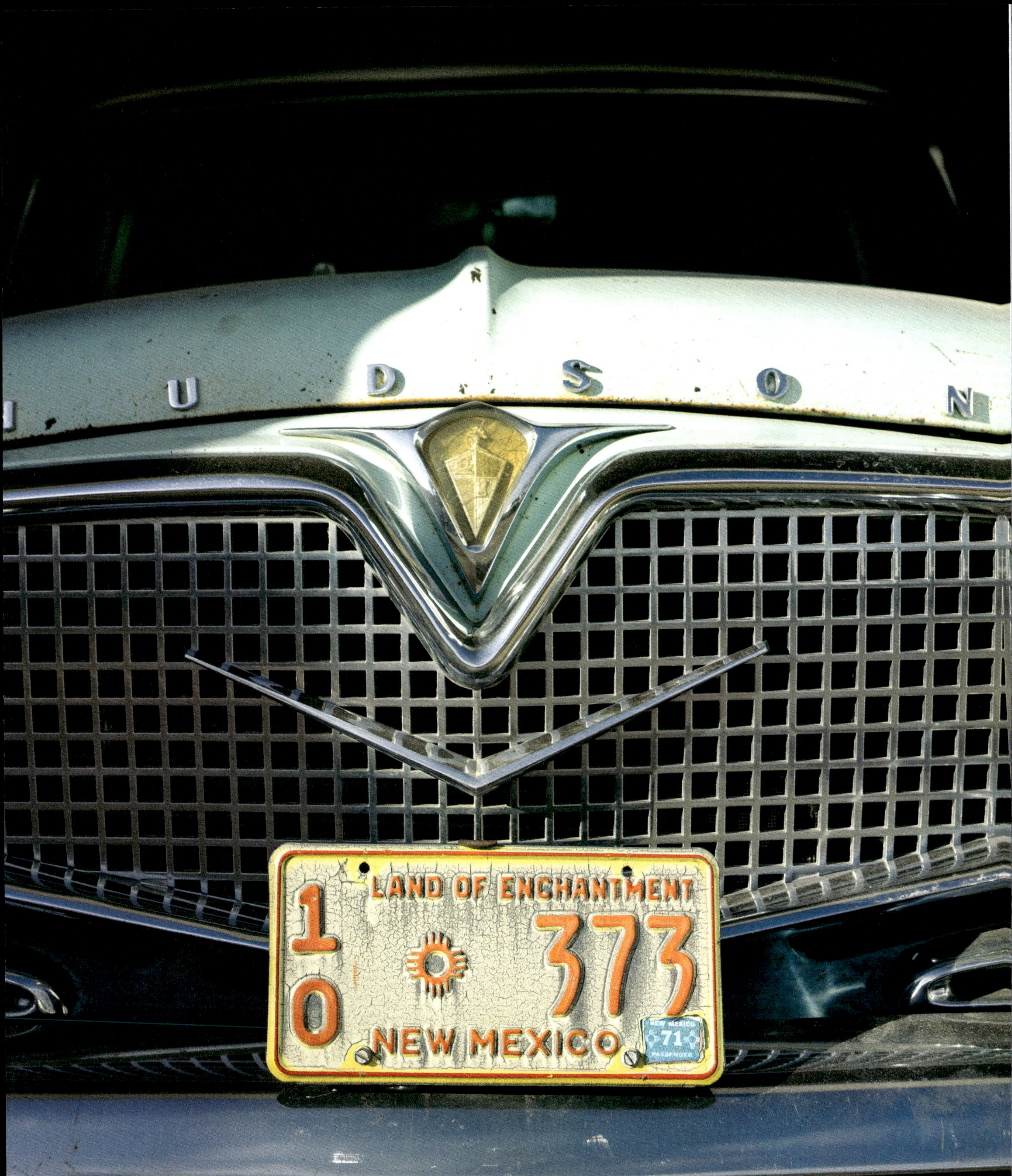
HUDSON
LAND OF ENCHANTMENT
10
373
NEW MEXICO
NEW MEXICO
71
PASSENGER

REMAINS OF THE DAY

In photographs, memorabilia, and the crumbling shells of abandoned buildings, Route 66 continues to tell stories of hope, grit, and inspiration.

By Alicia Romero

Route 66's centennial, like all anniversaries, affords an opportunity to reconsider the history of the road, both for what it signified for the past and what it means for us now. For many, Route 66 was more than a two-lane road—it meant opportunity, prosperity, and exposure to different cultures. Stretching across the state from east to west (and briefly from north to south), New Mexico's Route 66 once served as a vital corridor for travelers, businesses, and dreamers.

Today, much of Route 66 lives on as a trail of abandoned towns, shuttered trading posts, and forgotten attractions that tell stories of boom, decline, and reinvention. What remains in its architecture, ephemera, and memories helps us understand the significance of the Mother Road as a local, national, and even international story.

For those of us who never experienced Route 66 in its heyday, the glimmer of that neon-tinted past can be found in historic objects, photographs, and memorabilia in public and private collections. Vividly printed Curt Teich & Company postcards, for example, capture a Technicolor version of what life along the road was like during the bustling 1940s and 1950s. Nancy Tucker has donated thousands of her Route 66 postcards, cafe menus, matchbooks, historic images, and other collectibles to museums and libraries throughout the state. Tucker, who moved to Albuquerque as a preschooler in 1951, started collecting on eBay after a search turned up an old Albuquerque sanatorium postcard, which she instantly bid on. "Thus began my passion for Albuquerque ephemera," she says.

The road's stories can also be found in rusting gas station awnings, crumbling building shells, cracked pavement, and other relics of a bygone era still very much alive in the hearts and minds of those inspired by the roadway's promise.

Prior to Route 66, the railroad determined large-scale movement of goods and people throughout the country. As trains chugged into New Mexico in 1879, towns grew up to support this new labor force and economy. By the early 20th century, Glenrio, Endee, and San Fidel had become important stops along the tracks—before hitching their collective fates to an

R
The original orientation of Route 66 through Santa Fe passed by the Cathedral Basilica of St. Francis of Assisi.

PREVIOUS SPREAD:
A riot of vintage license plates, road signs, gas station advertisements, and other relics fill every space in the 1950s-themed 66 Diner in Albuquerque (left). A 1957 Hudson Hornet is often parked in front of the iconic Blue Swallow Motel in Tucumcari (right).

LIBRARY OF CONGRESS/JOHN COLLIER JR.

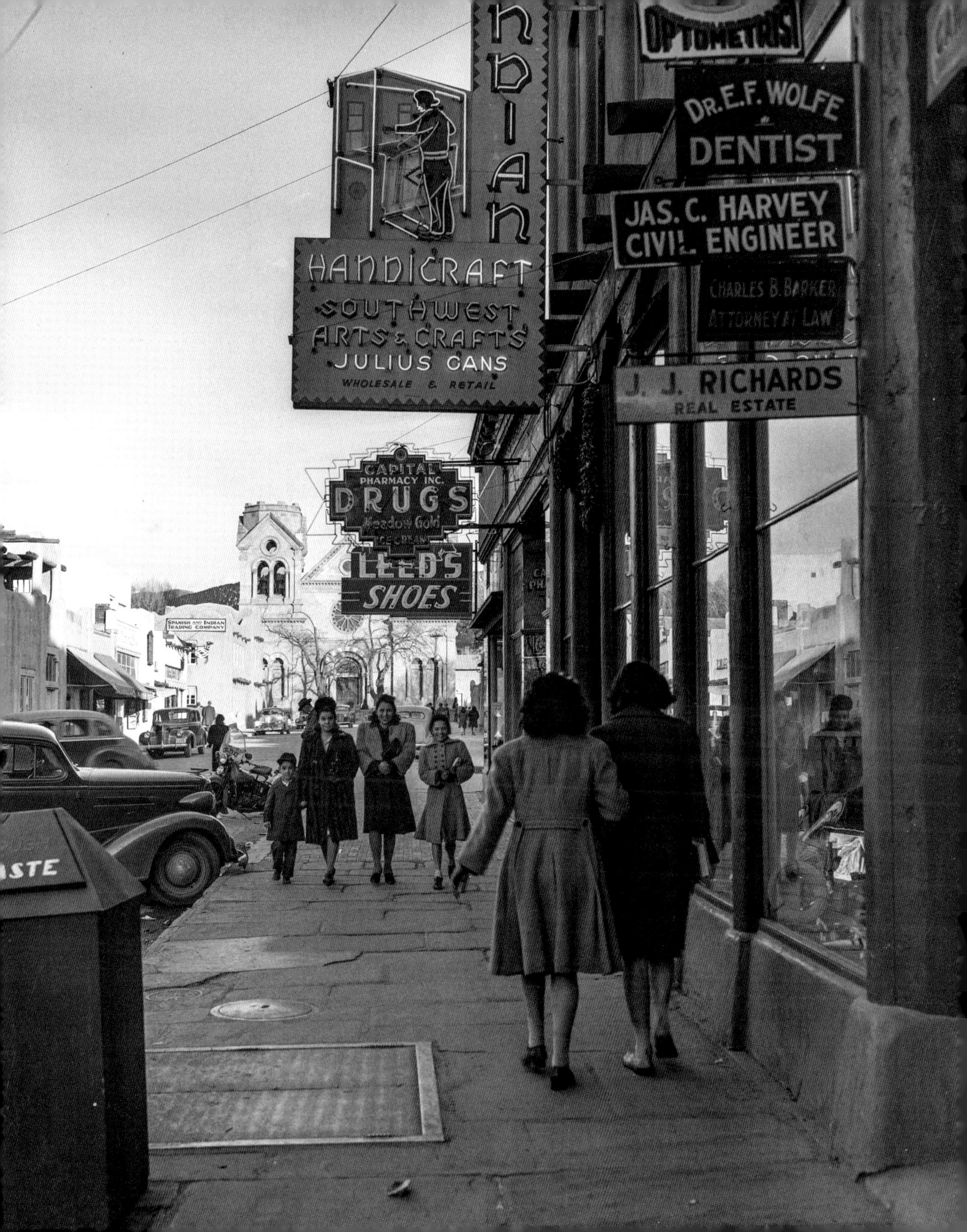
OPTOMETRIST
Dr. E.F. WOLFE
DENTIST
JAS. C. HARVEY
CIVIL ENGINEER
CHARLES B. BARKER
ATTORNEY AT LAW
J. J. RICHARDS
REAL ESTATE
HANDICRAFT
SOUTHWEST
ARTS & CRAFTS
JULIUS GANS
WHOLESALE & RETAIL
CAPITAL
PHARMACY INC.
DRUGS
Meadow Gold
LEED'S
SHOES
SPANISH AND INDIAN
TRADING COMPANY

1

RUST AND RELICS

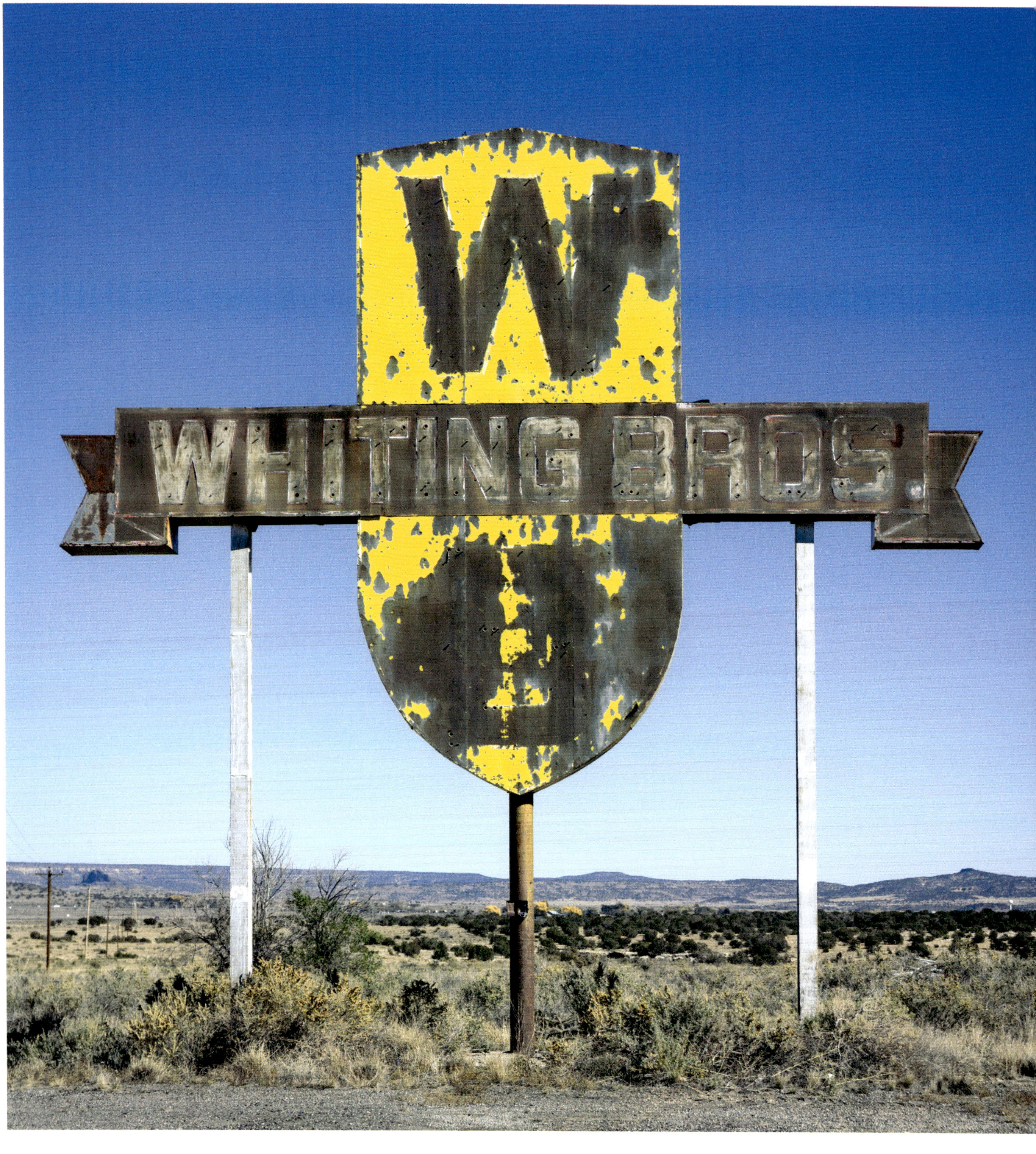

10

ROAD TO ENCHANTMENT

asphalt ribbon connecting the nation.

But when the Federal-Aid Highway Act was passed in 1956, it effectively ushered in faster, safer, and more direct passageways through the state, eliminating reliance on slower-paced roads such as Route 66 and other numbered highways. Route 66's cycle of boom and bust emptied out communities, leaving behind the forgotten amenities travelers and locals needed: restaurants and cafes, lodging, service stations, and maybe even a curio shop or trading post for a souvenir of the trip.

Places like Tucumcari, Santa Rosa, Albuquerque, Grants, and Gallup survived the decline of Route 66, but many others were left in the construction dust of I-40. Consider Montoya and Cuervo. Founded as railroad stops around 1901, the tiny towns between Tucumcari and Santa Rosa saw some growth in those early days and then again at the height of Route 66. But once the interstate bypassed the towns, the local economy dwindled and people left. What remains in these ghost towns—a crumbling shop with a fading "Cold Beer" sign on the side and the shell of an early 1900s stone homestead—stands as a reminder of how deeply Route 66 shaped local communities.

During the road's heyday, a variety of service stations fueled the constant flow of travelers along Route 66 in New Mexico. The Whiting Bros. gas station chain, founded in Arizona in 1926, was a familiar sight in the Land of Enchantment. Some of the most visible images of America's emerging car culture, these stations and their bright red-and-yellow signs offered not only fuel but also a comforting reliability for motorists crossing long, isolated stretches of desert.

A 1951 picture of a Whiting Bros. station on the east end of Central Avenue in Albuquerque offers a glimpse of the area before any significant development, just as families were starting to move to the Kirtland, Sandia, and Manzano military bases. Nothing remains of the station's six pumps or the L-shaped sign offering gas for 25.5 cents per gallon, but we can imagine what they meant for travelers making their way into Albuquerque with opportunity on the horizon.

Not all Route 66 attractions were practical necessities or aimed at the weary traveler. Some were imaginative attempts to create family fun as a break from the road. The Little Beaver Town amusement park in eastern Albuquerque was modeled on the popular *Red Ryder* comic strip, which ran from 1938 to 1965.

Little Beaver Town opened its swinging doors in July 1961, offering a highly stylized and romantic Wild West experience. The themed buildings and family-friendly attractions included an Indian Village with dances, novelties, and traditional arts and crafts made by Navajo, Hopi, and Pueblo tribal members. Despite the park's initial success, changing travel patterns and new appetites for entertainment forced its closure just three years later. Today the site has been reborn, transformed into Albuquerque's Route 66 Open Space Trailhead, a recreational site featuring horse hitches, a hilltop trail, picnic areas, and information on the history of the area, including its former life as Little Beaver Town.

Not all of Route 66's relics have such happy endings. Some abandoned places hide darker stories behind their crumbling walls. Take the Budville Trading Post near Cubero and the villages that make up Acoma Pueblo (Haak'u). Opened by husband and wife Howard Neal "Bud" Rice and Aurora "Flossie" Rice in 1928, Bud's Service Station catered to travelers in need of gasoline, food, and respite. Once the trading post was added, travelers could purchase other locally made goods, many of which came from the neighboring tribes. Bud, who became a local political figure, accumulated enough influence to have an exit ramp built off I-40 into Budville.

Unfortunately, the trading post was also the site of two separate tragedies: Bud and an elderly employee were brutally murdered there in 1967, and Flossie's brother-in-law was killed there in 1971. Still, Flossie continued to run the business until her death in 1979. Despite various attempts from new owners to reopen the trading post, the white shell remains largely empty. It serves as a tourist photo opportunity and a chilling reminder of the past.

Together, these ghost towns, gas stations, amusement parks, and trading posts form a mosaic of Route 66 in New Mexico. They illustrate how the road shaped lives, inspired creativity, and fueled local economies, only to be overtaken by new highways and changing travel habits. Although many of these places now stand empty or in ruins, they continue to attract local and international visitors seeking to understand the past and experience a glimpse of what slower-paced travel must have meant to thousands of motorists.

We are fortunate to have architecture, objects, ephemera, and oral histories documenting the history of Route 66 so that future generations can continue to learn about and love this road. Thanks to the many relics on its corridor, New Mexico's Route 66 exists as a living archive of American ambition, resilience, and impermanence. This book is a celebration of that history and its enduring significance in the American imagination. ✶

ALICIA ROMERO is the head curator at the Albuquerque Museum, which presents *The Other Route 66: 100 Years of People, Identity, and Place in Albuquerque*, on view from June 6, 2026, to January 3, 2027.

L
"Whiting Bros. signs for their motels and gas stations were arrayed from Tucumcari to Gallup," says historic preservationist Johnnie Meier. "But the gigantic shield-shaped sign at McCartys was the mother of all Whiting Bros. signs."

Willie Lambert

The Mother Road scholar has amassed a huge collection of vintage postcards and acts as an ambassador of the route.

ROUTE 66 HAS TAKEN WILLIE LAMBERT on the ride of a lifetime. For more than two decades, he's been documenting New Mexico's stretch of the iconic highway in photographs, notebooks, and some 500 hand-drawn maps. His collection of 1,500 vintage postcards fills more than 40 binders, arranged by location and in categories such as Gates & Fences, Bridges & Culverts, and Roadside Wildflowers. Lambert, who at 19 left home in Lakewood, New Jersey, for California, ended up in Santa Fe, where he's lived for much of his life. A gifted storyteller, he shares anecdotes about the Mother Road's unique history and culture on tours and in public presentations.

R
Willie Lambert shows off just a fragment of his Route 66 research in his Santa Fe home. Lambert's handwritten maps and vintage postcards are featured in his book, *New Mexico Route 66 Unpolished: From Santa Fe to Romeroville.*

When I was gone from Santa Fe, I was always wanting to get back as soon as I could. It's the perfect spot because of 66.

My sister said, "Willie, when I turn 66, let's take a cruise on Route 66." I said, "I'll look into it." That statement changed my life and gave me a direction. Not long after, we took two trips, driving from Santa Fe to California and then from Oklahoma to Santa Fe.

You can't just jump in your car and say, "I'm going to go drive Route 66." There's no signage, or there are signs that are misleading.

It's a puzzle, and we're still trying to understand or agree on where the original pieces are.

This whole thing has developed into research, search, find, and reward for where these fragments of the road are.

The postcards are so cool. I found a bunch of them in antiques stores in shoeboxes.

Now I search for them on eBay in the morning.

The postcards show motels, restaurants, and other places when they were state of the art. What's depicted on the postcards now exists in all different stages, from melting down to gone.

I put this research together for me to understand. This is how I had to digest it, to be able to understand it, to draw 500 maps, to touch it, to drive it.

I love to share the binders with people. By sharing these throughout the state, I meet people who have their 66 stories.

I never see Route 66 as being gone, simply because it was a path in the beginning, the line of least resistance, and it's gone through many changes through the years. There are new trees, new people, but where that 66 roadbed was will never be gone.

People ask me, "How the hell did you get into this?" "My sister," I say. They ask me, "When will you be done?" "Never." ✴

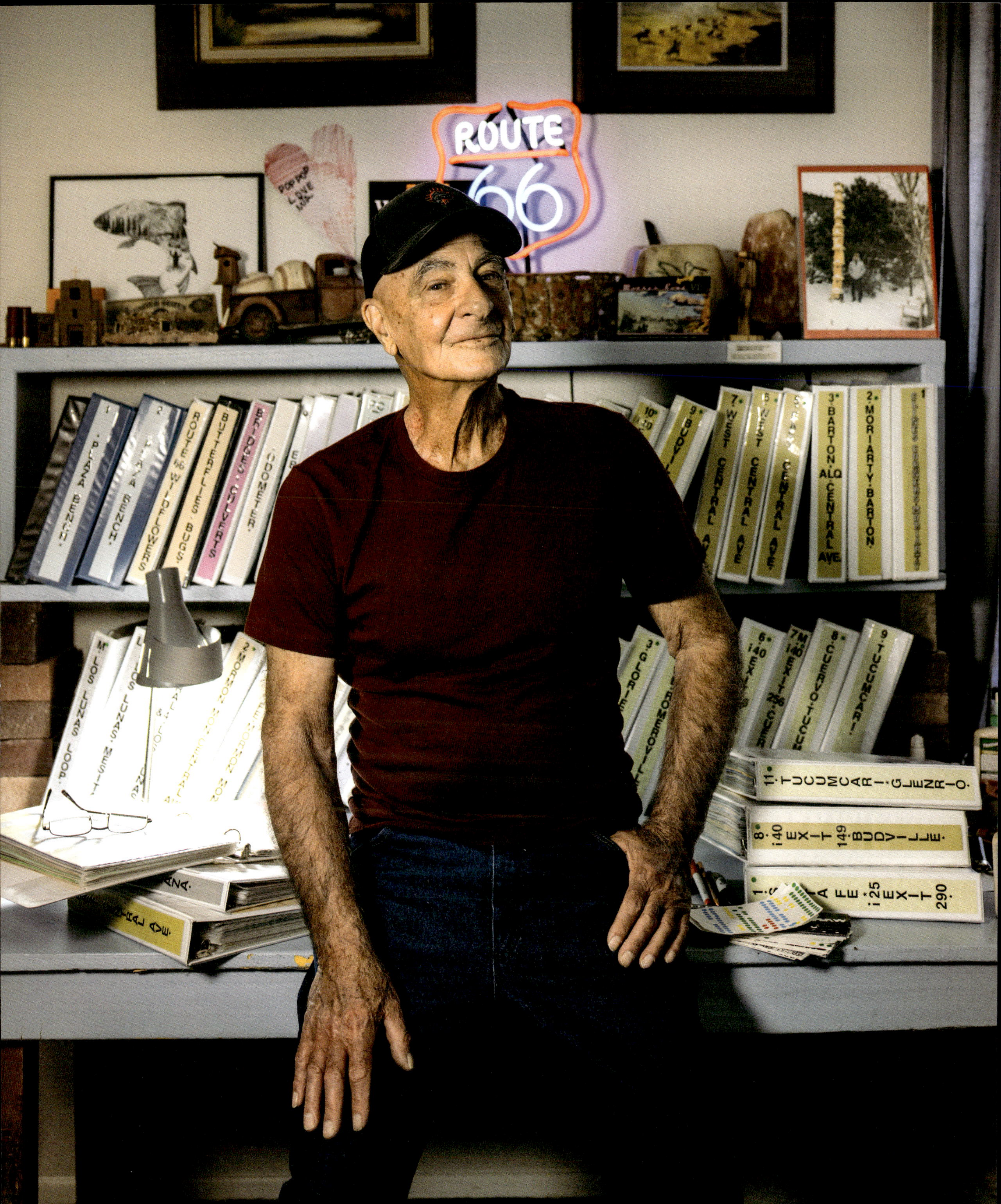
ROUTE 66
ROUTE 66 WILDFLOWERS
BUTTERFLIES, BUGS
BRIDGES, CULVERTS
ODOMETER
WEST CENTRAL AVE
2 MORIARTY-BARTON
3 BARTON-ALQ CENTRAL AVE.
9 TUCUMCARI
11 TUCUMCARI-GLENRIO
8 i40 EXIT 149 BUDVILLE

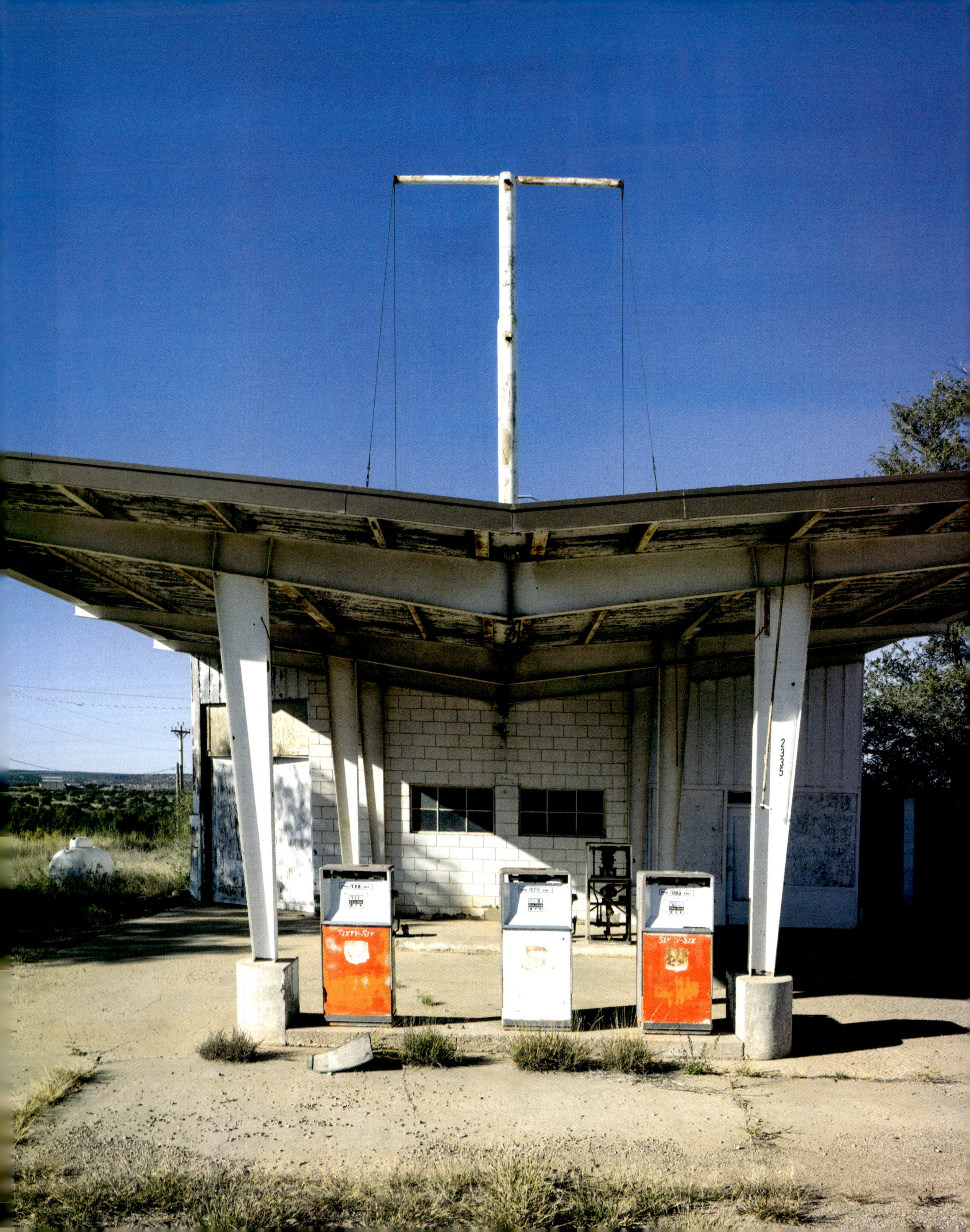
2335
SIXTY-SIX

1

RUST AND RELICS

L

Just down the road from Santa Rosa, a former gas station's rusted awning, old fuel pumps, and cracked pavement with weeds pushing through are reminders of yesteryear.

R

The ruins of a Whiting Bros. station in San Fidel allude to a once-booming business (top). A yellow 1930 Ford Model A drives visitors to Santa Rosa's Route 66 Auto Museum, where more than 30 vintage vehicles, gas pumps, and tons of memorabilia celebrate a bygone era (bottom left). Established in 1910, the roadside Montoya Cemetery lies midway between Tucumcari and Santa Rosa (bottom right).

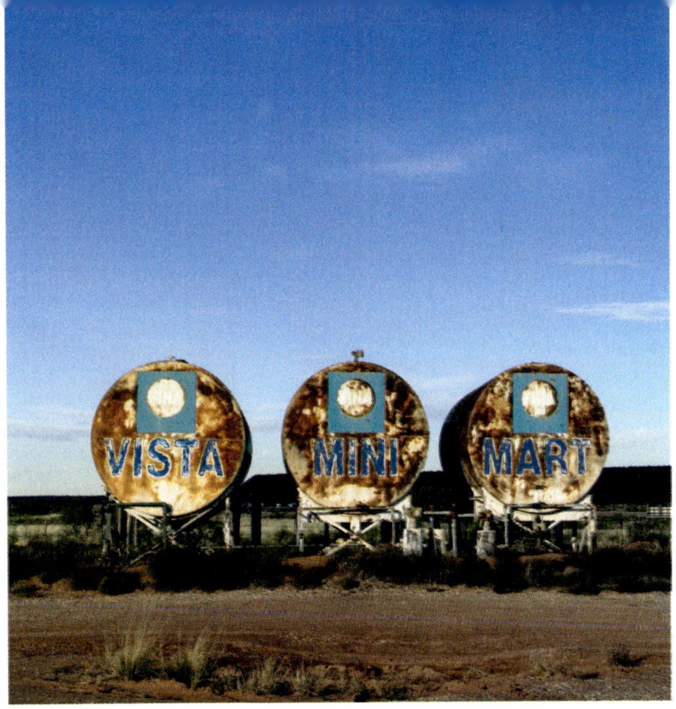

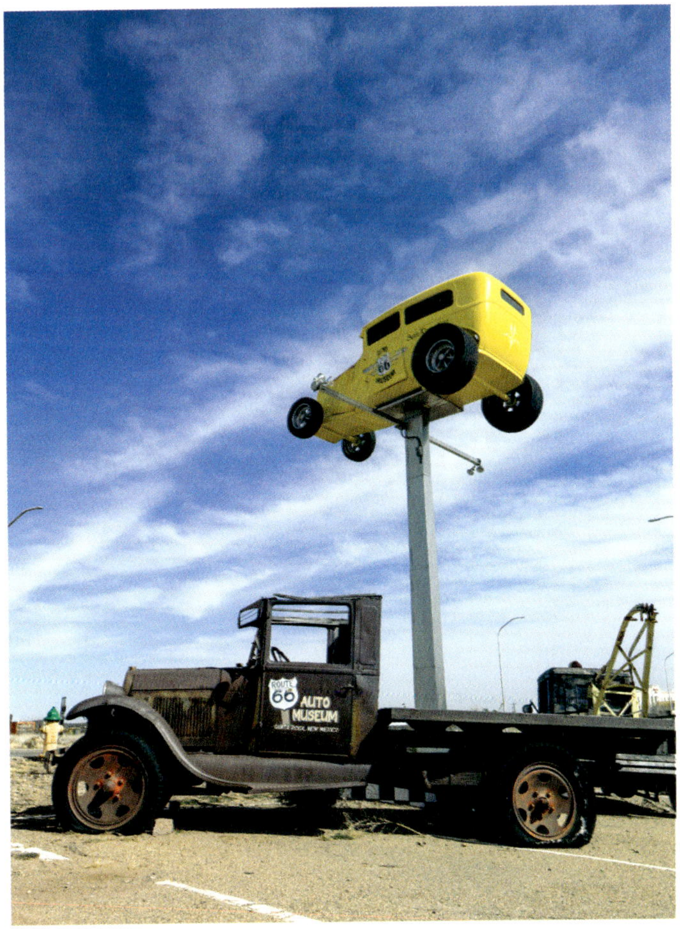

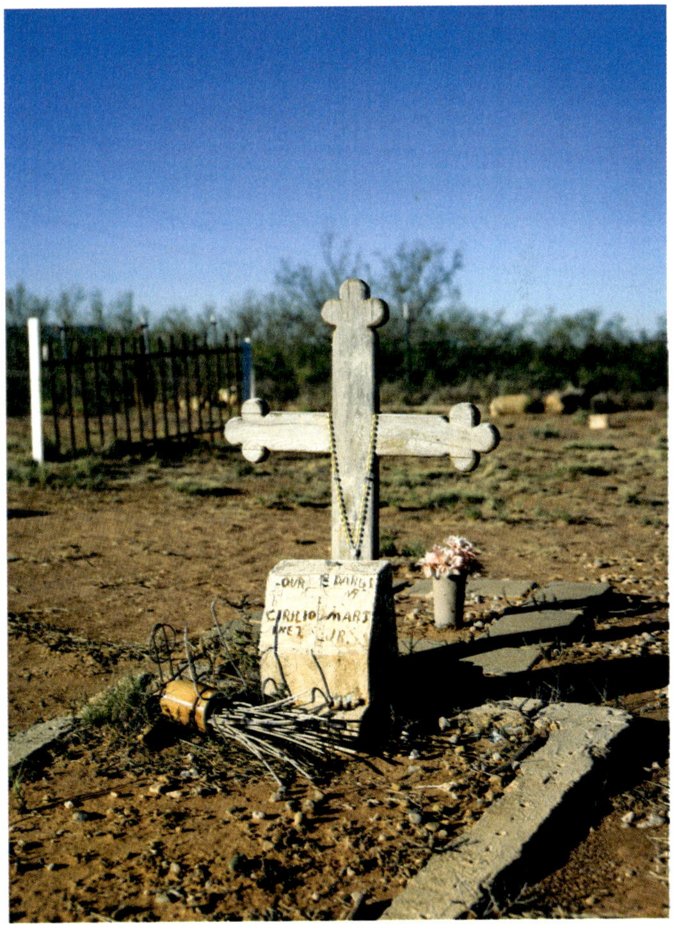

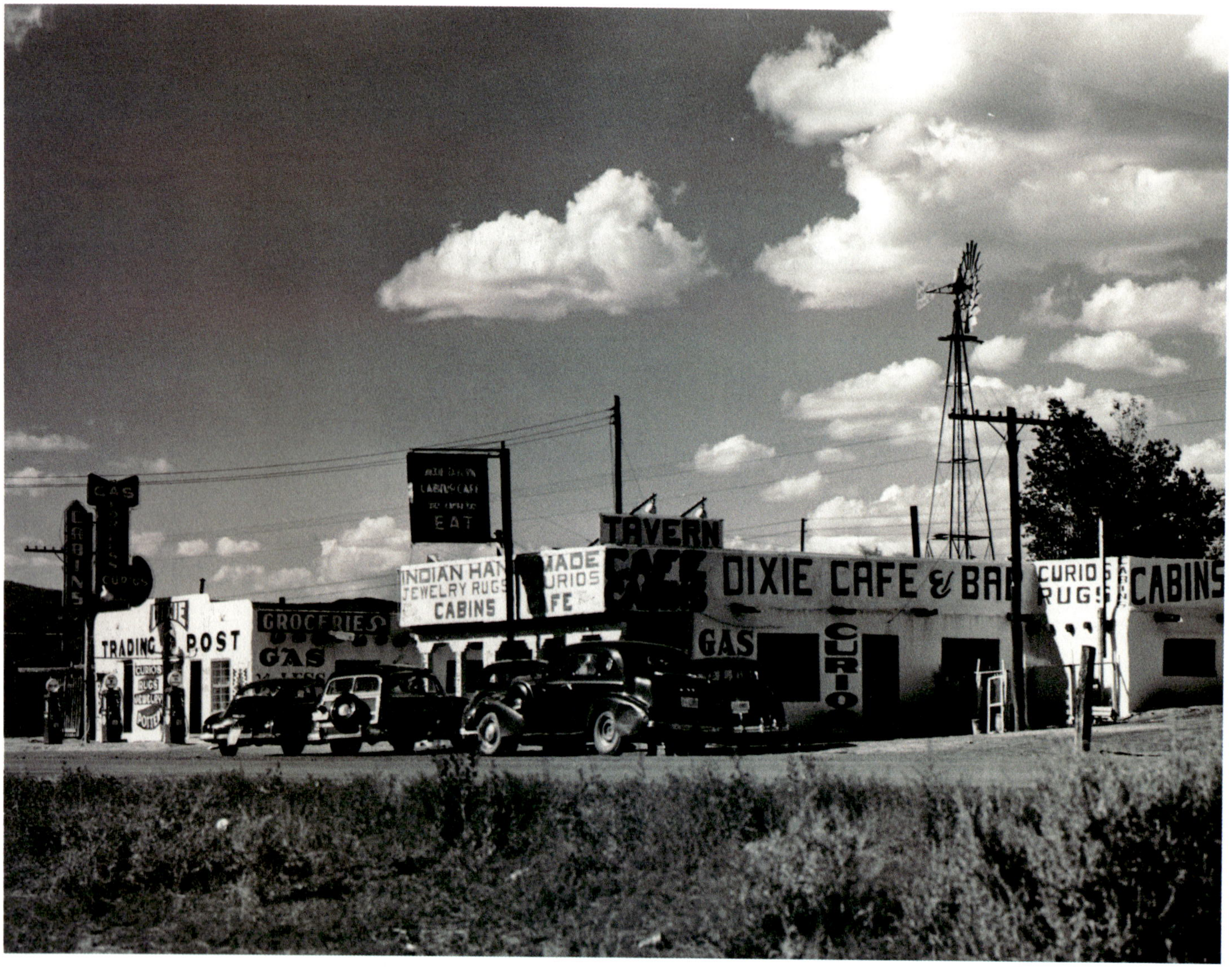

LEE MARMON, CENTER FOR SOUTHWEST RESEARCH, UNIVERSITY LIBRARIES, UNIVERSITY OF NEW MEXICO

L
Opened in 1936, the Dixie Cafe and Bar was a hub on Route 66 west of Laguna Pueblo, where motorists could grab a bite, service their car, rent a cabin, and buy Native rugs, pottery, and, jewelry.

R
Although many have tried to revive it, Budville's Dixie Cafe and Bar currently stands abandoned.

"

After World War II, people started purchasing modern, affordable cars, and once you purchased a brand new car, you wanted to go cruising. People started building motels, gas stations, and restaurants to provide for those travelers."

— **JOHNNIE MEIER, HISTORIC PRESERVATIONIST**

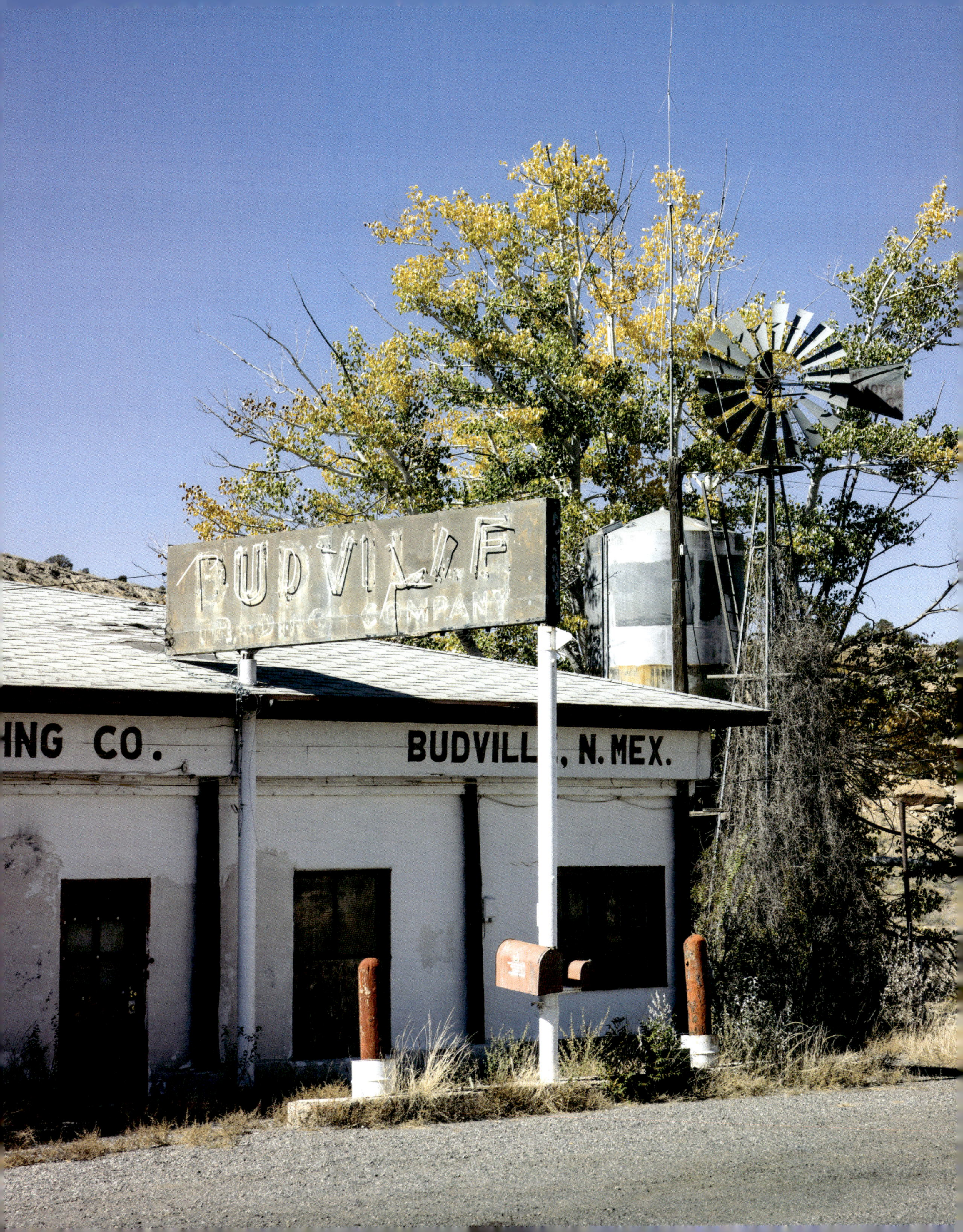
ING CO.
BUDVILL , N. MEX.

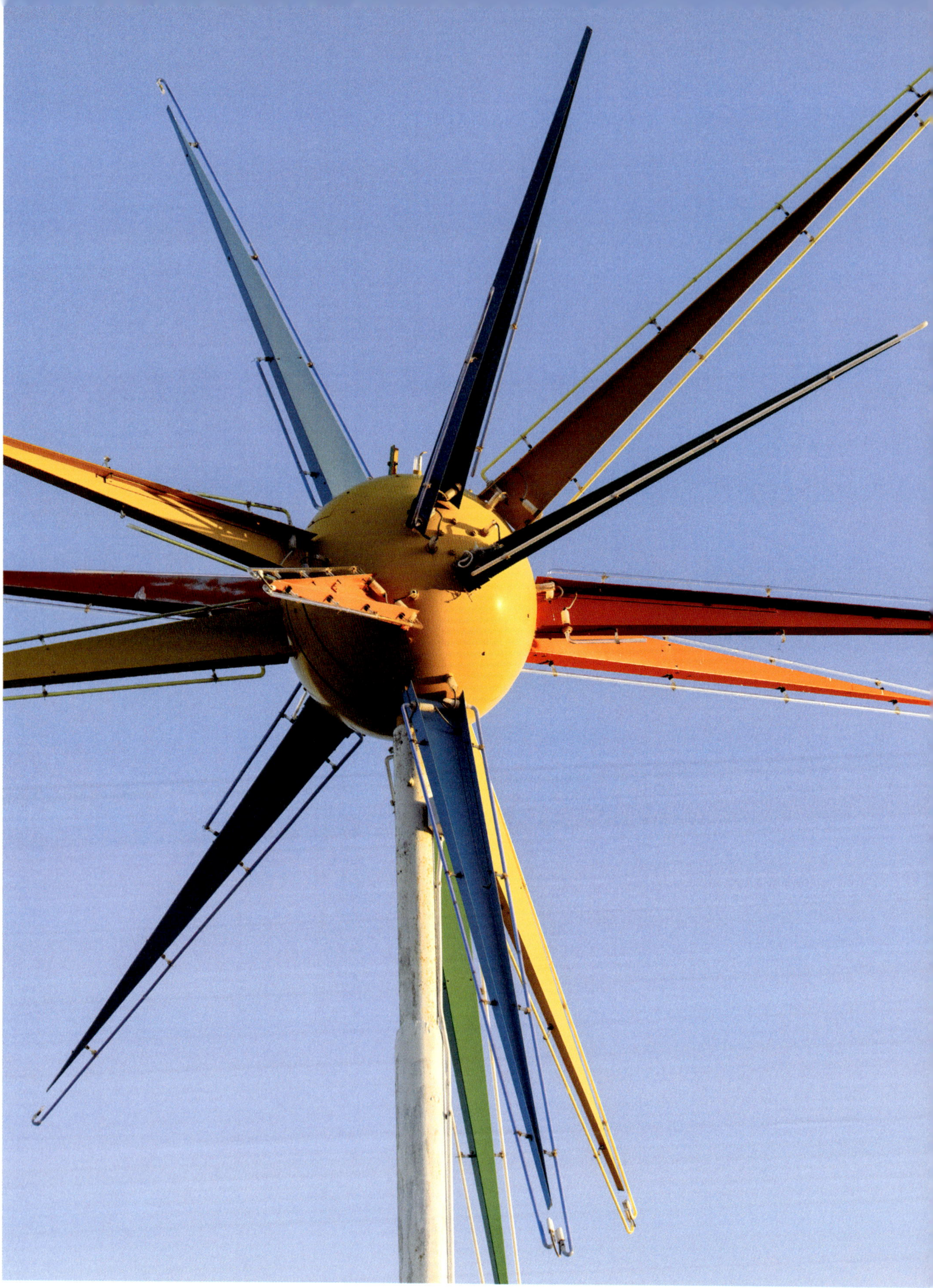

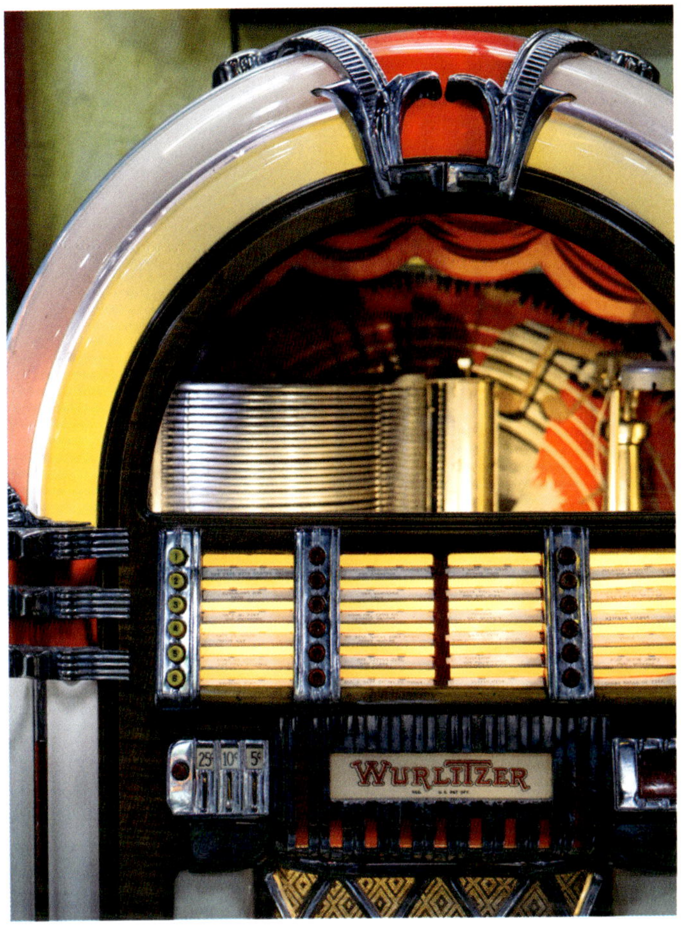

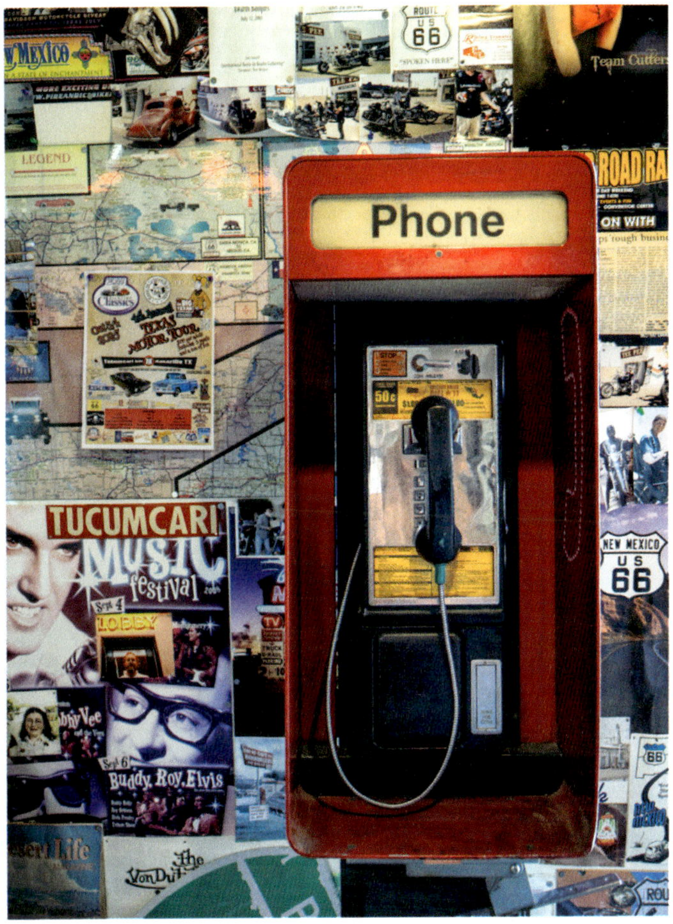

L

The 1960s Roto-Sphere in Moriarty spun in three directions at once when it hung above the old El Comedor de Anayas restaurant (now Country Friends Antiques), luring hungry motorists on Route 66.

R

Step into the golden era of Route 66 at Russell's Car and Collectible Museum in Glenrio. Packed with nearly two dozen shiny classic cars, vintage fuel pumps, service station signs, and an authentic Wurlitzer, the museum is a Route 66 fan's dream (above left). Get your kitsch on Route 66 at the Tee Pee Curios shop in Tucumcari, where you'll find Native American jewelry, T-shirts, license plates, and other souvenirs on every corner, shelf, and wall (above right).

"

Everybody notices it. More people stop and take pictures of that than anything in Moriarty."

— CINDY ARNETT, OWNER OF COUNTRY FRIENDS ANTIQUES, OF THE BUILDING'S ROTO-SPHERE

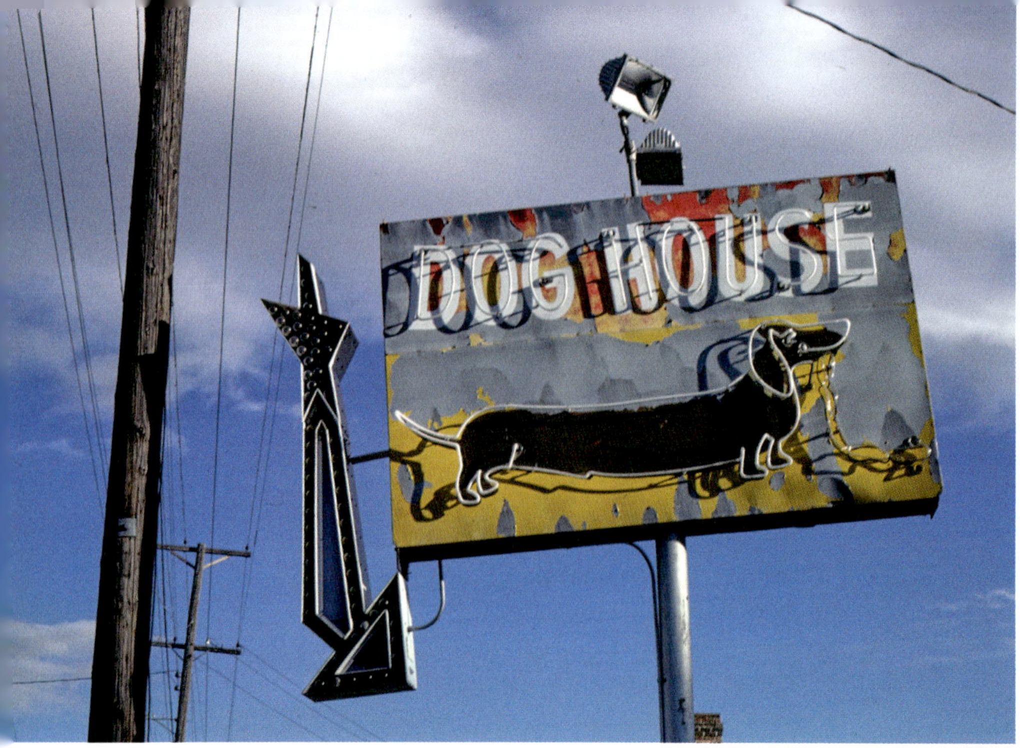

1
RUST AND RELICS

L
In Albuquerque, the Dog House's neon gets your tail waggin', circa 1979 (top). A billboard advertises the world-famous Ortega's Continental Divide Indian Market, in Grants, established in 1946 (bottom).

R
In Tucumcari, the Roadrunner Lodge playfully asks motorists to slow down and enjoy the pace of a Route 66 road trip. Those who stop are rewarded with mini whoopie pies upon check-in and radios tuned to oldies in each room.

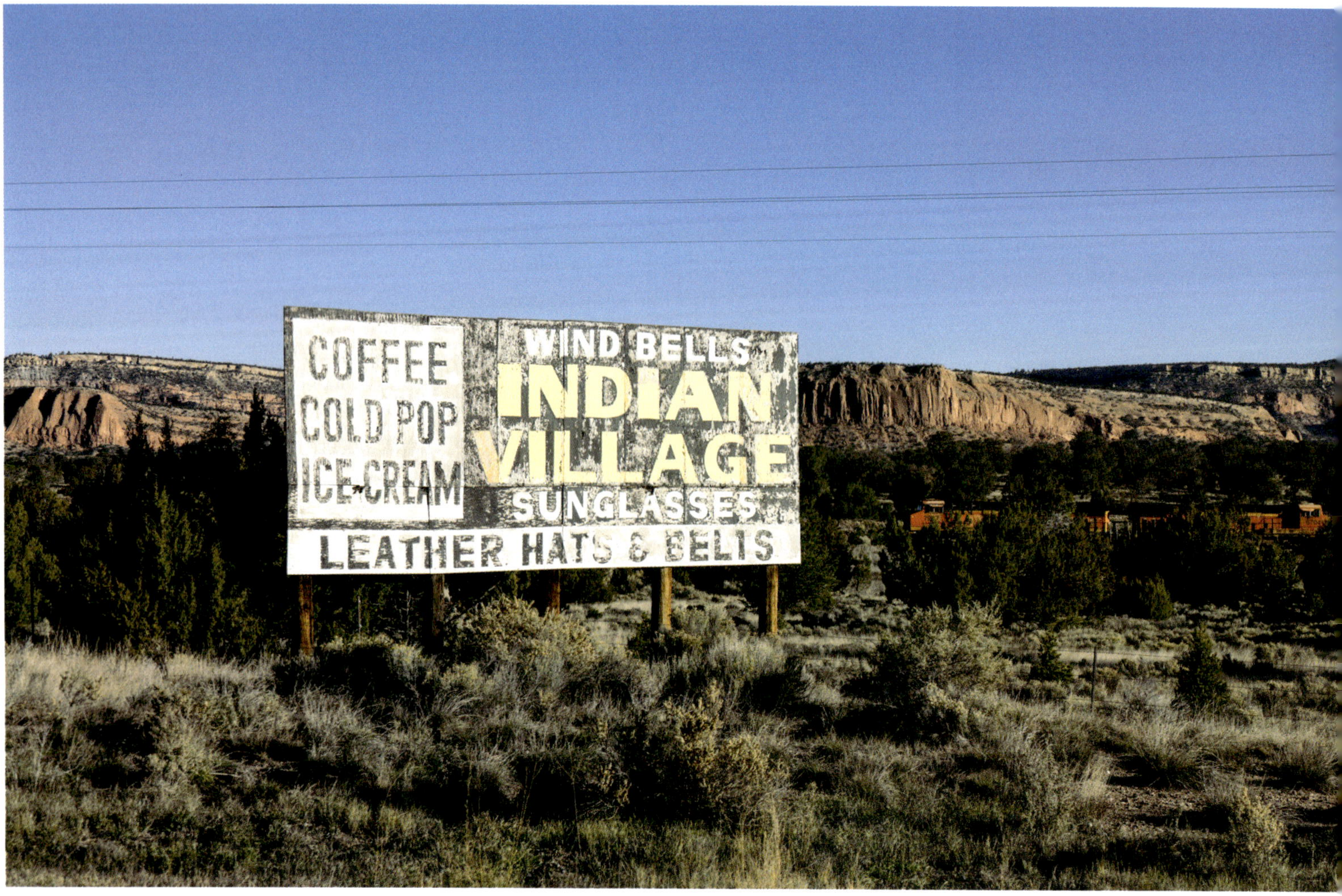

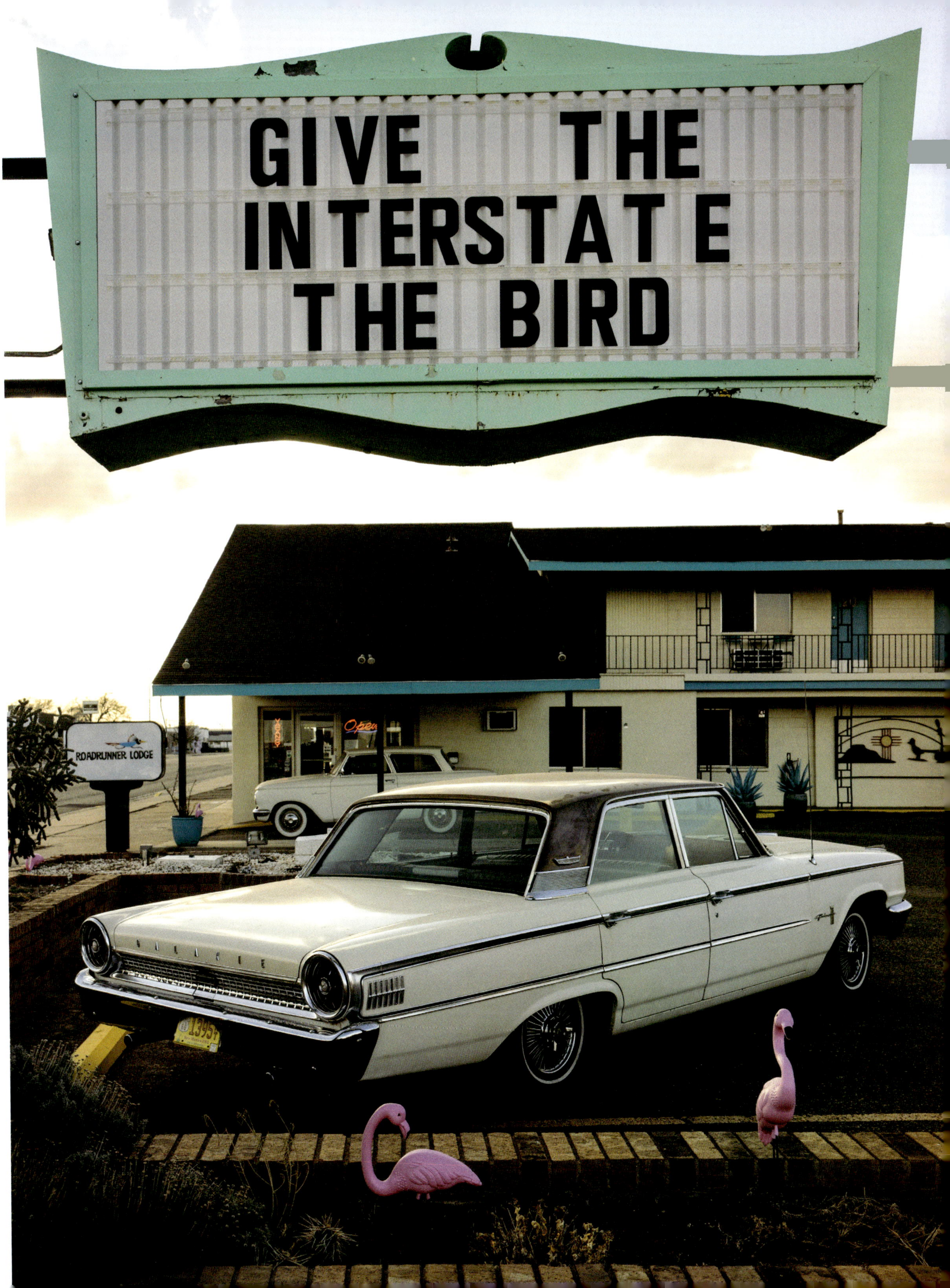
GIVE THE
INTERSTATE
THE BIRD
ROADRUNNER LODGE
Open

CHAPTER 2

LIGHT & COLOR

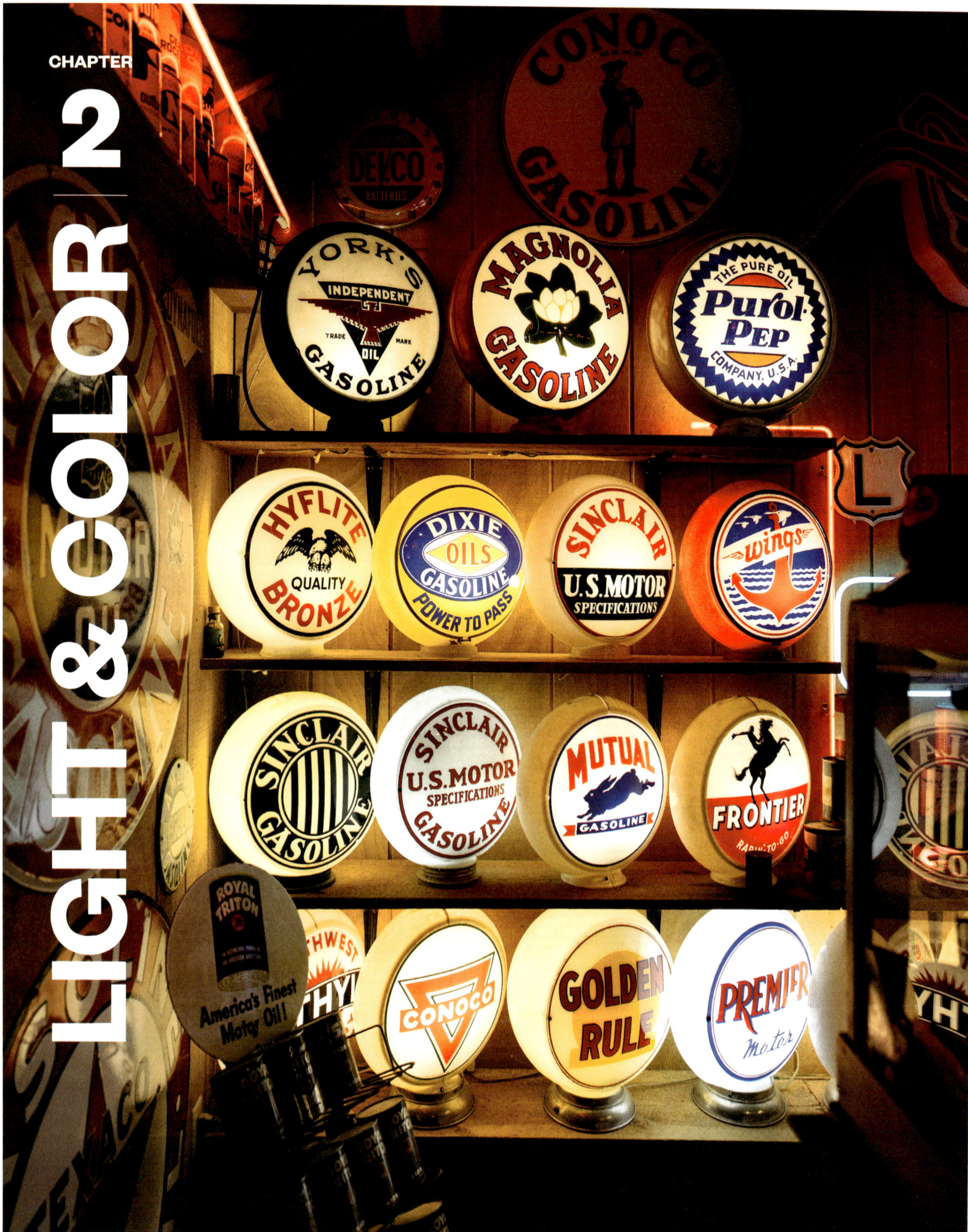

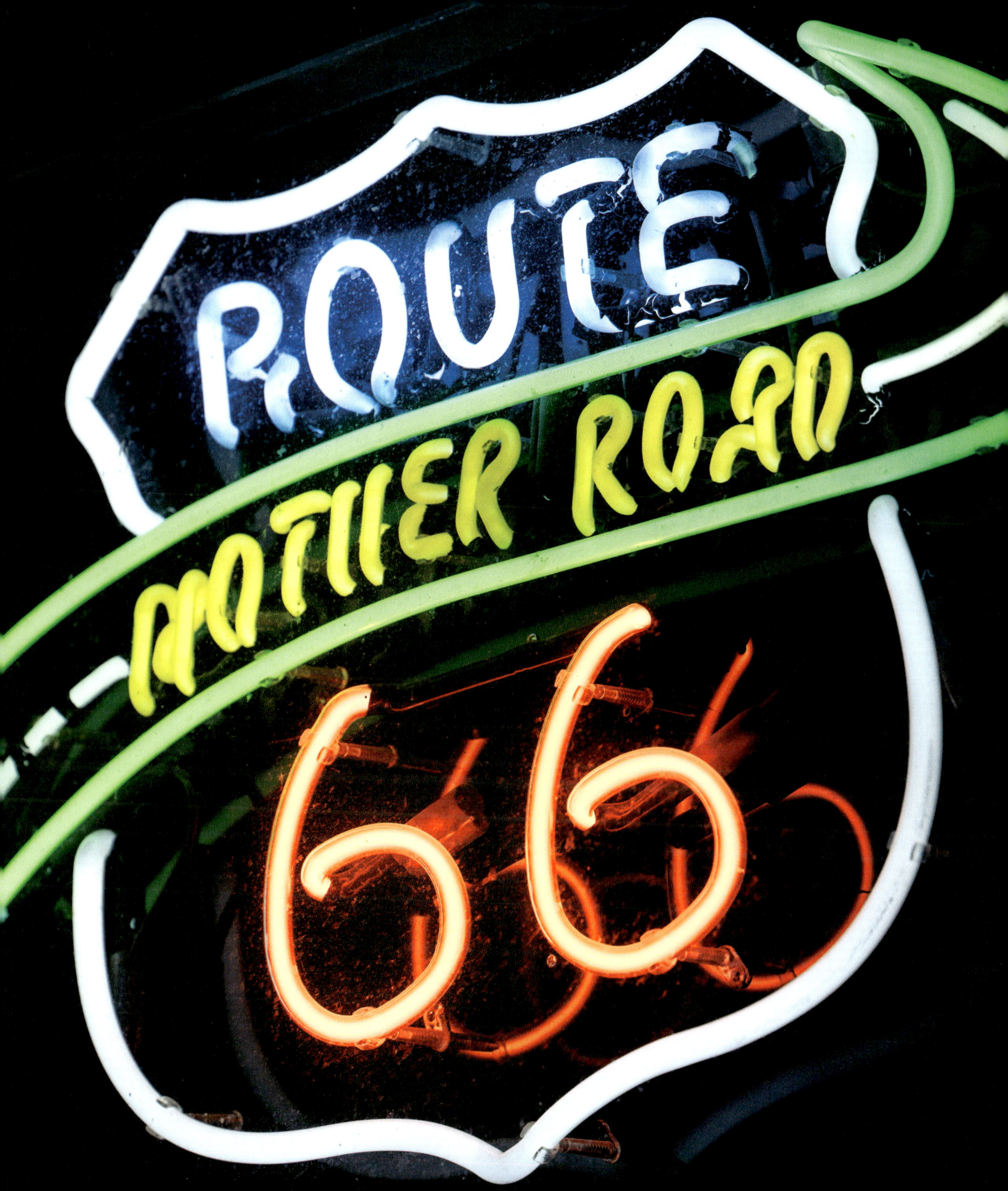
ROUTE
MOTHER ROAD
66

SHINING MOMENTS

Neon, murals, lowriders, and New Mexico's dynamic skies energize Route 66 and paint a portrait of the past.

By Nathaniel Tetsuro Paolinelli

Route 66 in New Mexico is not quiet. Even when the road itself goes still, when traffic thins and the wind takes over, light and color continue to speak. They glow, fade, flicker, and return. Neon hums against the night sky. Murals stretch across cinder-block walls. Chrome catches the last minutes of sunset. Here, light is not decoration. It is language.

I have spent years photographing New Mexico, drawn repeatedly to Route 66 not as nostalgia but as a living corridor. This stretch of road holds memory in layers: Indigenous homelands, railroad towns, wartime expansion, roadside commerce, decline, and reinvention. What binds these eras visually is light—how it strikes a sign, a wall, a windshield—and color—how communities choose to see themselves and be seen in the murals and public artworks on brick and adobe.

By the 1950s, Albuquerque had earned the nickname the Neon City, and it still fits. Neon arrived along Route 66 as a promise: vacancy, food, gasoline, and rest. Early signs were simple block letters bent into glowing declarations. Over time, they evolved into elaborate sculptures of light—animated and expressive. Today, neon artisans throughout the state continue that lineage, treating glass and gas as both craft and art. At the Classical Gas Museum in Embudo, historic signs are preserved not as relics but as living objects, still capable of stopping travelers in their tracks. Along Route 66, neon does more than advertise. It punctuates darkness and asserts presence in wide-open space.

Daylight tells a different story. In the clear high desert sun, murals have become one of the most powerful visual languages along the route. In Tucumcari, Santa Rosa, Albuquerque, Grants, and Gallup, walls act as public memory. Murals revive forgotten businesses, honoring labor histories and depicting the communities that built—and continue to sustain—the Mother Road. In Grants, large-scale murals, like the cactus growing out of a forgotten truck's hood on the side of 1912 Market, unfold like chapters of a shared story. Light plays a critical role here. Bold color palettes hold their own against intense sun, while shifting shadows alter the work throughout the day, giving it movement and life.

Public art along Route 66 extends beyond walls. Roadside sculptures rise unexpectedly from the landscape, catching light in ways that feel almost ceremonial. Contemporary works echo desert forms while reflecting the sky itself. In Tucumcari, Art City's immersive sculpture park invites travelers to linger after dark, when illuminated forms transform open land into a

R
The KiMo Theatre's restored neon sign was installed in 2011 during renovations to the Pueblo Deco building.

PREVIOUS SPREAD:
Lighted globe signs, such as these in the Classical Gas Museum in Embudo, were mounted on fuel pumps to establish branding for gas companies from the early 20th century through the 1970s (left). A neon Route 66 "Mother Road" sign hangs in the window of the Route 66 Welcome Center and Gift Shop in Tucumcari (right).

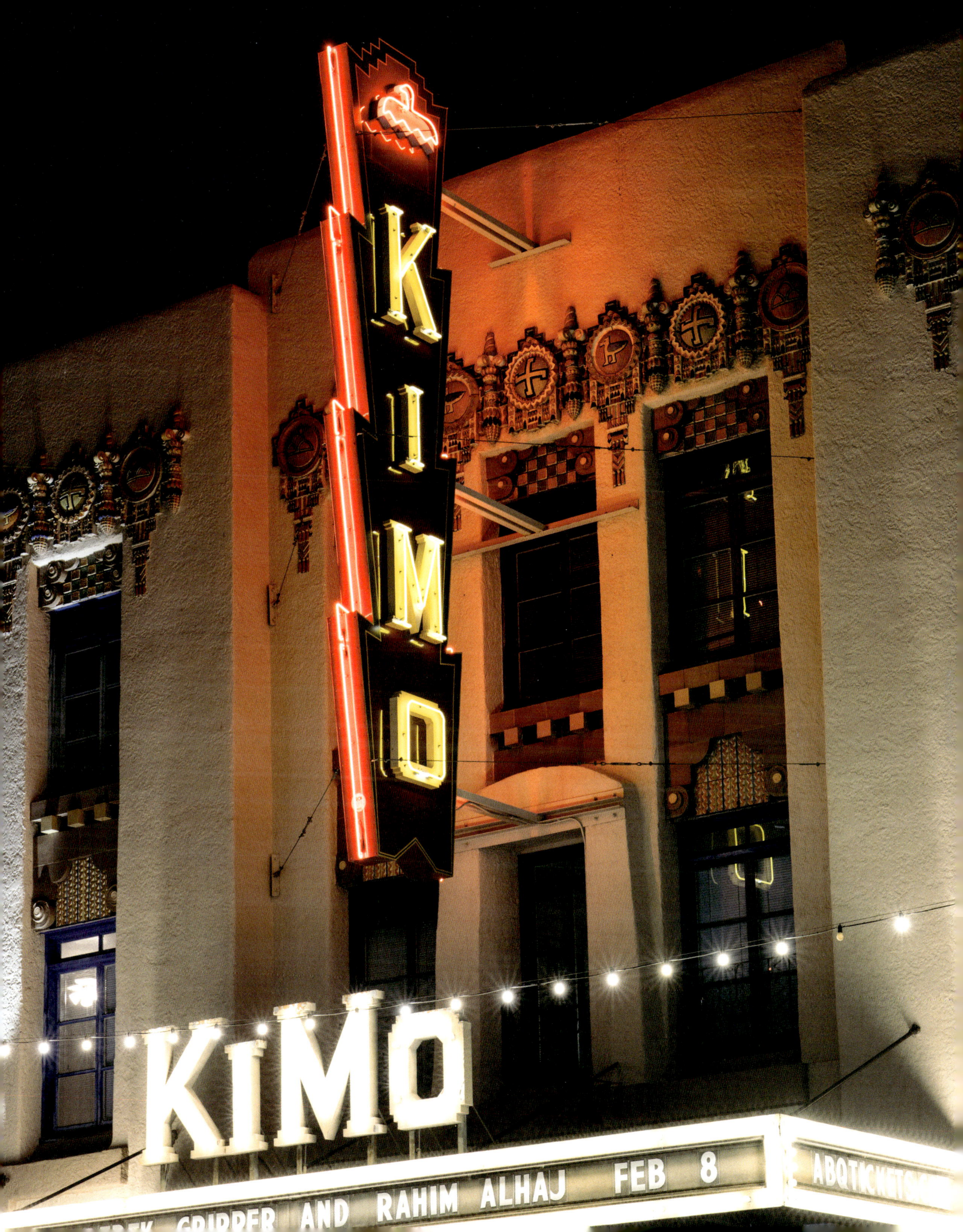
KIMO
KIMO
AND RAHIM ALHAJ FEB 8

2

LIGHT AND COLOR

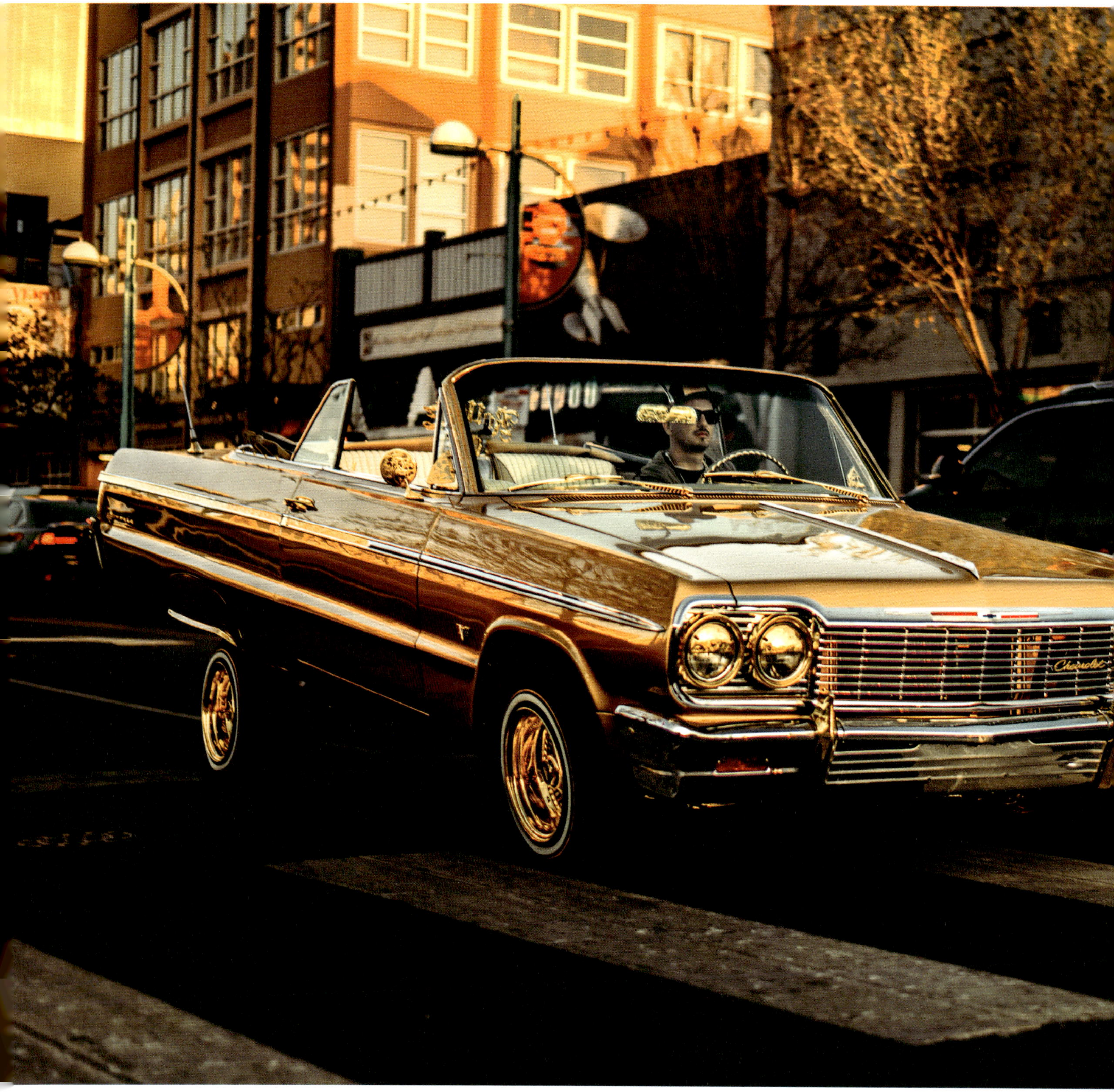

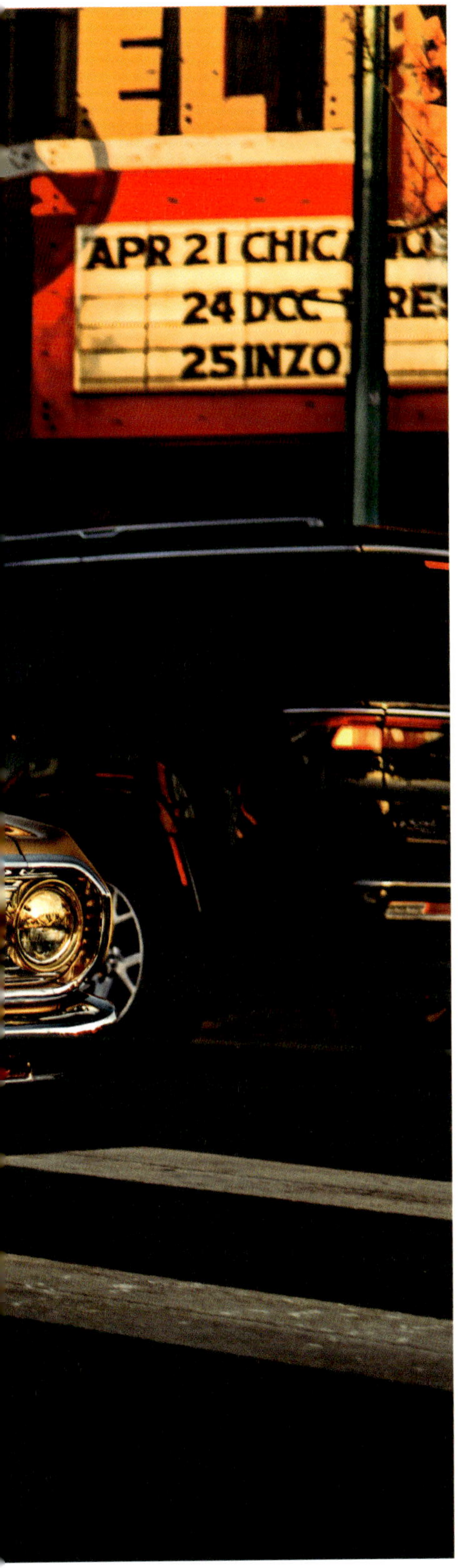

NATHANIEL TETSURO PAOLINELLI

shared experience. These works reinforce what Route 66 has always offered—not just movement but pause.

Car culture is inseparable from this visual landscape. In New Mexico, classic cars and lowriders are rolling expressions of light and color. Metallic paint is layered deep enough to mirror the sky. Chrome is polished to reflect neon. Interiors are stitched with care. Lowriders move slowly by design, allowing surfaces to fully engage with their surroundings. At sunset, they absorb color. At night, they glow.

Albuquerque is home to Duke's Car Club, the world's oldest lowrider club, with roots tracing back to Los Angeles in the 1950s and 1960s. What began as a response to exclusion has become a tradition grounded in discipline, craftsmanship, and community. Lowriders along Route 66 speaks to continuity: knowledge passed down, aesthetic standards refined, identity preserved in motion.

Builders and artists like Rob Vanderslice help sustain that lineage. Based in Albuquerque, Vanderslice has spent decades shaping the visual language of lowrider and custom car culture through paint. His work treats paint not as surface but as story, the colors and patterns responding directly to New Mexico light as it shifts from midday glare to evening glow. His role as a teacher and mentor has helped ensure that custom paint remains a living craft. For many within the lowrider community, the car is not a product. It is a reflection of time invested, relationships built, and lives reshaped.

Classic cars and lowriders alike speak to the optimism that once defined the open road. They echo the same impulse that built neon signs and roadside motels: a belief that presentation matters, that beauty can be functional, and that travel should feel meaningful. Even now, a polished hood catching a New Mexico sunset can feel cinematic, as if the road itself is briefly holding still.

That cinematic quality has helped Route 66 endure. Films and television have shaped how generations imagine the Mother Road, from scenes of early wanderlust and countercultural rebellion to those of family-friendly reinvention. Before the screen images, literature named the route's significance. John Steinbeck's *The Grapes of Wrath* cemented Route 66 as the Mother Road, a symbol of survival and movement through hardship. Across mediums, light and color remain emotional tools: sun-bleached highways, glowing signs, dusty horizons.

Route 66 in New Mexico is not frozen in myth. Contemporary initiatives such as Route 66 Remixed, a public art partnership between Meow Wolf and the Albuquerque Arts and Culture Department, demonstrate how new voices continue to shape the road's visual identity. Along the Duke City's 18-mile stretch of Route 66, paint mixes with the latest technology. Dale Deforest's augmented reality portal *Let's Not Forget, Albuquerque Is a Character, Too* appears in the ticket windows of the Guild Cinema to celebrate the city's television and film legacy. Jesse Littlebird and Thomas Christopher Hagg's colorful *Buffalo Return to Route 66* brings bold graphics inspired by Pueblo pottery motifs to the El Rey Theater.

These projects add to Route 66's story, layering Indigenous perspectives, experimental forms, and community-driven narratives that reflect the present moment.

Route 66's power lies in its ability to bridge eras. Neon recalls midcentury ambition while inspiring contemporary makers. Murals honor the past while inviting present-day participation. Cars connect generations through shared craftsmanship. Together, they form a visual ecosystem that keeps the road alive.

To travel Route 66 in New Mexico is to move through a gallery without walls, curated by time, place, and the people who call this corridor home. Light changes constantly here, and color responds in kind. That ongoing conversation between history and reinvention is what continues to draw me back. The Mother Road does not simply reflect light. It carries it forward. ✴

L
A gold Chevy Impala cruises along Albuquerque's Central Avenue in the remnants of daylight.

NATHANIEL TETSURO PAOLINELLI is an Albuquerque documentary photographer. His book *Seventh and Central* (University of New Mexico Press) was published in 2026.

Johnnie Meier

The owner of the Classical Gas Museum in Embudo has spent decades restoring the Mother Road's neon glow.

HISTORIC PRESERVATIONIST Johnnie Meier is an alchemist of sorts, restoring the magical glow of yesteryear's neon signs along New Mexico's Route 66. He's also the owner of the Classical Gas Museum in Embudo, a quirky collection of colorful vintage gas pumps, old vehicles, neon signs, and other artifacts of America's roadside culture that's hard to miss on NM 68 between Santa Fe and Taos. He helped restore the dazzling neon signs at the KiMo Theatre in Albuquerque and most of the neon in Tucumcari, including signs at Tee Pee Curios and La Cita Restaurant.

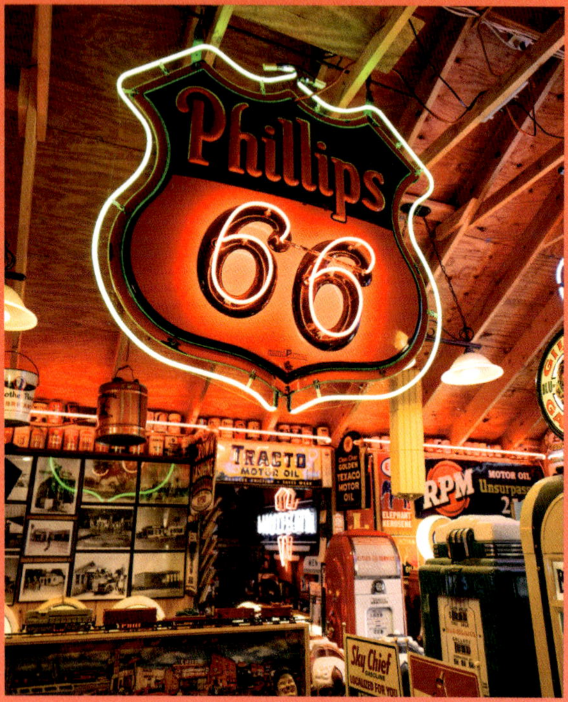

L
This rare Phillips 66 sign lights up the Classical Gas Museum in Embudo.

R
While Johnnie Meier had always tinkered with classic cars, he began collecting what he calls "roadside culture artifacts" in 1987.

I spent 25 years at Los Alamos as a scientist, and my specialty was lasers.

There's little difference between gas lasers and gas tubes. I understood immediately how neon signs worked, down to the atomic level.

It's such simple technology, and that's why neon proliferated all over the country.

I really responded to the art of it and then the history.

There's a postcard that describes Central Avenue in Albuquerque as "a galaxy of neon." I love this phrase.

The signs played such a cultural role in representing the history of New Mexico. They had meaning. I didn't want to see that meaningfulness lost.

About 20 years ago, I spearheaded a project with a $50,000 grant from the National Park Service. We went to a local PBS affiliate to film the restoration of 10 classic neon signs in the state. The project resulted in the Emmy-winning PBS documentary *Route 66: The Neon Road.*

These one-of-a-kind neon signs have come to be appreciated as great examples of American folk art.

They are sculptures, very figural in their representation. They were snapshots of culture.

What you have are pearl whites, ruby reds, emerald greens, and sapphire blues all wrapped in crystalline. It's street jewelry.

These brightly lit signs welcome you to the properties. You feel drawn in.

I think *Route 66: The Neon Road* was a catalyst. It generated a lot of interest in restoring the signs.

These signs are touchstones for a lot of communities. They contribute to the identity of the communities. When they lose these touchstones, the whole community is impacted.

Some towns along 66 in other states celebrate the single neon sign that's still standing. But go to Tucumcari—they have nearly a dozen. Albuquerque has more than a dozen.

New Mexico really has the premier collection on all of Route 66. ✴

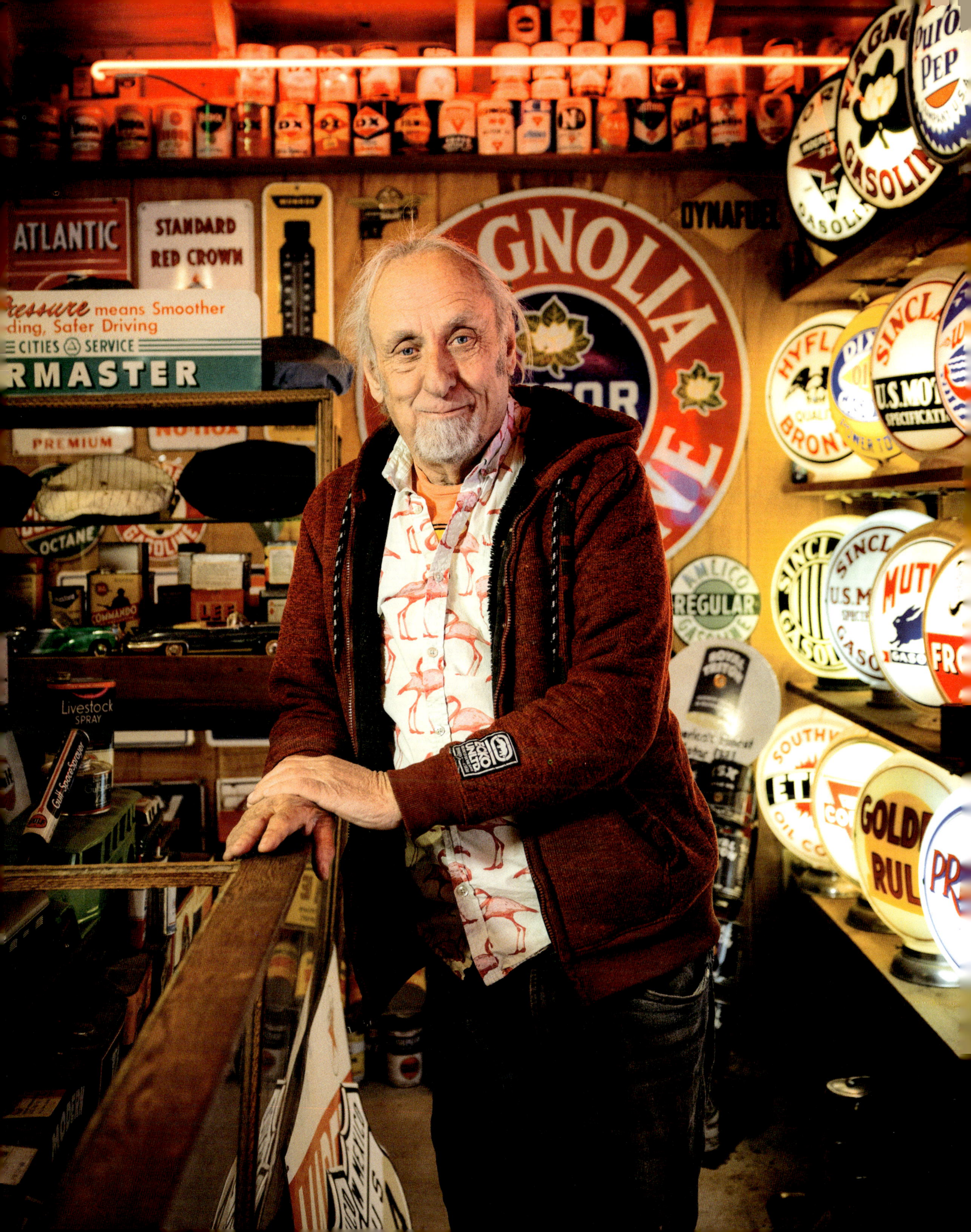
ATLANTIC
STANDARD
RED CROWN
DYNAFUEL
GNOLIA
Pressure means Smoother
ding, Safer Driving
CITIES SERVICE
RMASTER
PREMIUM
OCTANE
REGULAR
Livestock
SPRAY
GOLD
RUL
Puro
PEP

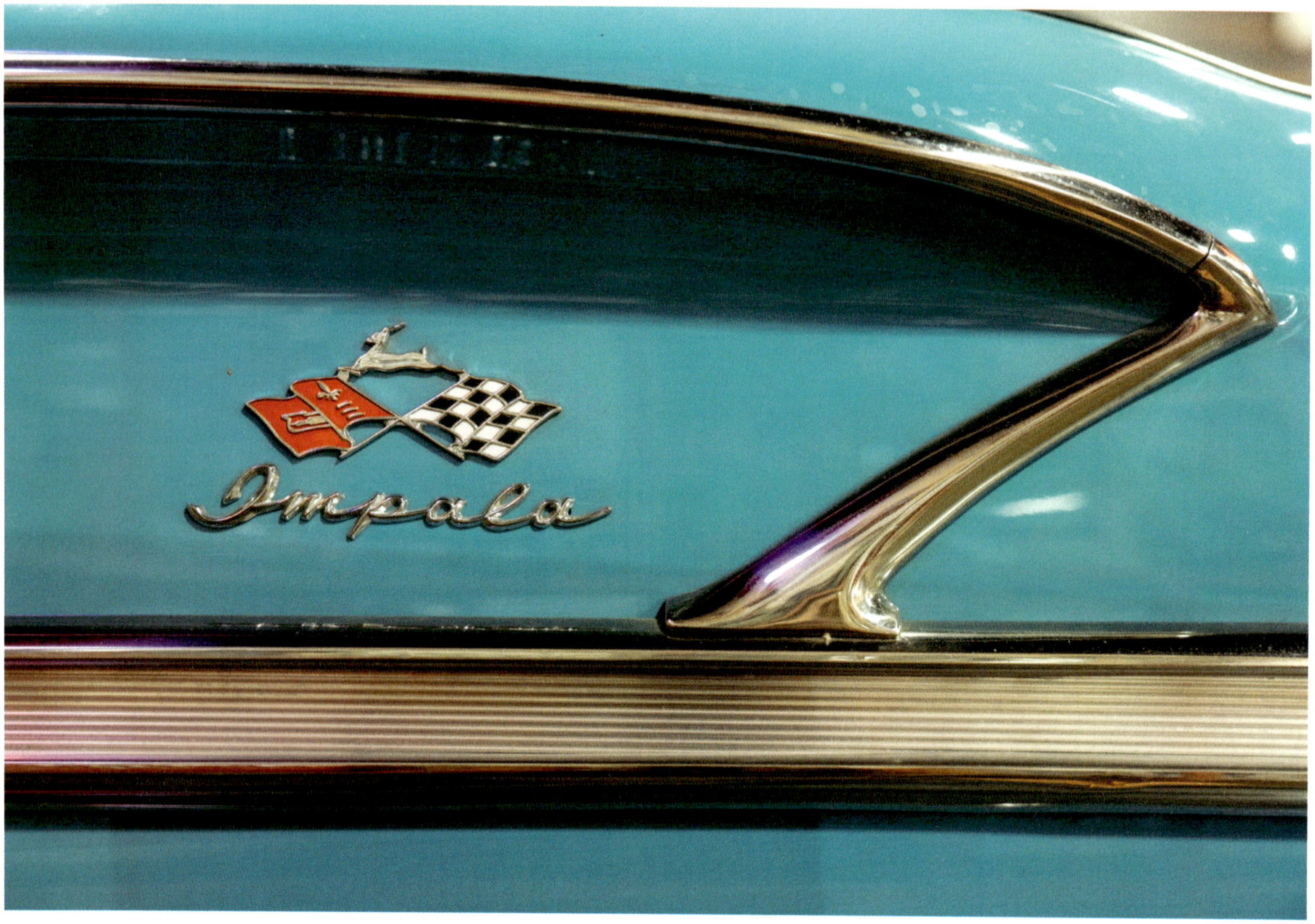

L
This turquoise Chevy Impala is one of more than 30 vintage vehicles in the collection of the Route 66 Auto Museum in Santa Rosa.

R
With a year-round temperature of 61 degrees, the Blue Hole in Santa Rosa is a cool spot to stop on any Route 66 road trip.

"We've become good friends with people from all over the world who are making the Route 66 trip. We take the time to talk to people. People are so happy when they leave."

— ANNA CORDOVA, WHO OPENED THE ROUTE 66 AUTO MUSEUM IN SANTA ROSA MORE THAN 20 YEARS AGO WITH HER HUSBAND, JAMES "BOZO" CORDOVA, A PASSIONATE RESTORER OF VINTAGE CARS

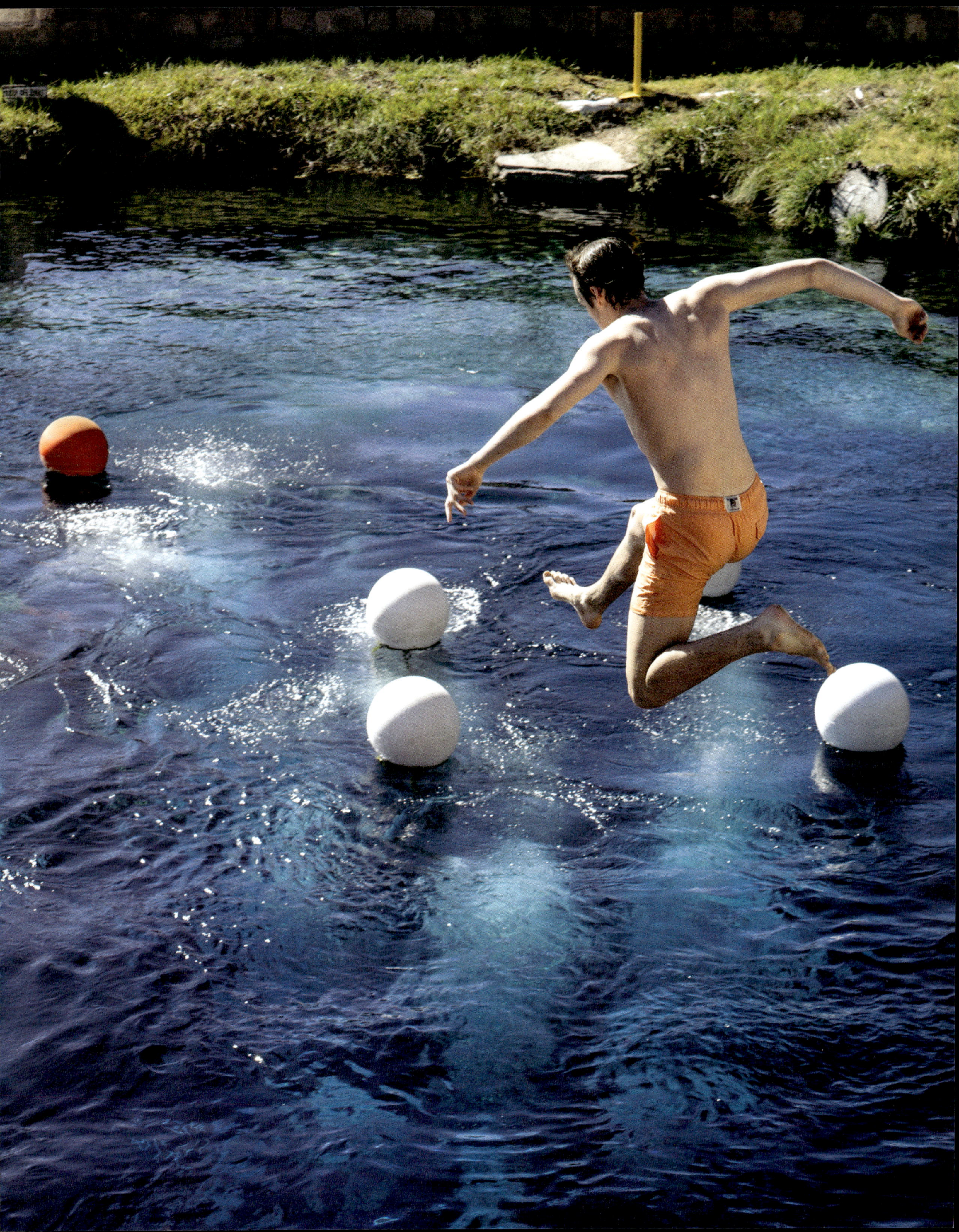

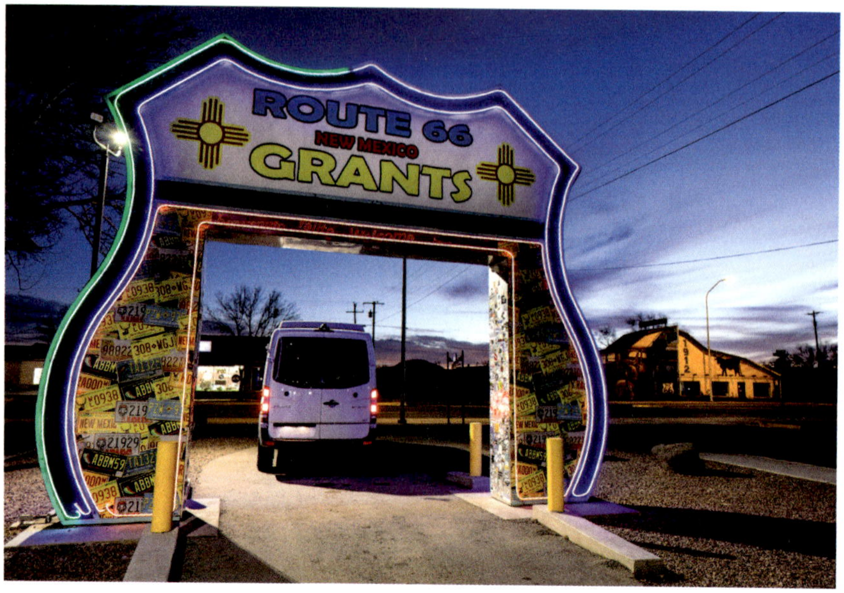

L

The colorful Route 66 drive-through arch in Grants is made for taking selfies (top). Created by artist Victor Ving and his partner, Lisa Beggs, the vibrant, vintage postcard-style *Greetings from Burque* mural can be found in Albuquerque's Nob Hill neighborhood (bottom).

R

Artist Jesse Littlebird (pictured with his 1973 Dodge Dart, known as Petrolglyph) collaborated with Thomas Christopher Haag for *Buffalo Return to Route 66* at El Rey Theater as part of Albuquerque's Route 66 Remixed project.

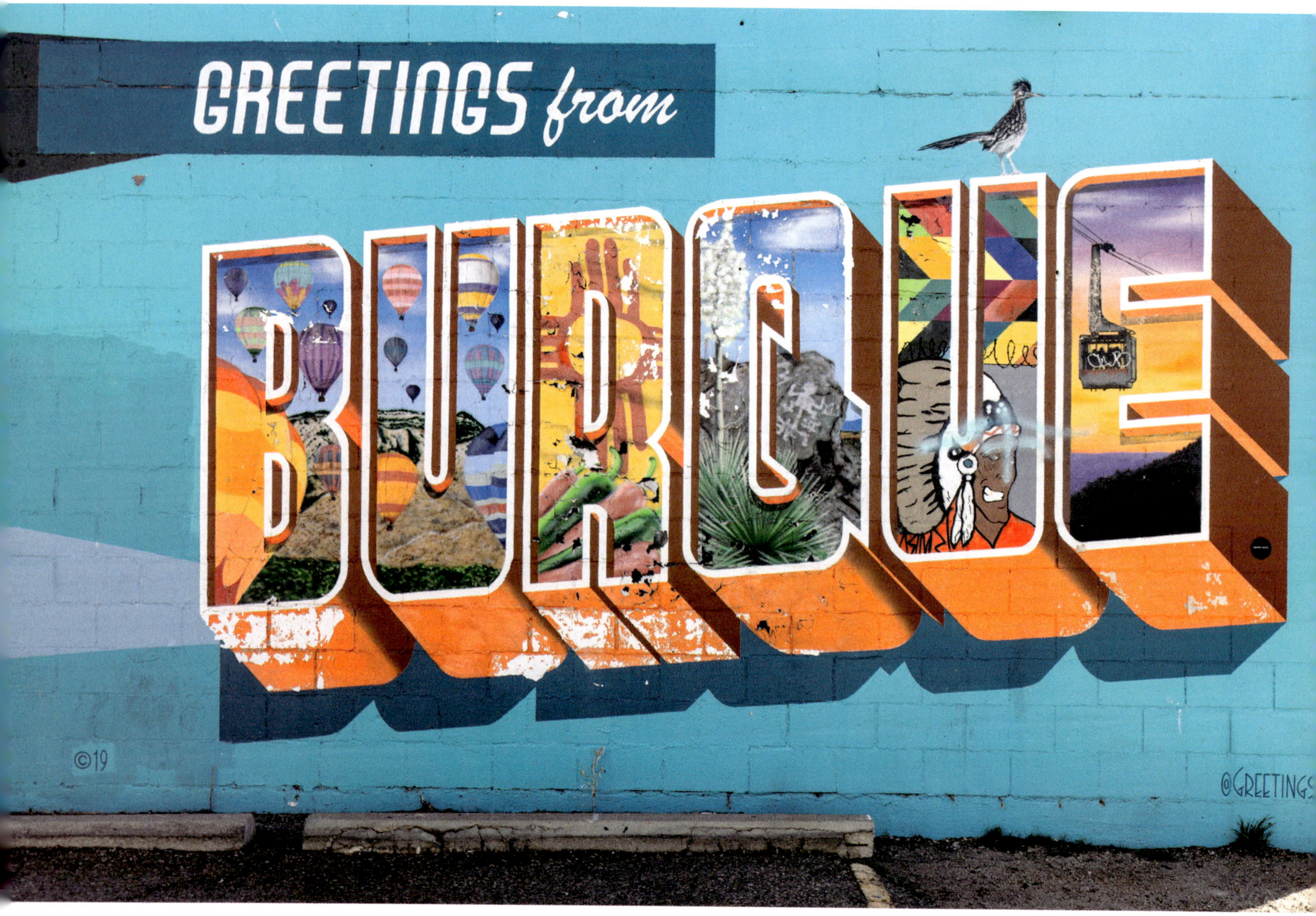

2

LIGHT AND COLOR

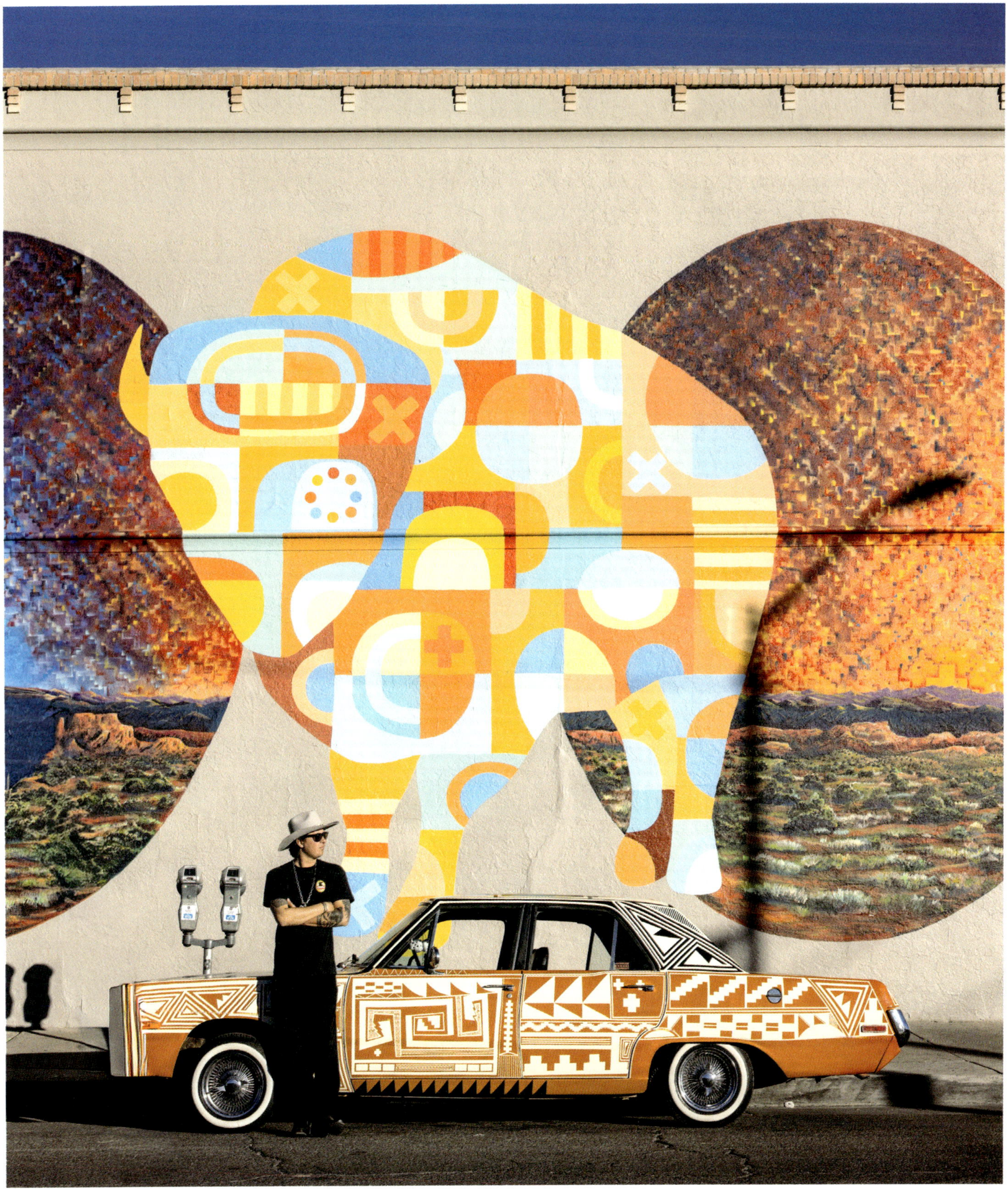

33

ROAD TO ENCHANTMENT

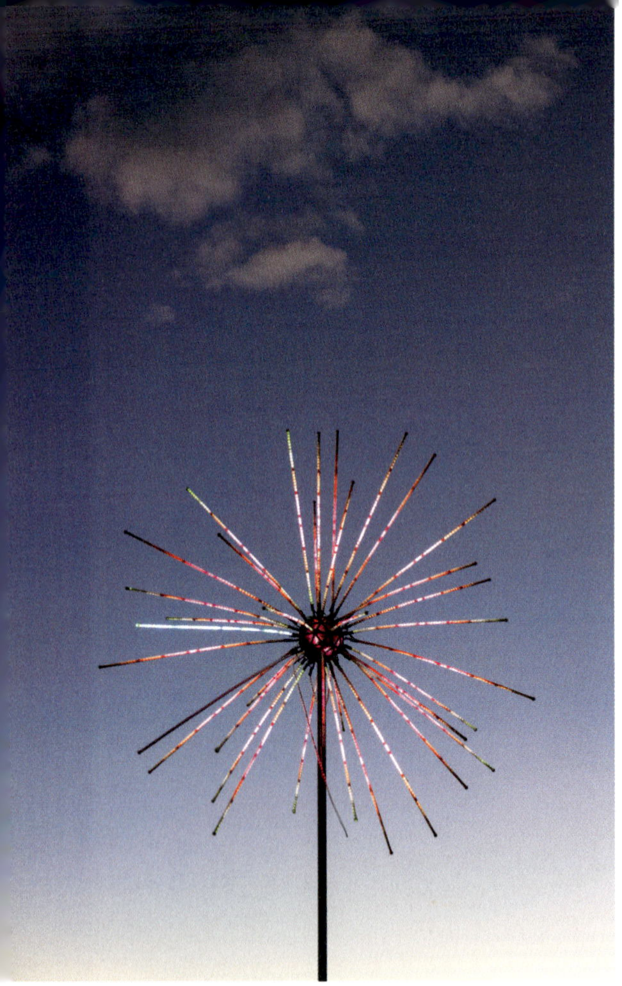

2

LIGHT AND COLOR

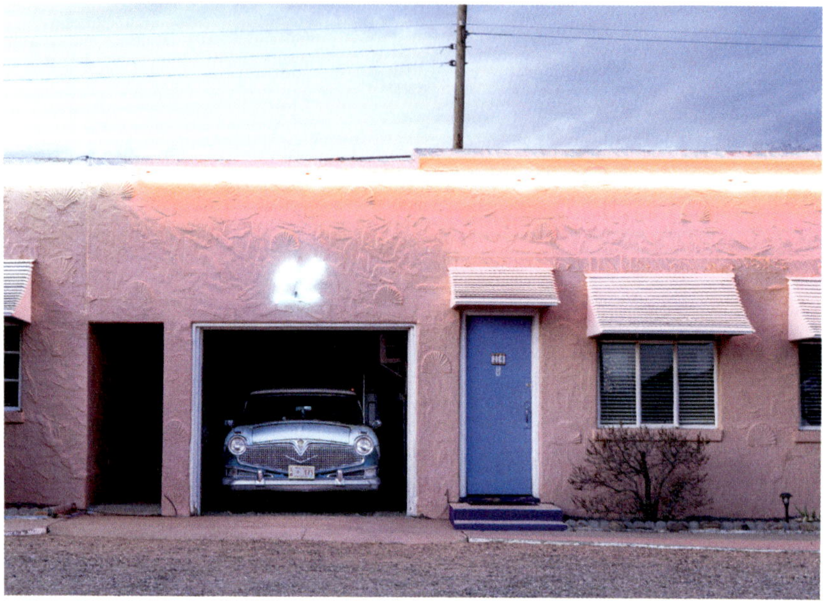

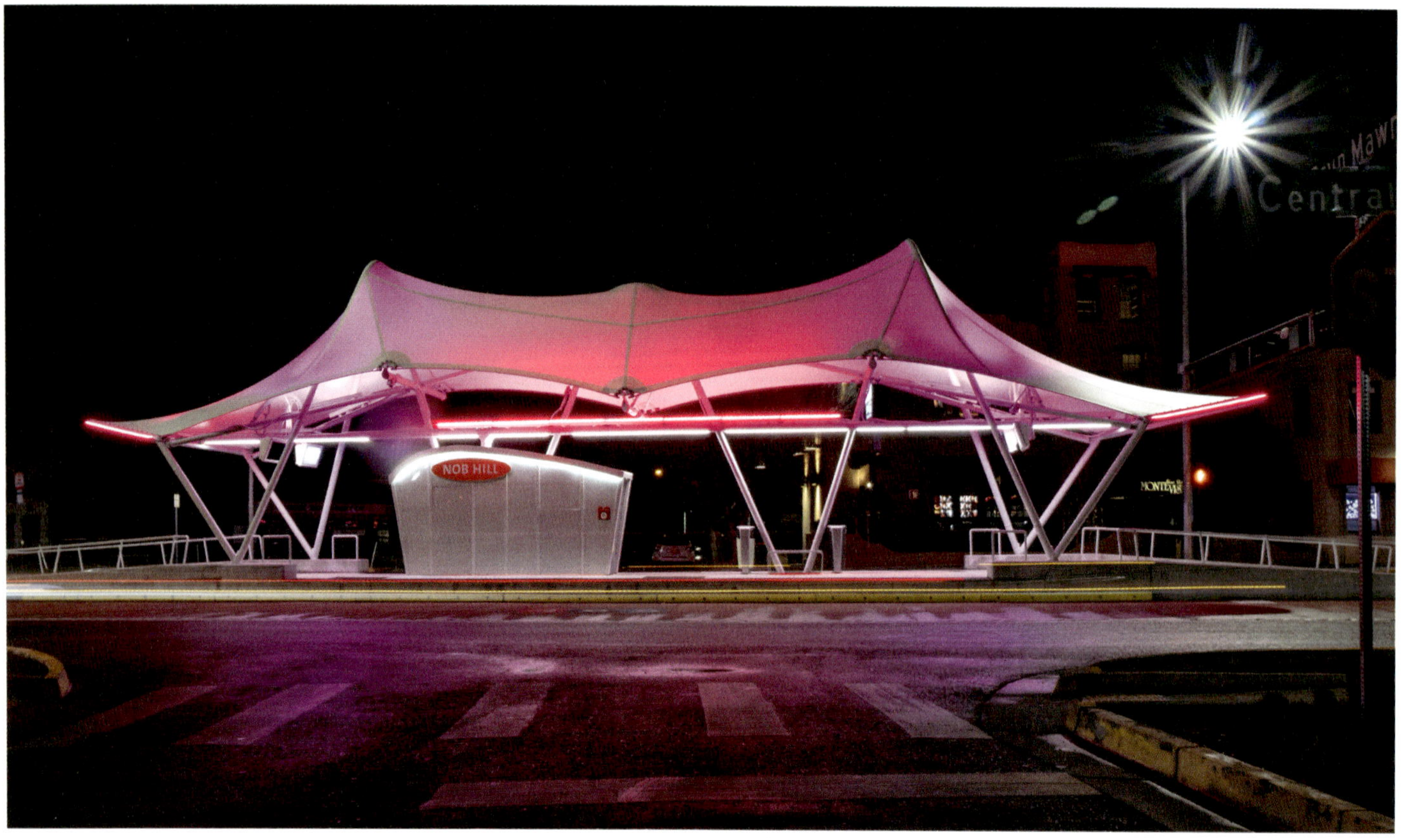

BOTTOM: NMTD

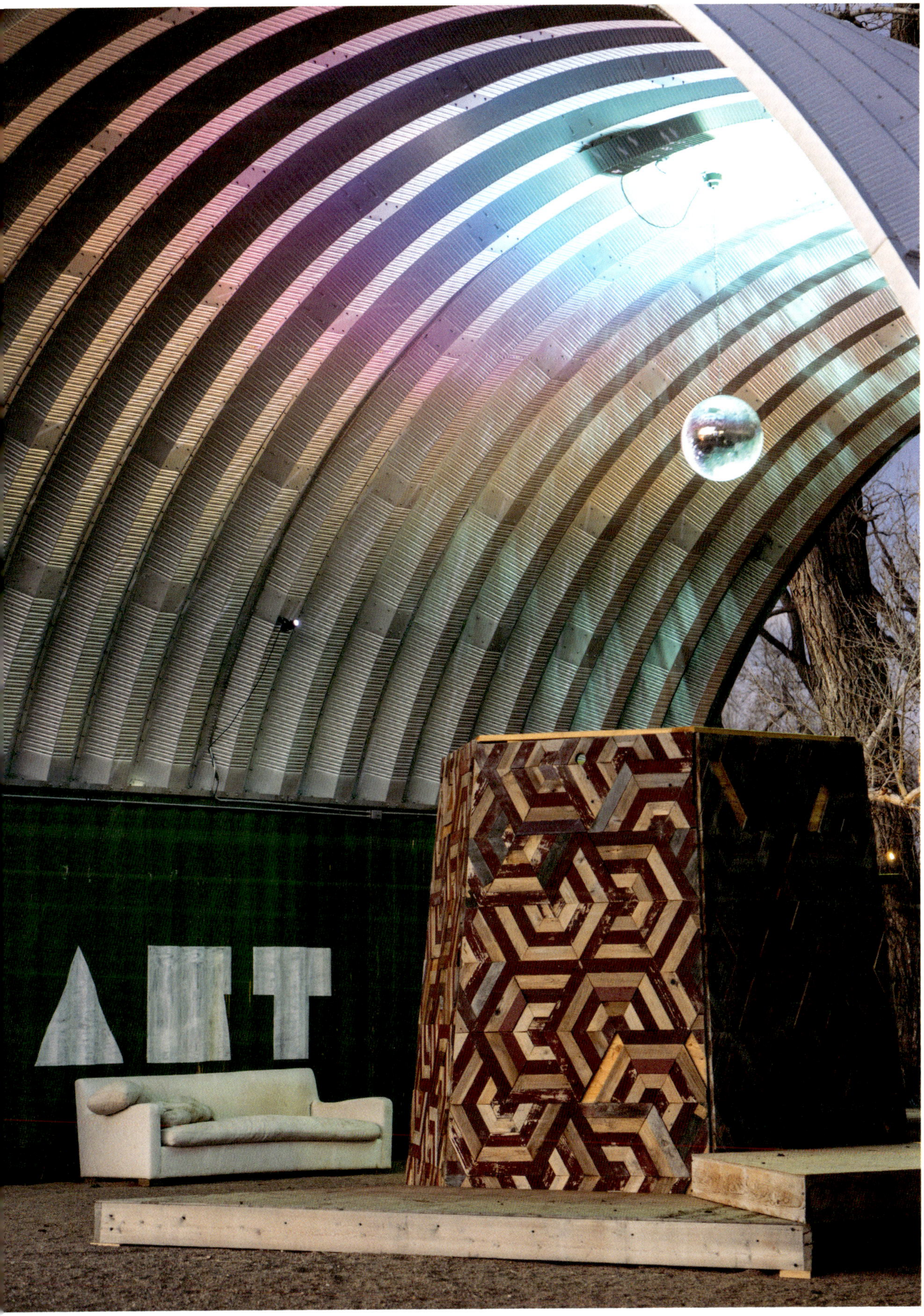

R
At Art City's 40-acre sculpture park and glamping resort in Tucumcari, artists and guests camping in cabins, tents, RVs, and vans can relax and get to know each other at the large main hub.

L
Abram Santa Cruz's 28-foot-tall steel and LED light sculpture *Electric Dandelions* lights up the night skies at Art City in Tucumcari (top left). A 1957 Hudson Hornet is right at home in one of the historic garages at the Blue Swallow Motel in Tucumcari (top right). The Albuquerque Rapid Transit (ART) system, which runs along Central Avenue and connects to Downtown, Midtown/University, and Uptown, includes this bus stop in the heart of Nob Hill (bottom).

James Emory

The muralist has left his mark on Grants—and Route 66 travelers.

IN A SINGLE YEAR, brothers James and Blake Emory painted 30 murals along a five-block stretch of Route 66 in Grants. Their bold imagery pays tribute to the northwestern New Mexico town's ranching, farming, mining, and Native heritage. Painted in 2024, the murals are part of the Grants MainStreet District, one of 10 New Mexico districts devoted to the revitalizwation of historic Route 66. In neighboring Milan, James, who recently moved to an off-grid solar ranch in Santa Fe, created a mural of a historic gas station and installed a "muffler man" sculpture painted in New Mexico's signature yellow and red.

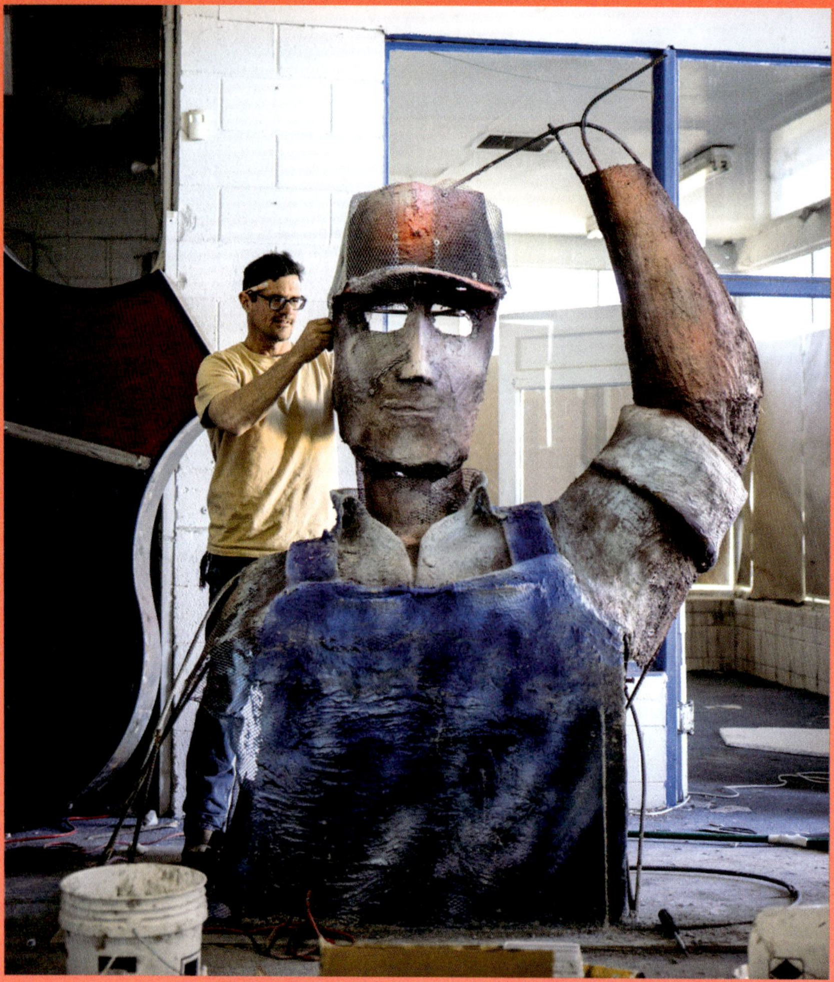

We did the very first mural on the 1912 Market on Route 66. Immediately after it was done, a couple from Italy in a Lamborghini passed by, did a U-turn, pulled over, jumped out in their leather and sunglasses, and said, "This is so awesome, bro."

Now, thousands of visitors have taken pictures.

The murals give the community something to share.

I'm a freehand artist. There's no research; it's just pure imagination. You see a spot, you imagine what needs to be there, and after doing this for 30 years, you get good at projecting.

Working on the murals gave me the understanding of how powerful America's first highway to the West is.

It also gave me the idea that this is an untapped territory. I have created an art district on Route 66.

I see it as an economic development opportunity for multiple states. ✶

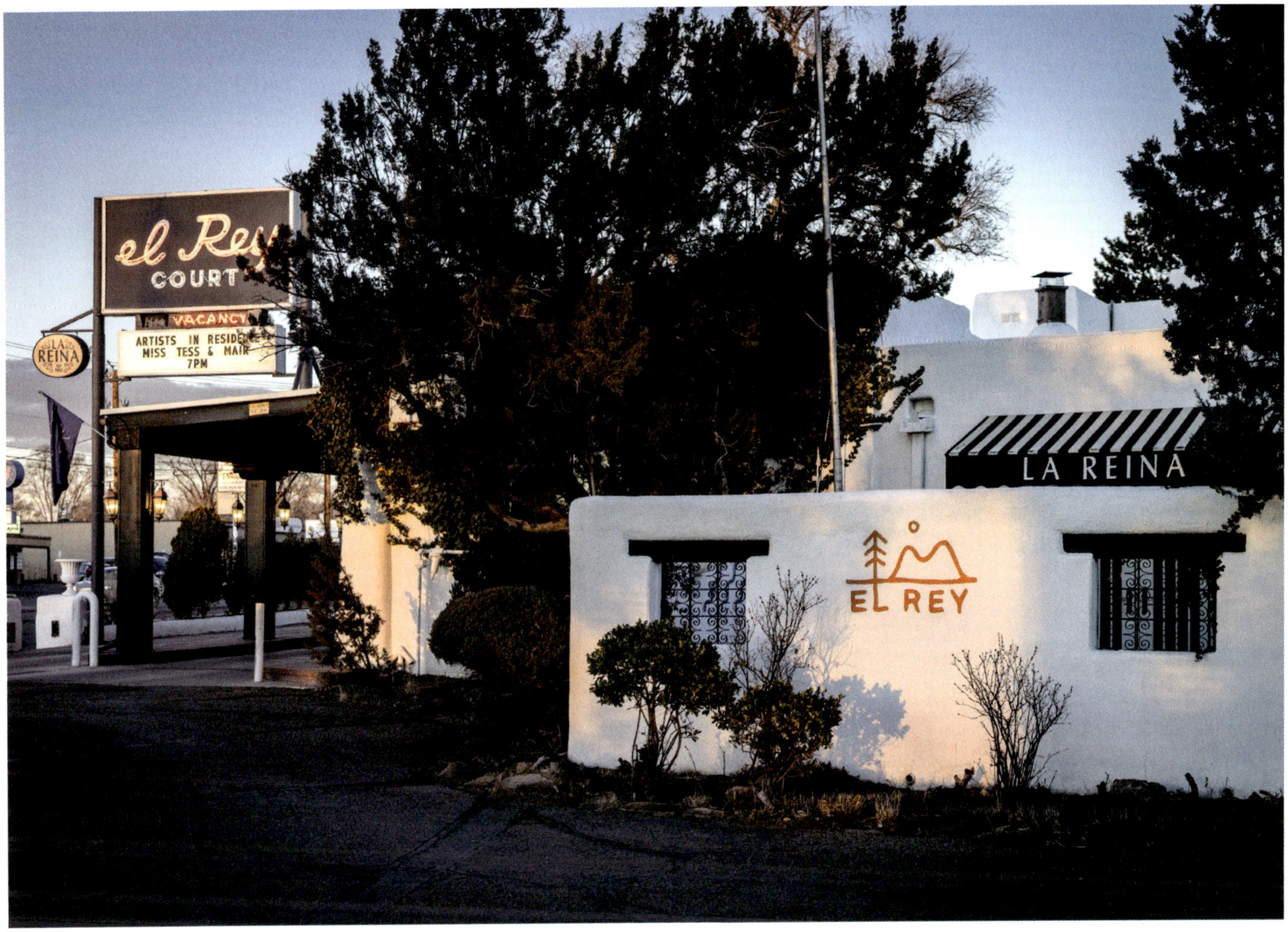

L

Artist James Emory, in his Grants studio, creates vibrant murals, sculptures, and other works that honor history in Route 66 towns. This "muffler man" can be found in Milan.

R

Reopened in 2018, Santa Fe's El Rey Court has a modern Southwestern vibe and La Reina bar, where locals and travelers gather over live music and cocktails.

HOMECOMING COURT

Santa Fe's El Rey Court is the queen of the roadside motels.

The landmark white adobe building on the original 1926 alignment in Santa Fe has been a mainstay since 1936, when it opened as a 12-room motor inn. Over the years, the inn expanded with an outdoor pool, hot tubs, and incorporation of the 1950s Alamo Lodge. The original neon sign still glows, but El Rey has kept pace with the times. The trendy 86-room hotel features a happening pool scene, live music from local and touring musicians, and creative tequila and mezcal cocktails at La Reina bar just off the lobby. "It is a true oasis from the daily grind," says Gabrielle Cruz, director of rooms. "The property has served as a welcoming respite for travelers and artists alike for nearly a century." ✴

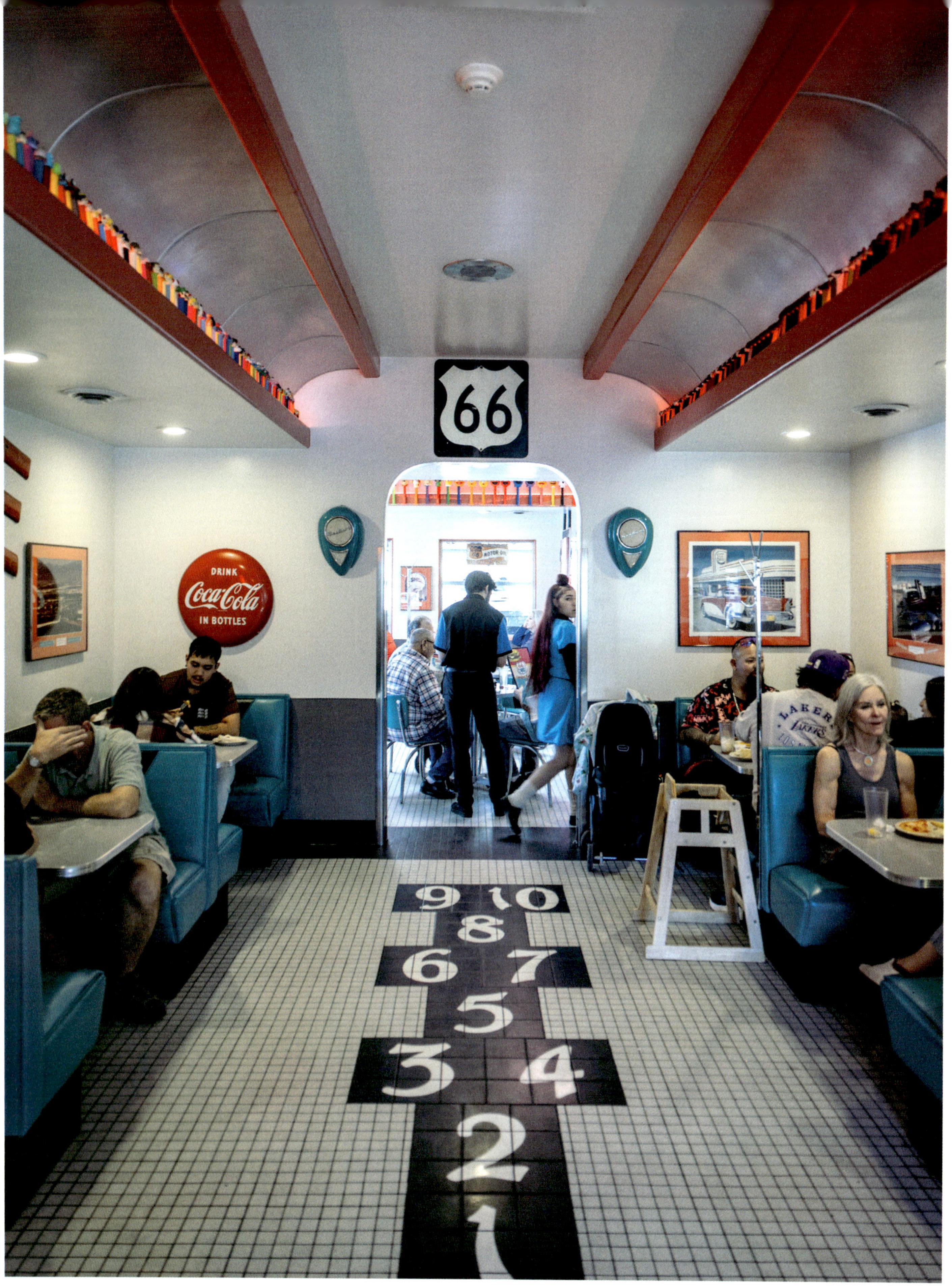
66
DRINK
Coca-Cola
IN BOTTLES
9
10
8
6
7
5
3
4
2
1

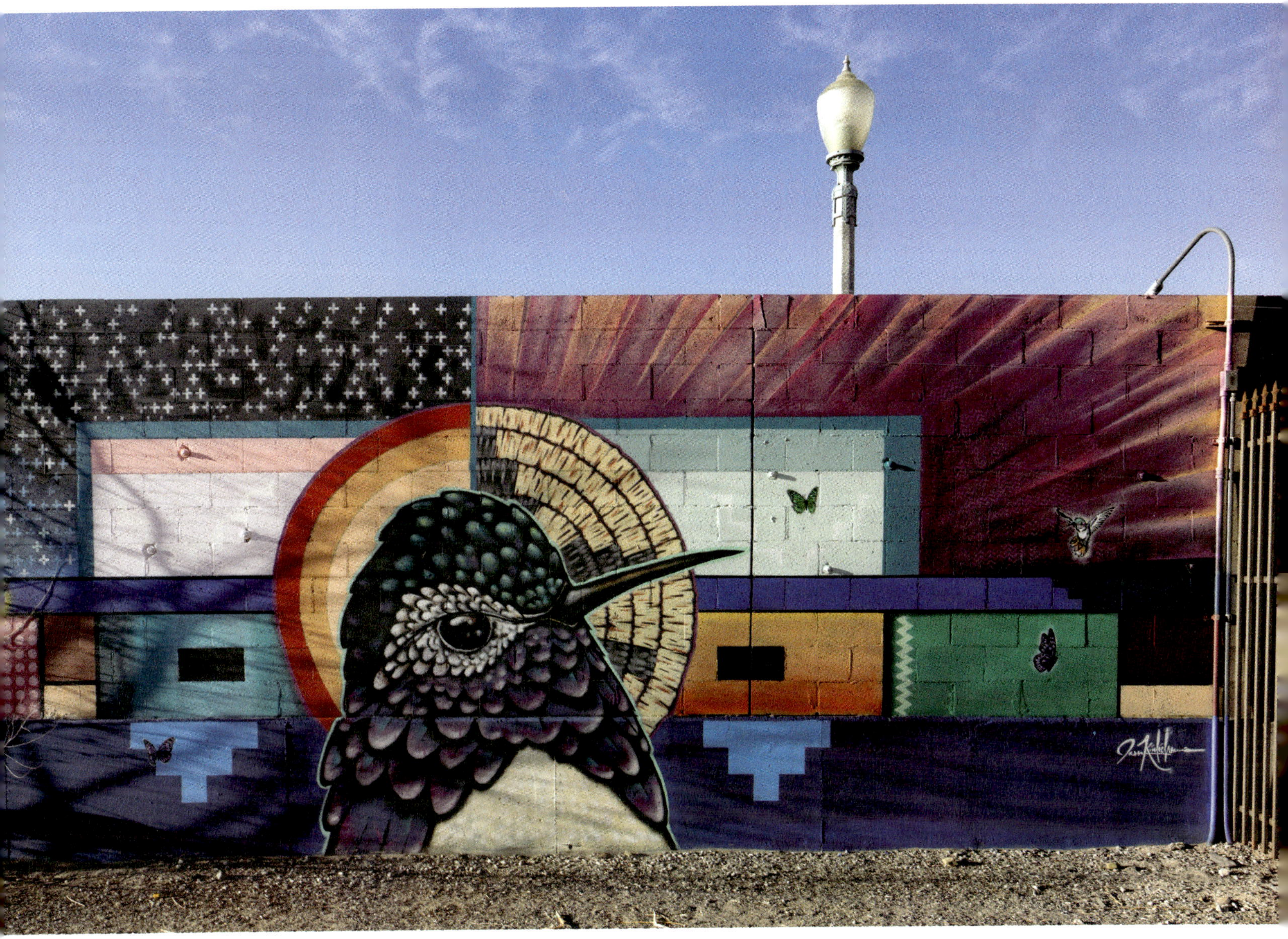

L
Housed in a former 1945 Phillips 66 gas station, the 1950s-themed 66 Diner in Albuquerque is a throwback with a soda fountain, a vintage jukebox, license plates, and other memorabilia. The diner has been an icon since it opened in 1987.

R
Diné artist Jason Kinlicheenie's mural is one of more than 30 bright, bold public art pieces celebrating the history and heritage of Gallup, which offers a self-guided Downtown Mural Walking Tour.

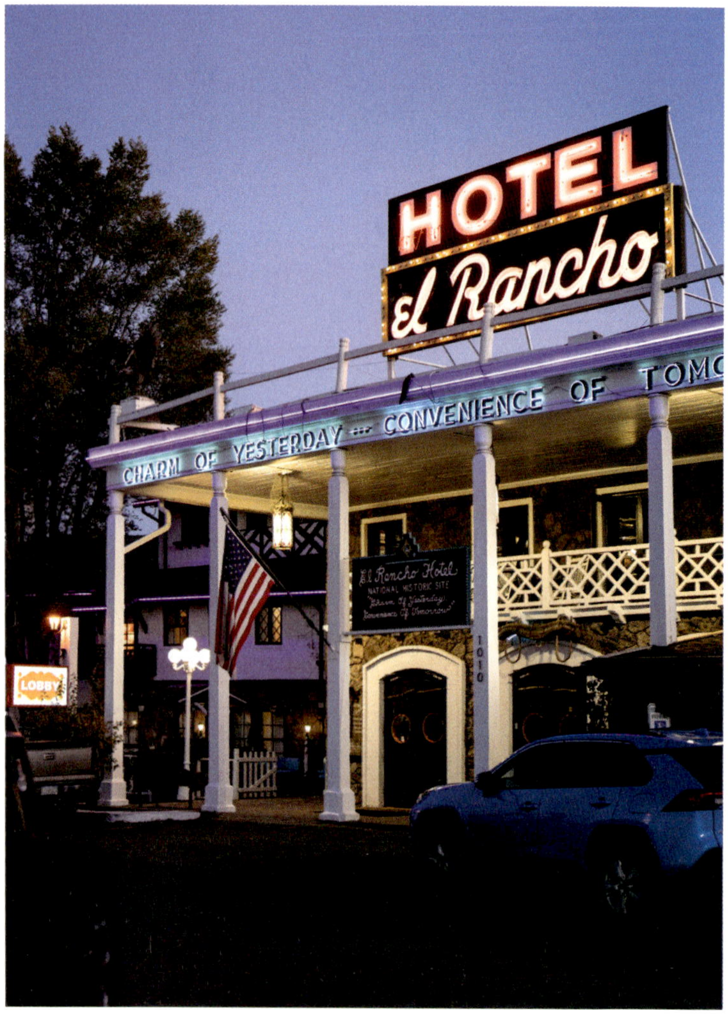

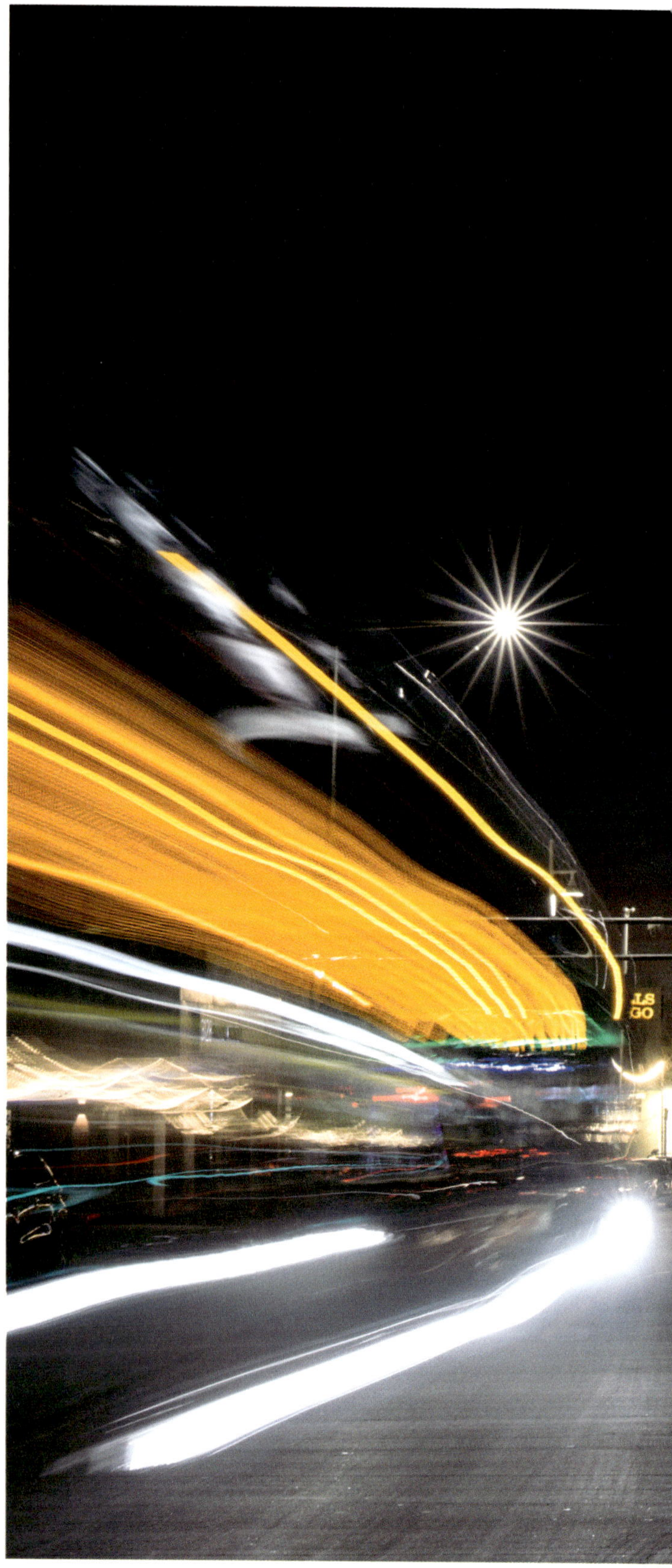

L

During Hollywood's golden age, Katharine Hepburn, John Wayne, and other stars stayed at Gallup's El Rancho Hotel while filming Westerns and other movies. A multiyear renovation has added some glitz to the 1936 hotel.

R

Albuquerque's 18-mile stretch of the Mother Road is bathed in color and light. The Nob Hill neighborhood mixes authentic old and new vibes, with vintage shops, trendy boutiques and restaurants, giant murals, and enough neon to light up the night.

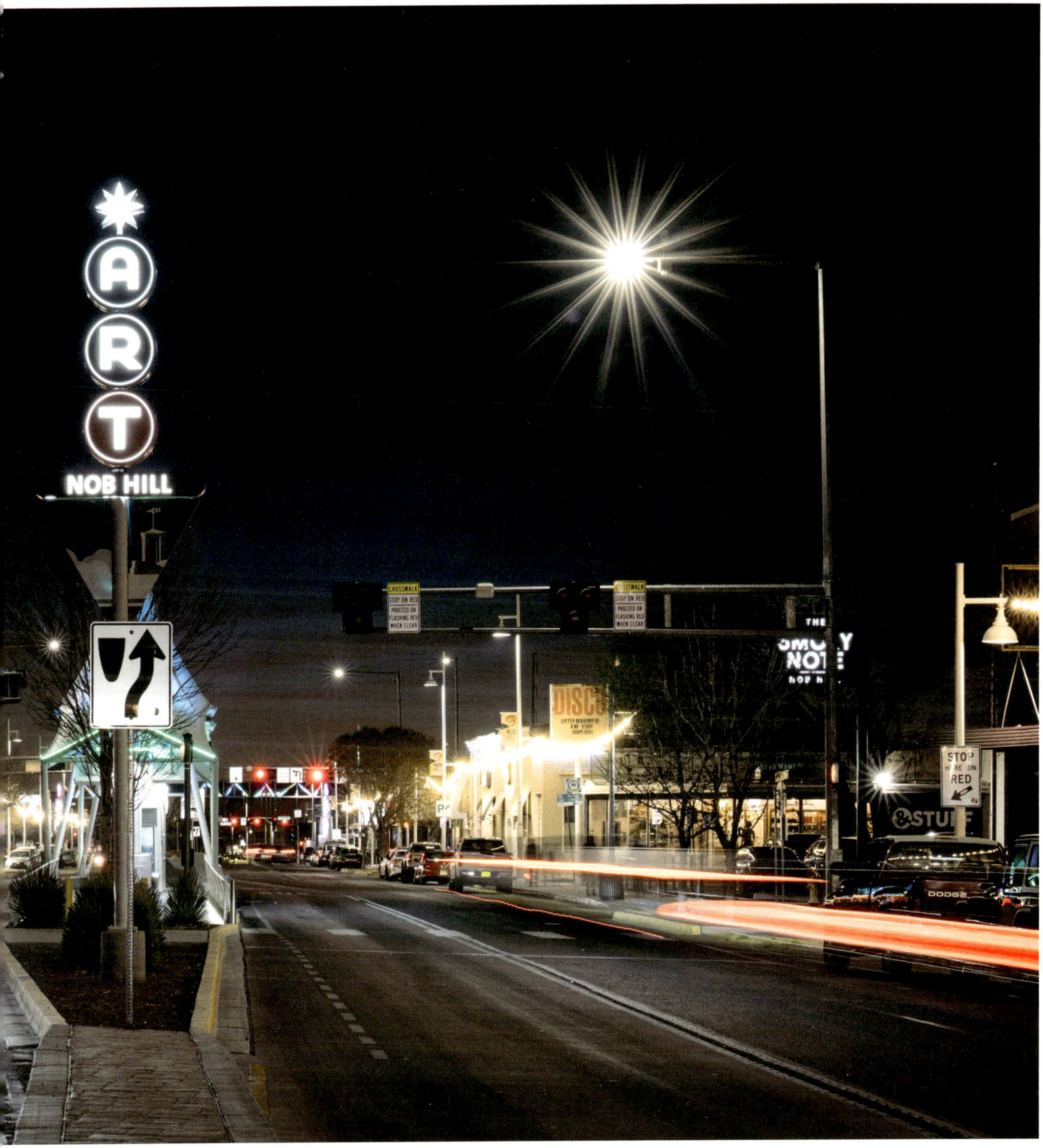
ART
NOB HILL
CROSSWALK
STOP ON RED
PROCEED ON FLASHING RED WHEN CLEAR
STOP HERE ON RED

CHAPTER

3

COMFORT & JOY

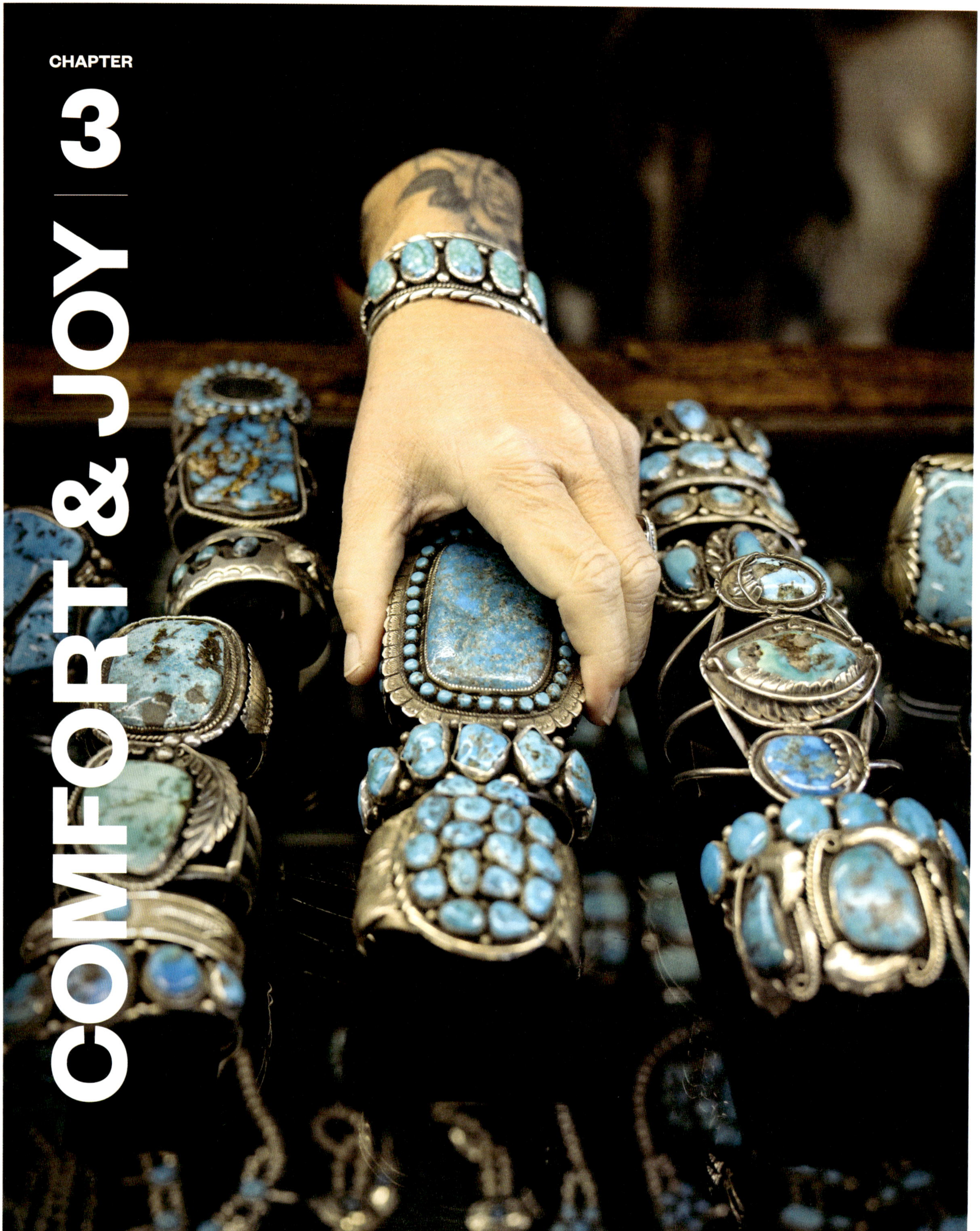

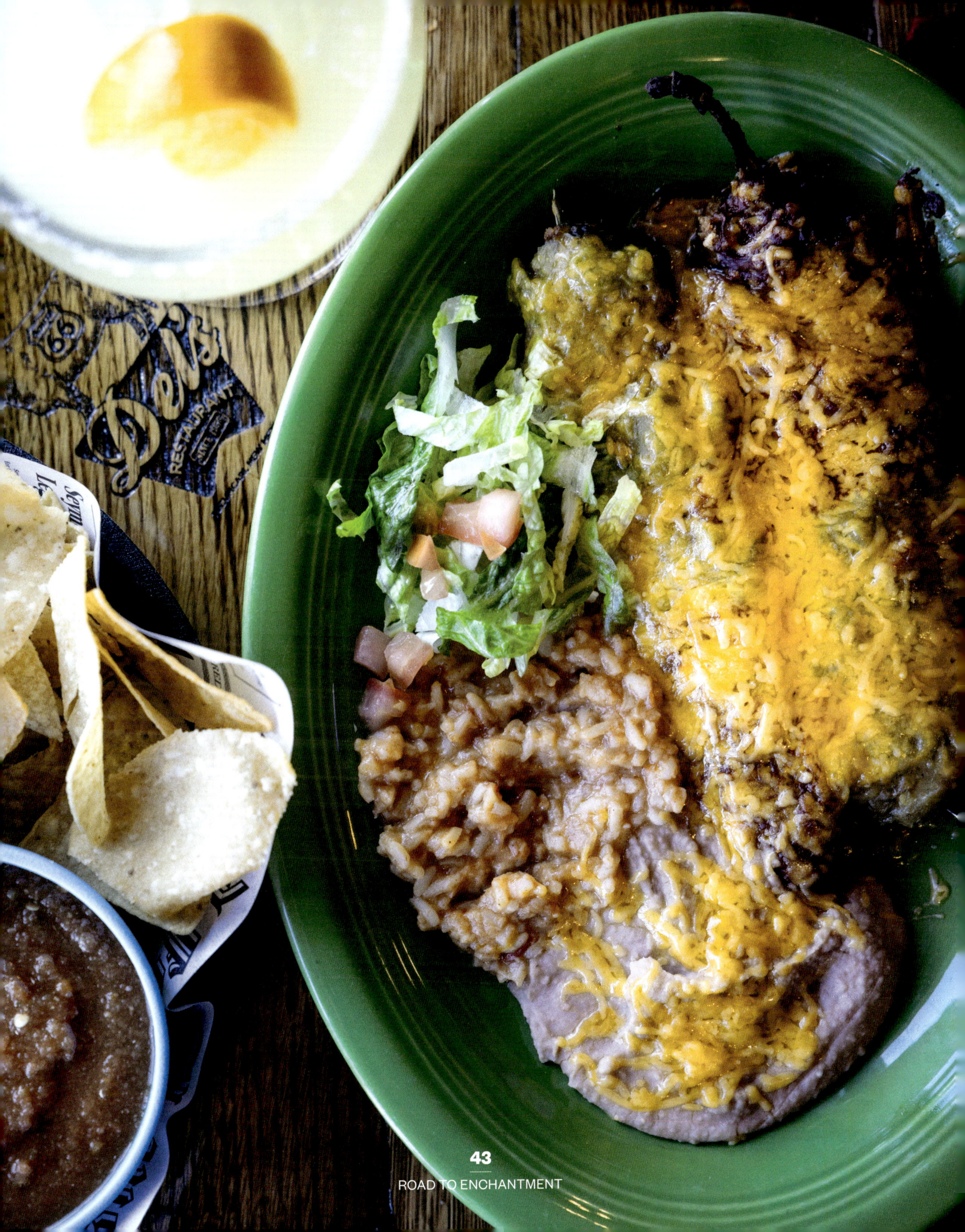
RESTAURANT

3

COMFORT AND JOY

SOUL MATES

Comfort food, pit stops, and road trips make the miles more enjoyable.

By Gwyneth Doland

I was 20 years old when I first cruised into Albuquerque on Route 66, the ribbon of pavement pulling me toward the desert horizon. I arrived road-weary but mesmerized by the neon glow of the diners, shops, and motels along the city's historic 18-mile stretch of the Mother Road. I was wandering the country on a six-week road trip with no itinerary, hunting kitschy souvenirs and 35mm photo ops with every fiberglass dinosaur, giant ball of string, and roadside oddity I could find.

But mostly, I was out for the food.

For two weeks, I rambled all around New Mexico, gorging on green chile cheeseburgers, washing them down with cherry limeades, and dunking sopaipillas in honey and red chile. Somewhere between Tucumcari and Gallup, I got *enchanted*.

I don't know if it was the road, the food, or the people, but all of it felt like the real deal, and it hooked me. A year later, I packed up, drove straight to Albuquerque, rented a house in the South Valley, and landed a job I still brag about: carhop at Mac's Steak in the Rough. More than 30 years later, I drive down the Mother Road every day—and I still think it's cool.

From its earliest years, the road offered a lively mix of diners, cafes, curio shops, and motor courts. Many of the diners served classics like burgers, shakes, and chicken-fried steak. In New Mexico, the star of the menu has always been our beloved chile. From enchiladas and chiles rellenos to carne adovada and burritos, all could be slathered with red, green, or both. Today, it's surprising how many of the road's original diners, restaurants, and cafes are preserved in all their glory, sitting alongside newcomers that deliver fresh thrills.

Not far past the Texas border, Tucumcari overdelivers on the promise of roadside fantasy. On "The Boulevard," as the locals call it, neon still glows at night, buzzing over the Blue Swallow Motel, Motel Safari, and the Roadrunner Lodge Motel. Pop into Tee Pee Curios and you'll get a feel for the town's notorious hospitality: quirky, unhurried, and appreciative of visitors' enthusiasm for this movie set of a town. Dig into a chicken-fried steak at Del's Restaurant or chiles rellenos at the sombrero-shaped La Cita Restaurant for a first real taste of how New Mexico does comfort food.

Down the road in Santa Rosa, car buffs brake for the Route 66 Auto Museum but also for Joseph's Bar and Grill, where the sparkly vinyl booths and chrome-edged tables set the scene for a classic diner spread, including green chile cheeseburgers, root beer floats, and, if you're doing it right, a slice of chocolate cream pie. This is the promise of Route 66: No matter how long the drive, there's always a booth waiting somewhere up ahead.

Now, if I'd been riding the original route in the 1920s or '30s, Santa Rosa is where I'd have veered north toward Santa Fe. I can picture it: rattling along a barely paved track in the rumble seat of a Ford Model A. No doubt I

R
Motorists have long been drawn to Tucumcari's iconic Tee Pee Curios for souvenirs, Native jewelry, and neon razzle-dazzle.

PREVIOUS SPREAD:
Listed on the National Register of Historic Places, Richardson's Trading Post in Gallup is filled with 3,000 Navajo rugs and case after case of jewelry, pottery, and tooled leather saddles (left). Since 1956, Del's Restaurant in Tucumcari has been serving heaping helpings of comfort food, including the best-selling chile relleno plate (right).

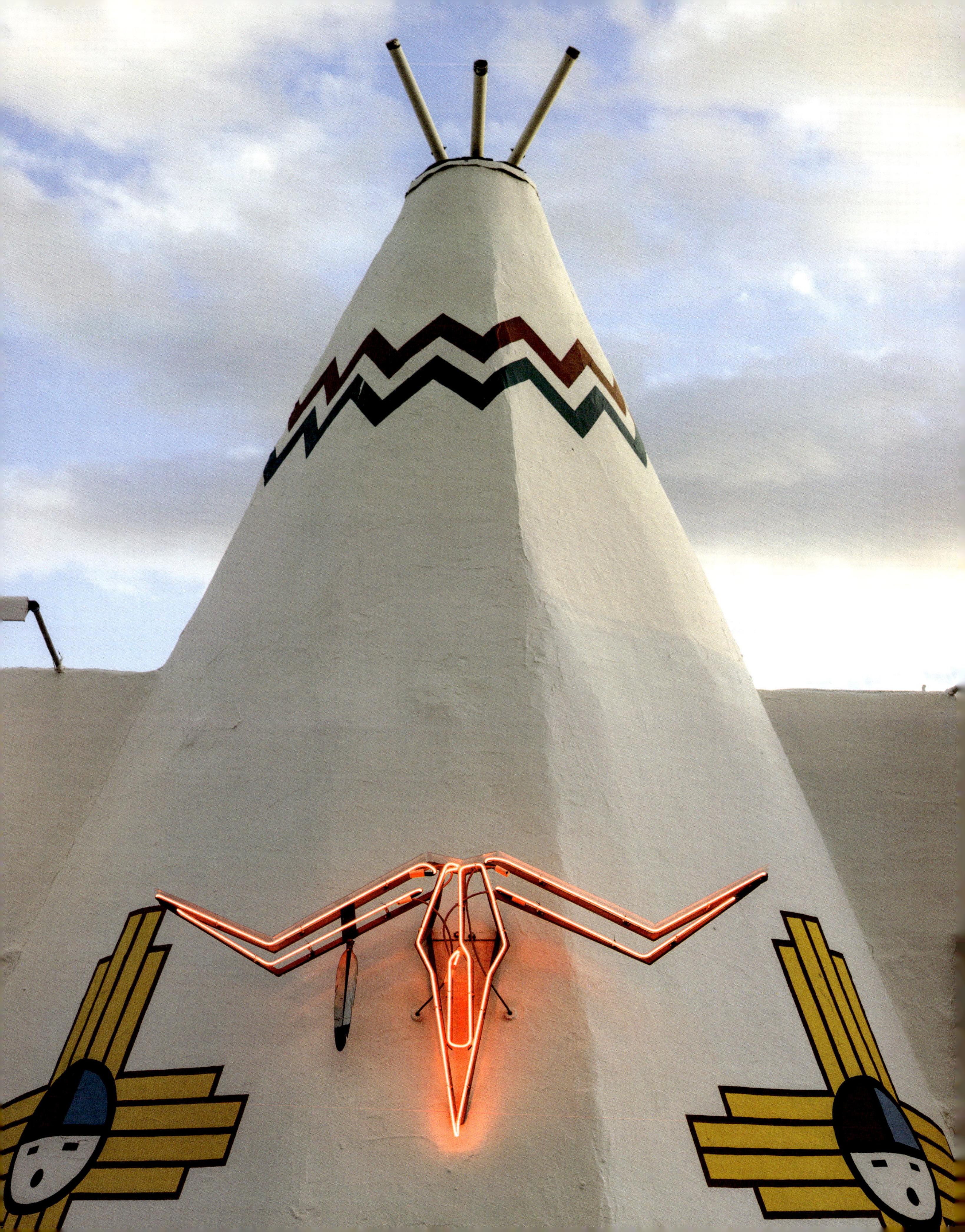

3

COMFORT AND JOY

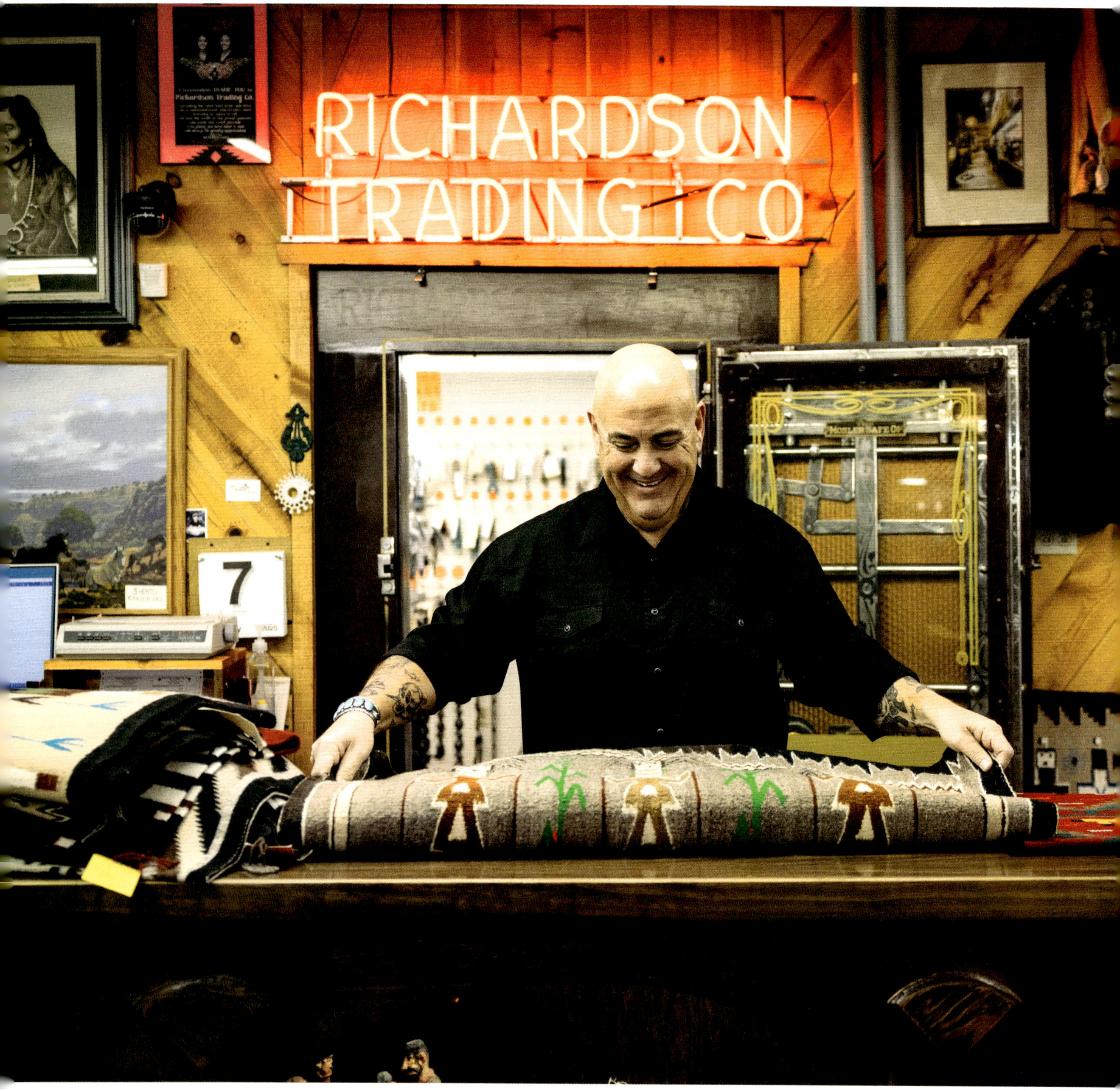

46

ROAD TO ENCHANTMENT

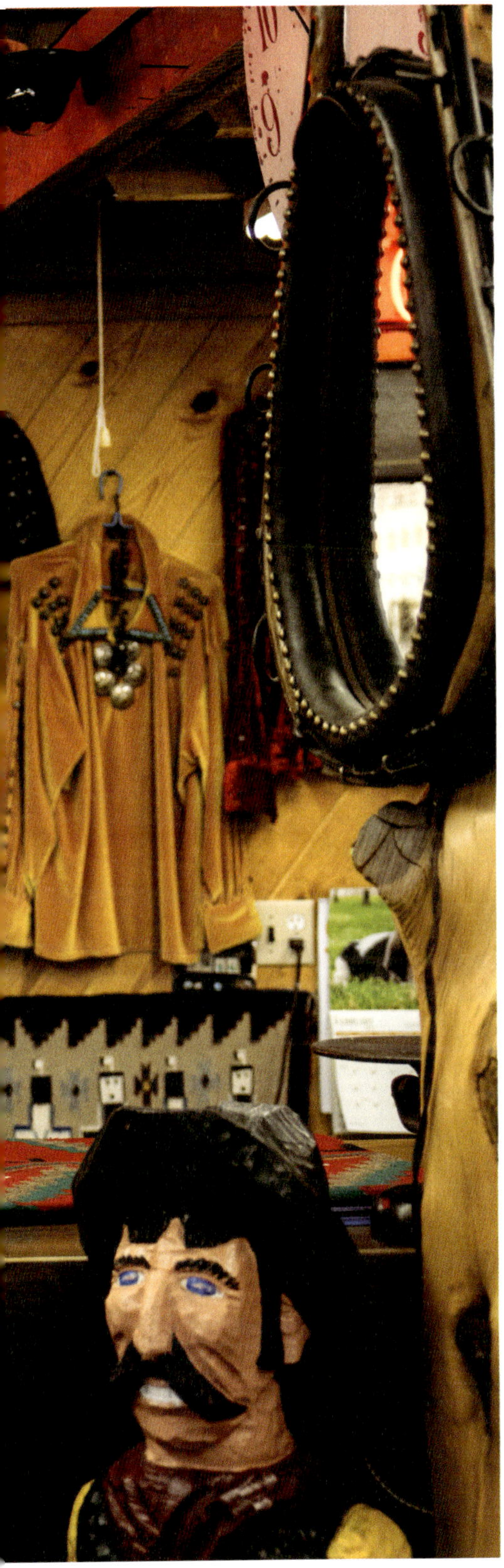

would have ached for the rare pit stops along the way. Today, Harry's Roadhouse inhabits one of those old gas stations, and I always feel restored by a plate of Harry's blue corn waffles or famous turkey enchiladas. It's the same vibe at the Pink Adobe's Dragon Room, where I've had many a much-needed cheeseburger and margarita after a long day of reporting at the Roundhouse. I especially love La Plazuela, the interior courtyard cafe at La Fonda on the Plaza, where I can't resist the chiles rellenos.

Although Santa Fe is where I've spent a lot of my time working, Albuquerque has always been home. The day after I moved here, I had lunch at Lindy's Diner, which tearfully closed in April 2026. For me, the next best thing to home cooking is the food at mom-and-pop spots like Mary & Tito's Cafe, the Barelas Coffee House, and Mac's La Sierra—places where the chile hits strong and the coffee is mild enough to drink by the carafe.

When I was young, I'd stumble into the western-themed Frontier Restaurant at 2 a.m. after seeing bands play nearby; now I work across the street at the University of New Mexico and am more likely to meet a colleague for huevos rancheros under my favorite John Wayne fan art.

In the decade since I moved to the North Valley, things have changed a lot along Albuquerque's stretch of Route 66. Midcentury fervor has sparked multimillion-dollar renovations of roadside motels like the Imperial, now home to a sparkling dive bar and mini food hall, and Arrive, with its poolside DWTNR Cocktail Bar & Lounge. On bring-your-own-vinyl night at Hotel Zazz, the scene spills easily toward dinner. Maybe that's at my special splurge, the James Beard–nominated Mesa Provisions.

My favorite glow up is El Vado Motel, the first place I ever stayed in Albuquerque, back when the neon was glitchy and a tiny, spare room cost $30 a night. In 2018, the motel reopened with upscale rooms and suites with historic touches. Even better, the parking lot is now a patio gathering space and some rooms have been converted into a tap room, mini restaurants, and artisan shops.

Albuquerque's burgeoning speakeasy revival has repurposed old Route 66 gas stations and restaurants into cozy, cool hangouts. I love the secret/semi-secret/not-at-all-secret cocktail bars Teddy Roe's, Fat Frank's, Founders Speakeasy, and the fabulously retro Daydream Rum Bar, where I recently ended a brutal workday with a shockingly good tropical old-fashioned.

Back in the golden age of the old road, the trek west of Albuquerque offered natural and cultural wonders, quirky trading posts, and cozy cafes, and much of that remains. In Grants, El Cafecito has been serving local classics for more than 40 years. The newer Junkyard on 66 is a busy brewery and barbecue restaurant decorated with hubcaps and devoted to the Mother Road.

Long a center of hospitality and commerce for western New Mexico, the Navajo Nation, and nearby pueblos, Gallup is also home to some of the best Native arts in the country. Dozens of trading posts, including standouts such as Perry Null Trading, Ellis Tanner Trading, and Richardson's Trading Post, have deep ties to Navajo, Hopi, and Zuni artists, with knowledgeable salespeople eager to help deliver a little retail endorphin rush.

On a recent drive through Gallup, my family and I stopped at the historic El Rancho Hotel, which is decorated with headshots of Hollywood stars who stayed here while shooting Westerns in the 1940s and '50s. My son rolled his eyes as I swooned over a snap of dreamy Kirk Douglas, but the kid sure slayed a plate of chicken fingers in the hotel cafe.

Maybe the highlight of your trip will be a perfectly puffed sopaipilla, a crunchy chicharrón, an epic sunset, or a scorpion immobilized in a resin paperweight. At the very least, you'll leave New Mexico with a full belly and a bursting camera roll. At most, we'll see you sporting some fresh turquoise and carrying a six-pack from Marble Brewery on your way to the cookout.

Route 66 has a way of pointing you back this way every time. ✶

L
Billy Keeler, owner of Richardson's Trading Post, continues the family business started in 1913.

GWYNETH DOLAND is a writer, traveler, lover of chicharrones, and professor of practice in journalism at the University of New Mexico.

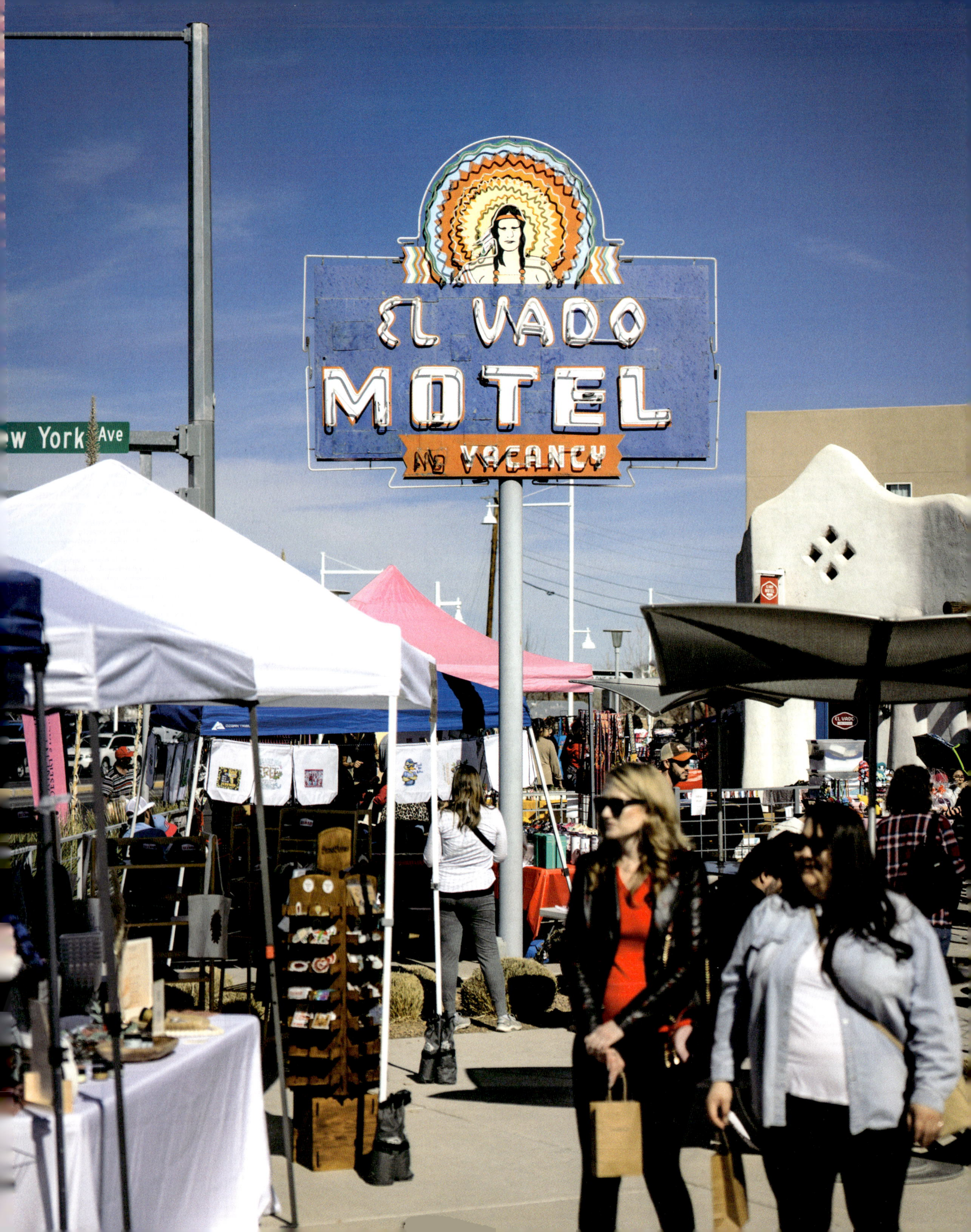
EL VADO
MOTEL
NO VACANCY
w York Ave

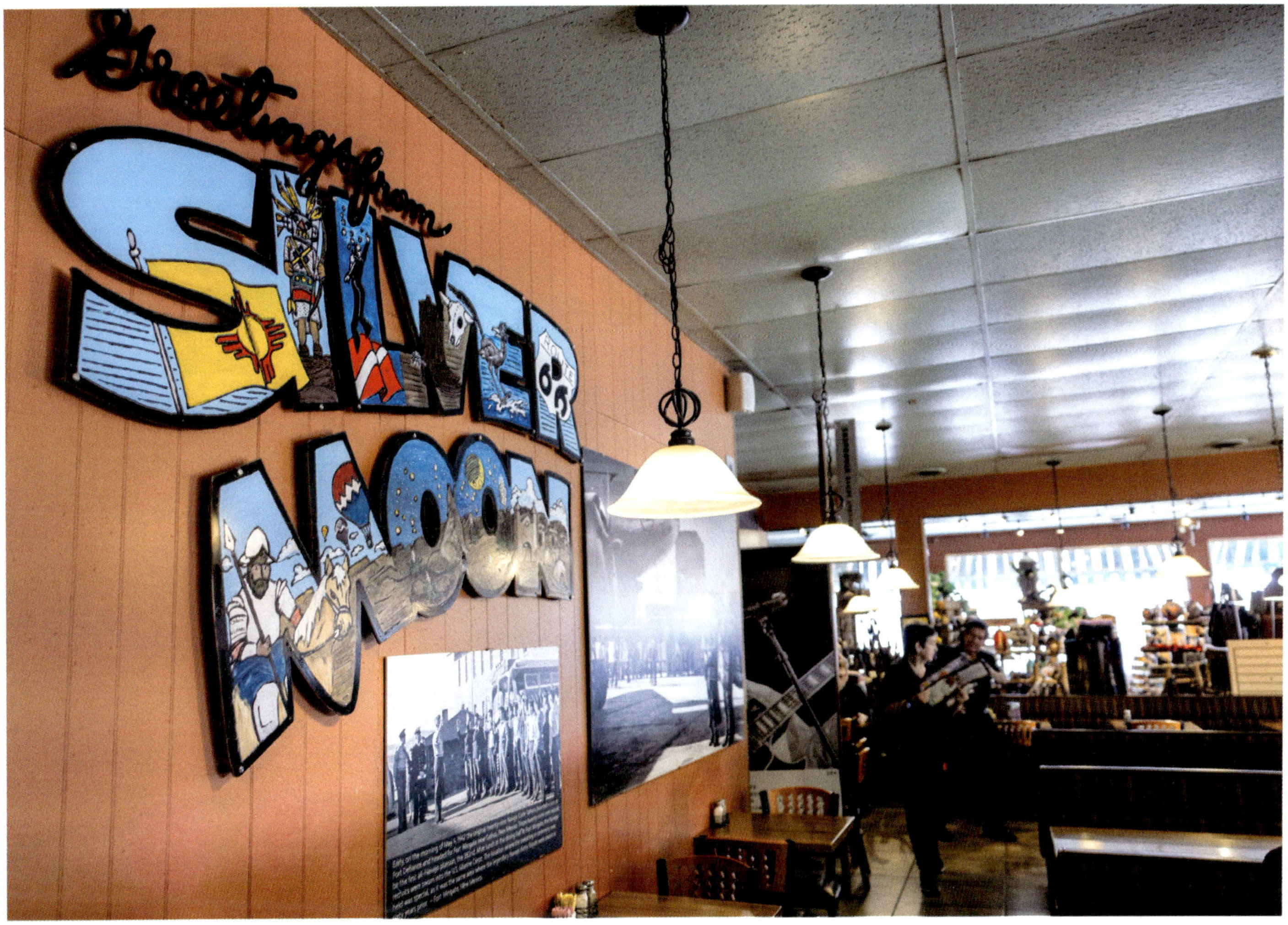

L
With a tap house, mini food pods, and live music on the busy patio that once served as a parking lot, the renovated 1927 El Vado Motel is an Albuquerque hot spot.

R
After filling up on blue corn chicken enchiladas or a double-patty Route 66 Burger at the Silver Moon Café in Santa Rosa, head to a gift shop overflowing with jewelry, books, and souvenirs.

> “Our mantra is ‘community first.’ We wanted this to be a community gathering place, a hip and cozy neighborhood hangout where people can bike in, grab a beer, and relax.”
>
> **— NATE VALDEZ, FORMER AREA GENERAL MANAGER FOR PALINDROME, WHICH OWNS EL VADO MOTEL**

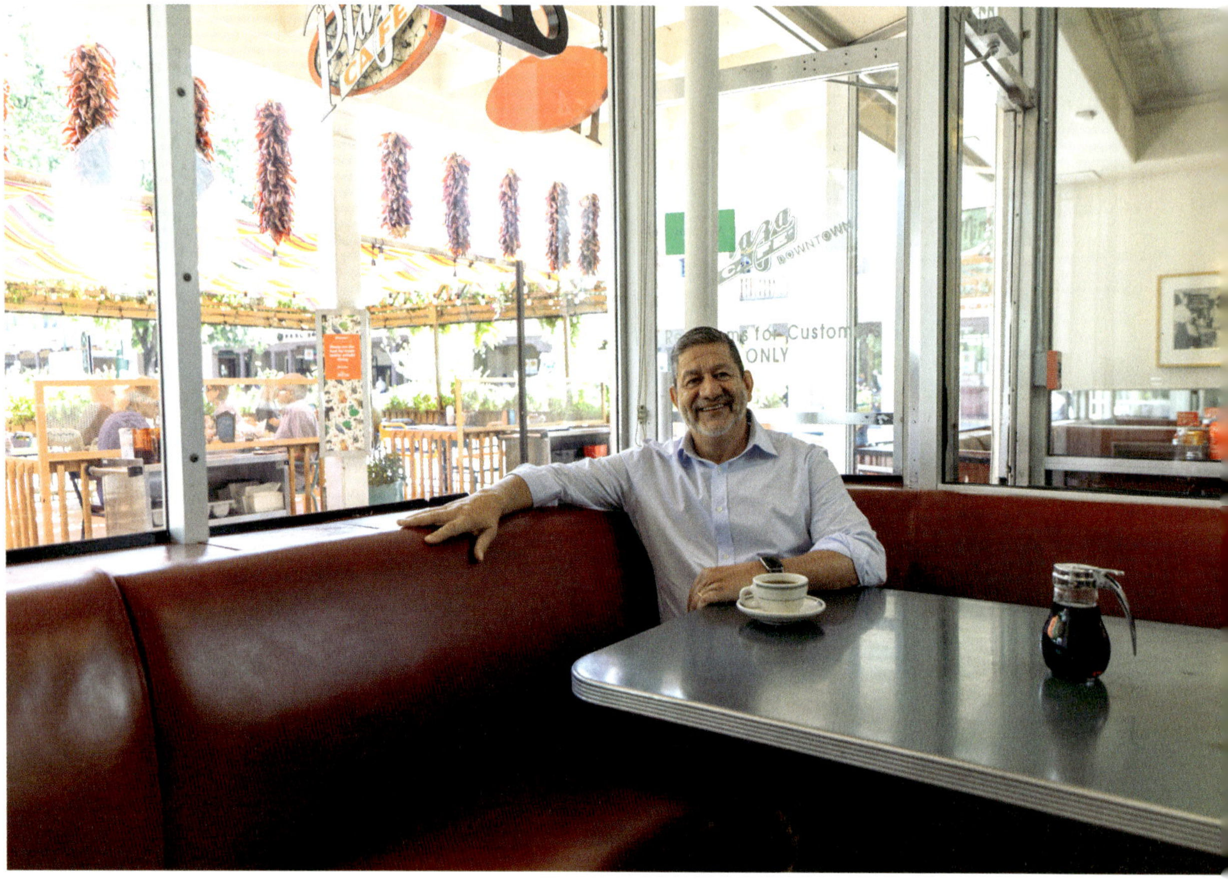

L
Plaza Cafe owner Leonardo Razatos's family has operated the downtown Santa Fe restaurant since 1947, serving traditional New Mexican and Greek dishes (top). Leticia Romero, chef and owner of Isleta Grill on Isleta Pueblo, has twice won the New Mexico State Fair Green Chile Cheeseburger Challenge (bottom left). Romero insists there is no secret ingredient in Isleta Grill's burger (bottom right). "I think it all comes back to heart and love," she says.

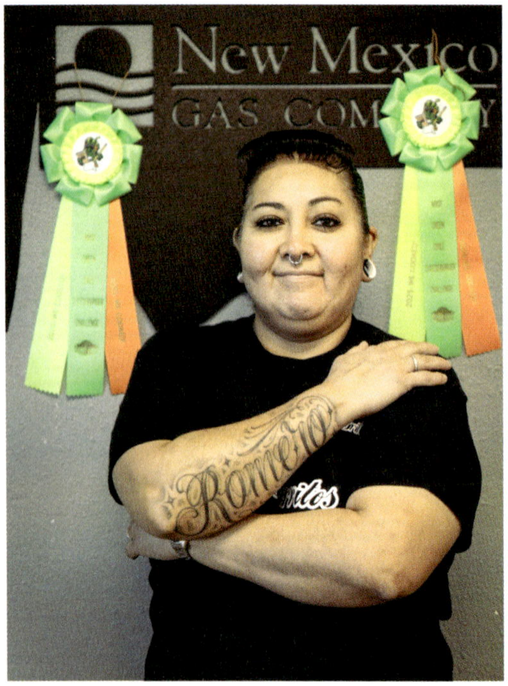

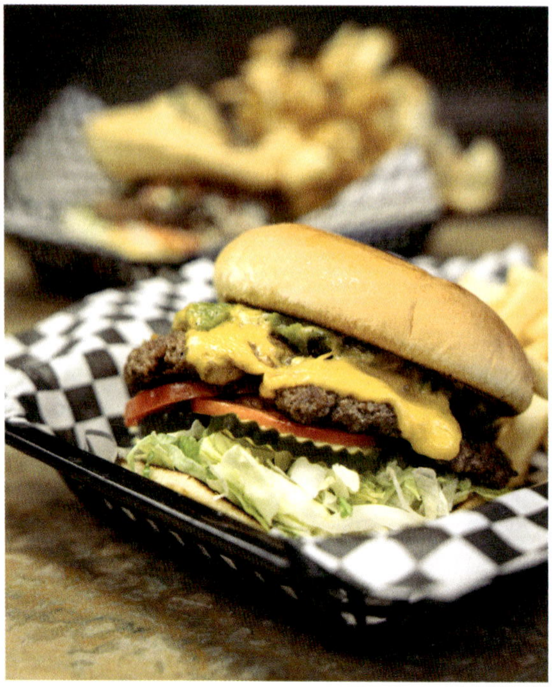

R
In 2019, Jacob Fox opened the quirky And Stuff Retail Collective on Central Avenue in Albuquerque's Nob Hill neighborhood. "There are so many makers doing cool stuff in Albuquerque and New Mexico," he says. "We want to highlight them and support them as much as we can."

PLAZA CAFE: GABRIELLA MARKS

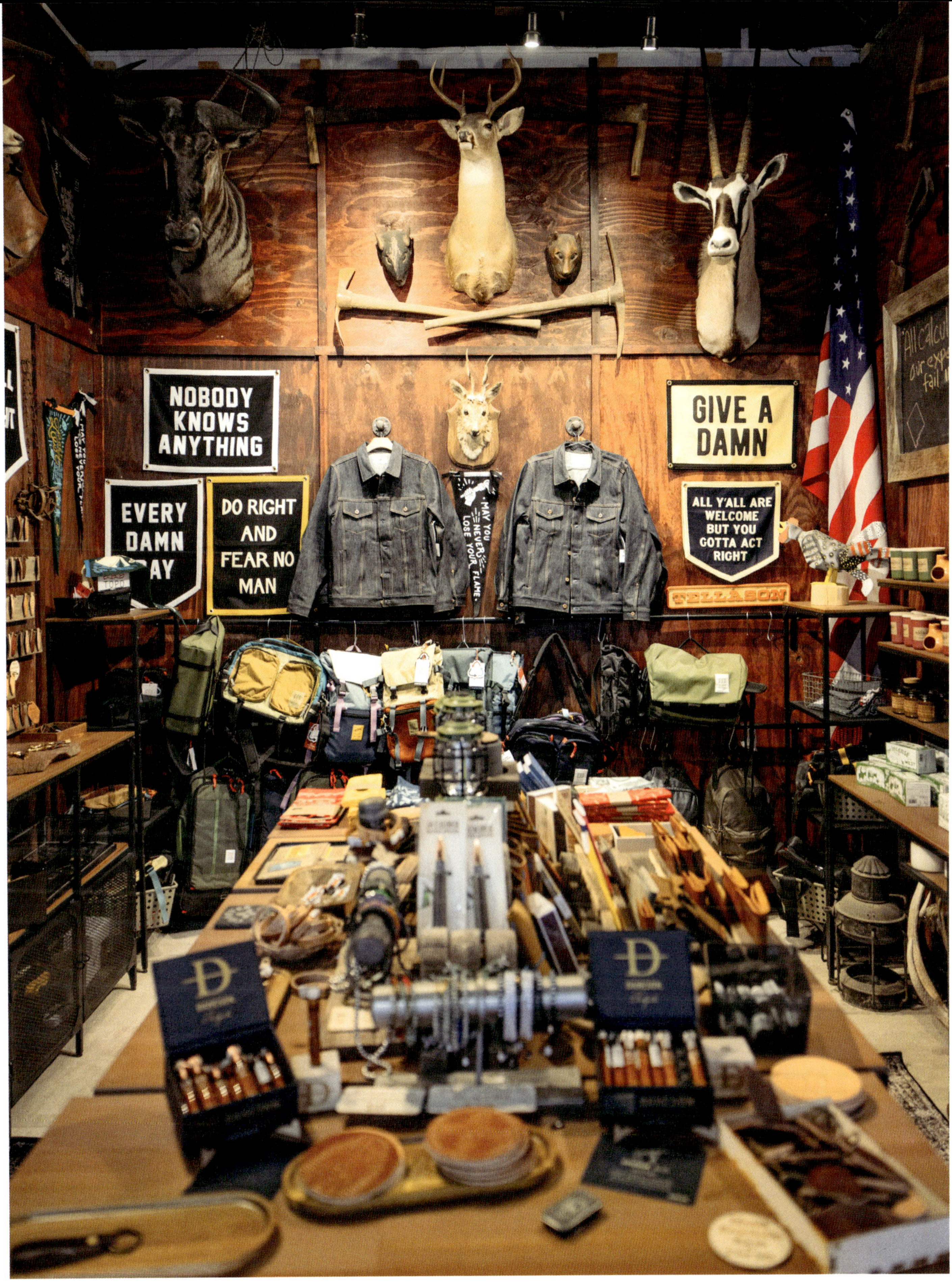
NOBODY KNOWS ANYTHING
EVERY DAMN
DO RIGHT AND FEAR NO MAN
MAY YOU NEVER LOSE YOUR FLAME
GIVE A DAMN
ALL Y'ALL ARE WELCOME BUT YOU GOTTA ACT RIGHT
TELLASON

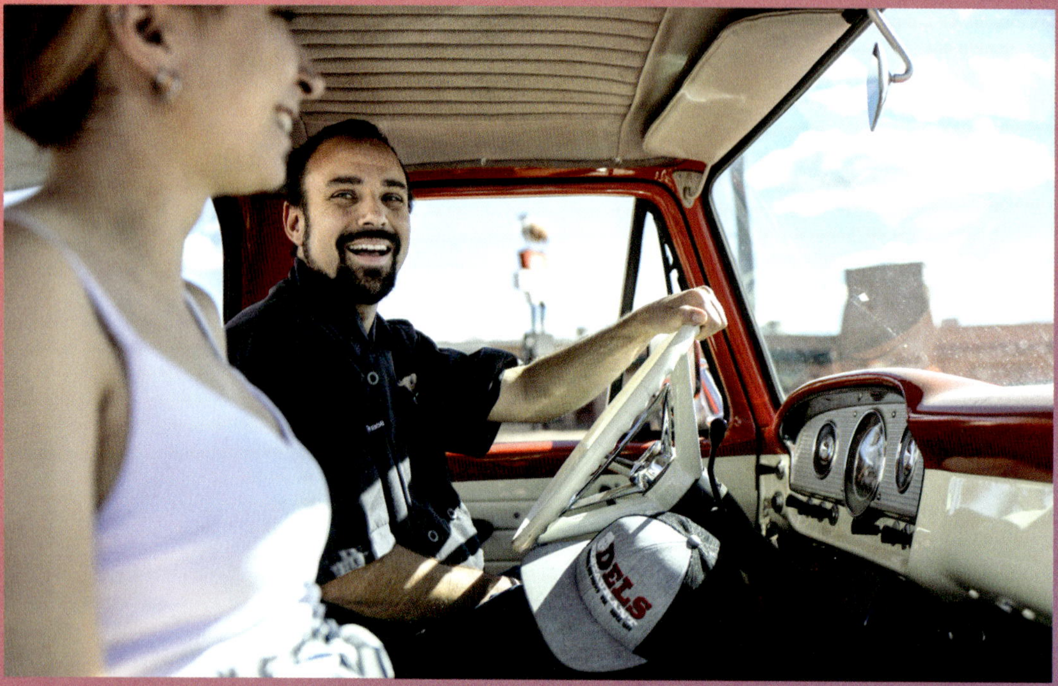

Chase Waters

The former Del's Restaurant employee has not changed much about the Tucumcari landmark since taking over.

CHASE WATERS WAS A TEENAGER when he started working at Del's Restaurant in Tucumcari, opened by Del Akin in 1956 and still serving its signature chicken-fried steak and other home-cooked food. Del's original neon sign, topped by a Hereford bull, still beckons travelers to this community hub. Route 66 travelers stop in for directions, information, friendly recommendations on what to do and see, and plates piled high with food. Waters, whose family has deep roots in Tucumcari, bought the restaurant in 2021 because he'd always loved it. He's hardly changed a thing, except to bring back breakfast. "Del's is a big part of Route 66 history and our town's history," he says.

L
Chase Waters and his wife, D'Naylie, ride in his vintage Ford F-100.

R
Shake off any dust from the road with a refreshing margarita at Del's Restaurant in Tucumcari.

Our chicken-fried steak is popular, but depending on where people are from, they'll lean more toward our New Mexican–style chile relleno.

We call Route 66 "The Boulevard" here.

It's always been the same, dating back to when my parents were in high school and used to cruise The Boulevard in the evening, with all the neon glow. It's still a thing that high schoolers do as well as tourists.

My grandfather owned a Phillips 66 station here on Route 66. I know about the devastation and hurt that came upon his business and other businesses around here when I-40 came in.

Route 66 lets people slow down and take in the beauty of the land, all across the state. People enjoy their time, slowing down and appreciating the small things instead of always going, going, going.

I still have my grandfather's old pickup truck, a Ford F-100. He bought it brand new, and sometimes I park it in front of the restaurant. ✴

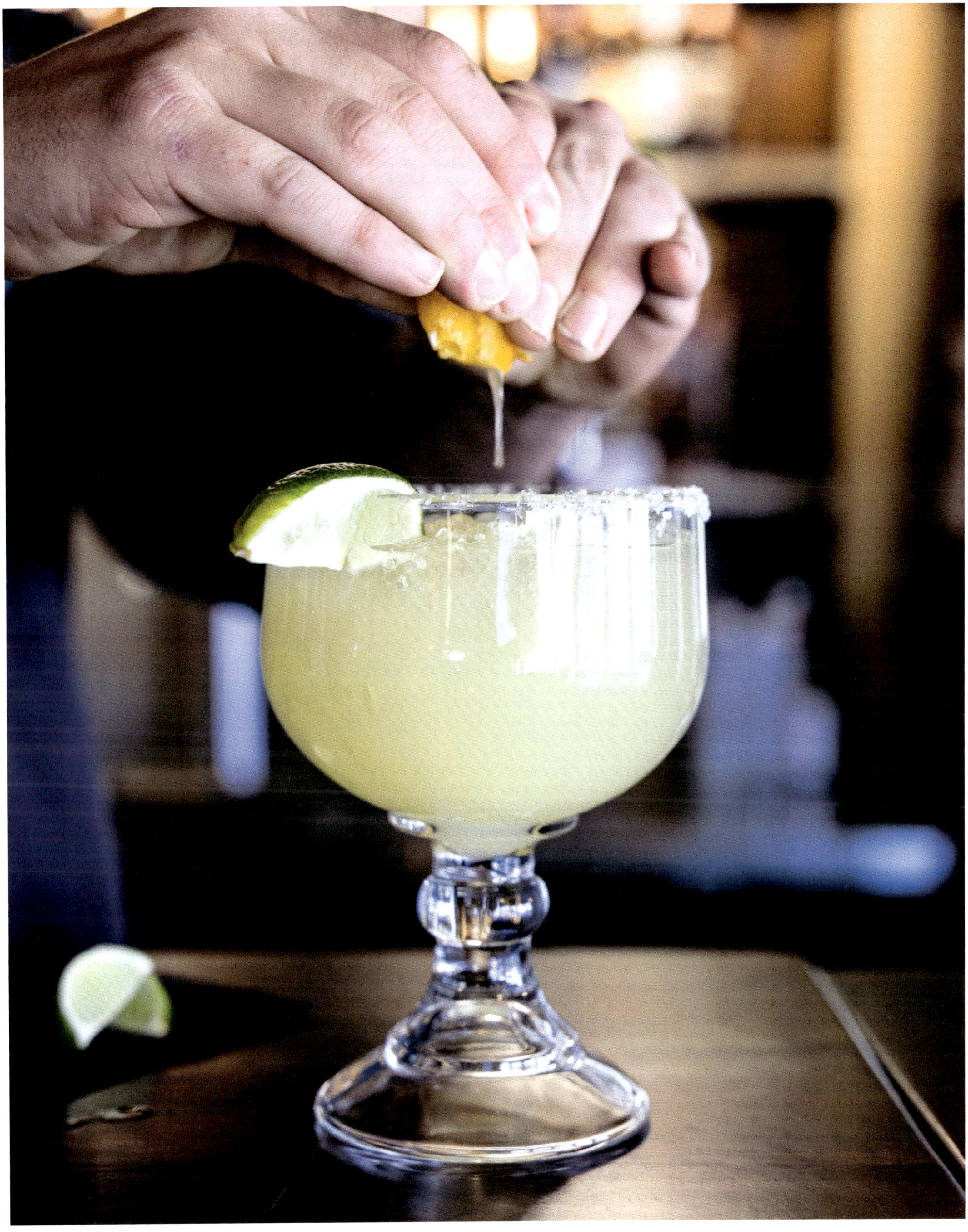

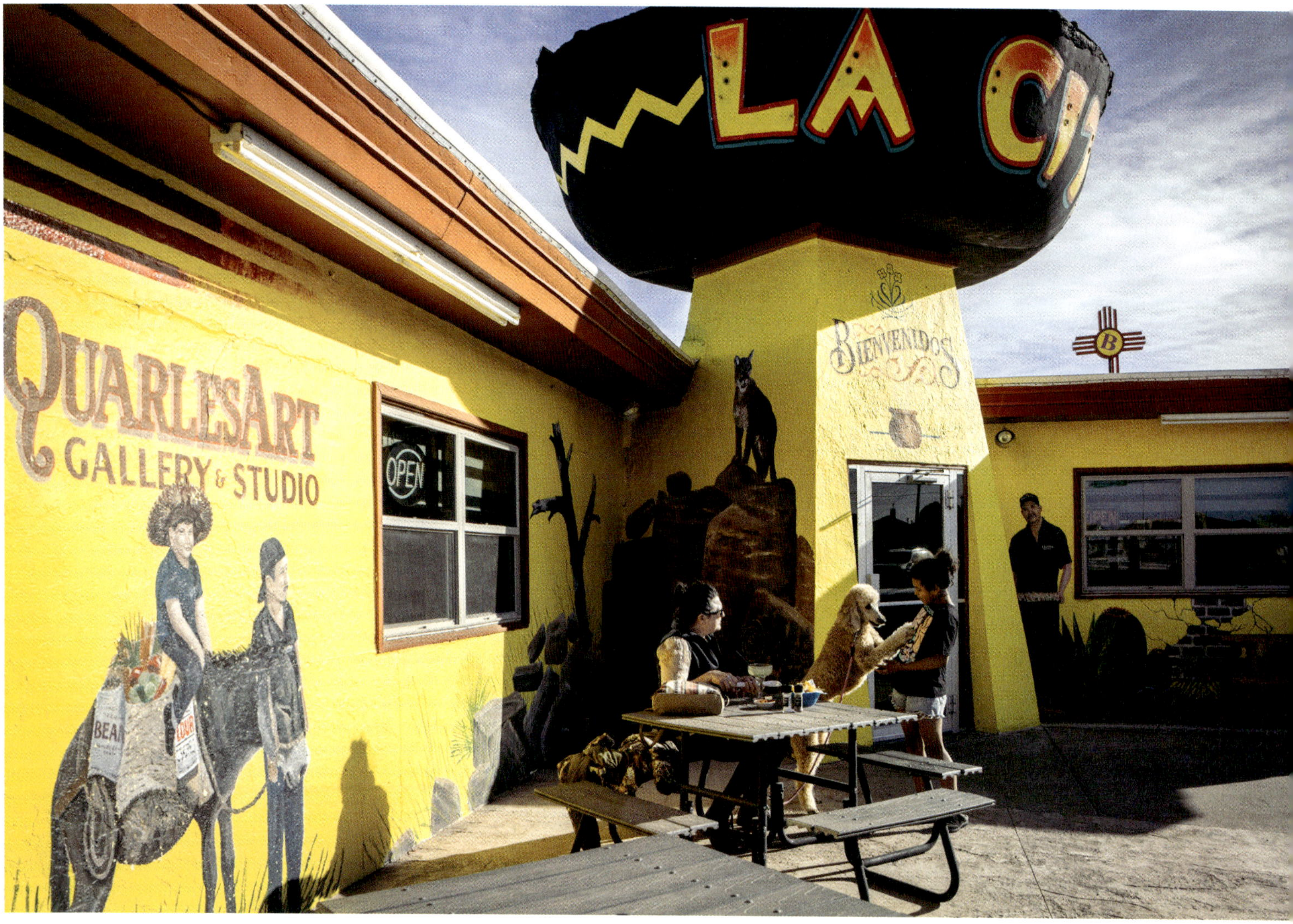

L
Even with all of Tucumcari's neon bling, the sombrero-shaped La Cita Restaurant still stands out for its red and green—chile, that is.

R
The recipe for carne adovada at Joseph's Bar and Grill in Santa Rosa has been passed down for generations.

"

The most famous dish we have with Route 66 travelers, especially those who can handle the heat of New Mexico chile, is our carne adovada. It's an old recipe from the founding owner, Joseph Campos Sr."

—RICARDO MARTINEZ, WHO'S WORKED AT JOSEPH'S BAR AND GRILL IN SANTA ROSA FOR 14 YEARS

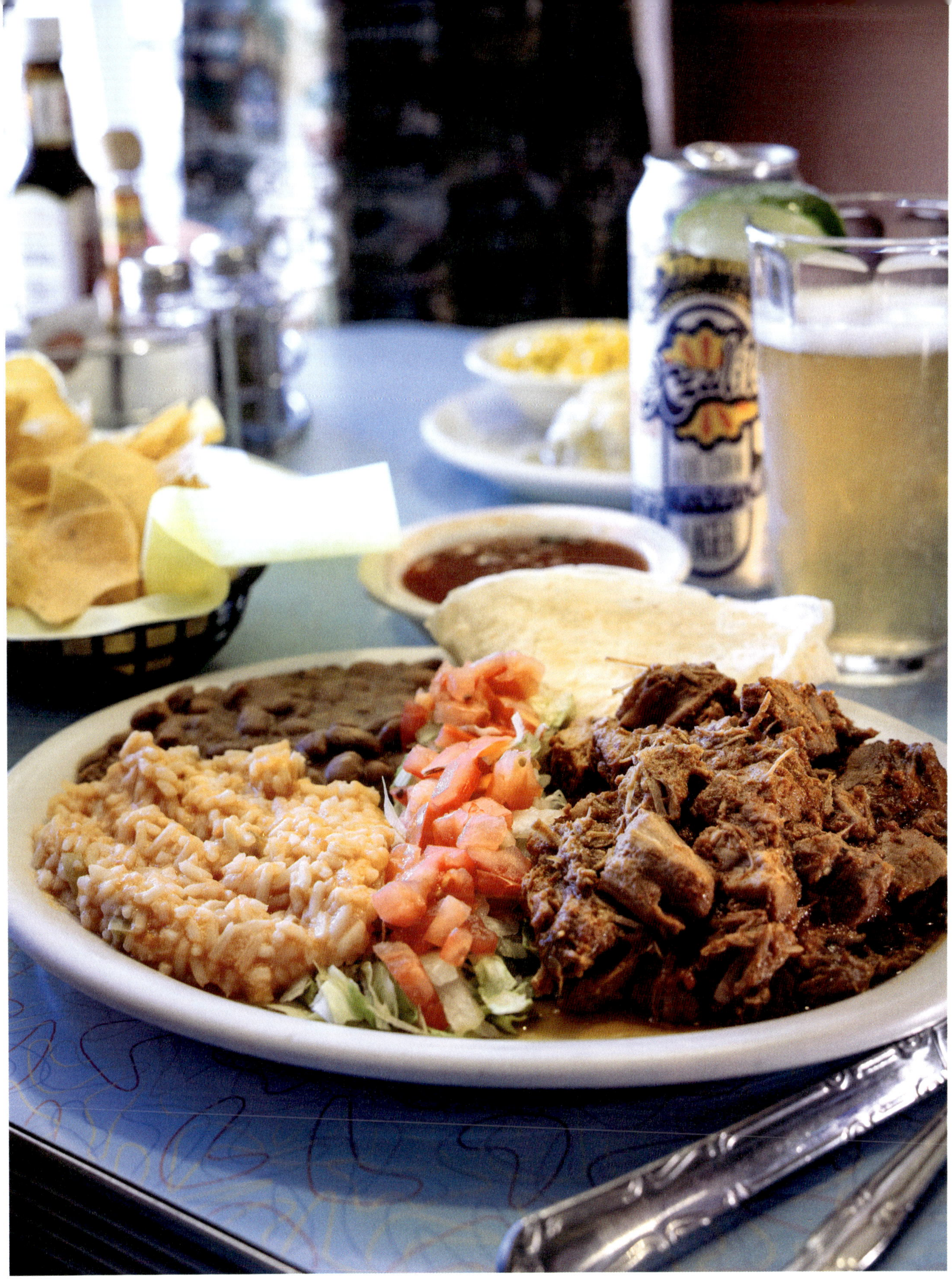

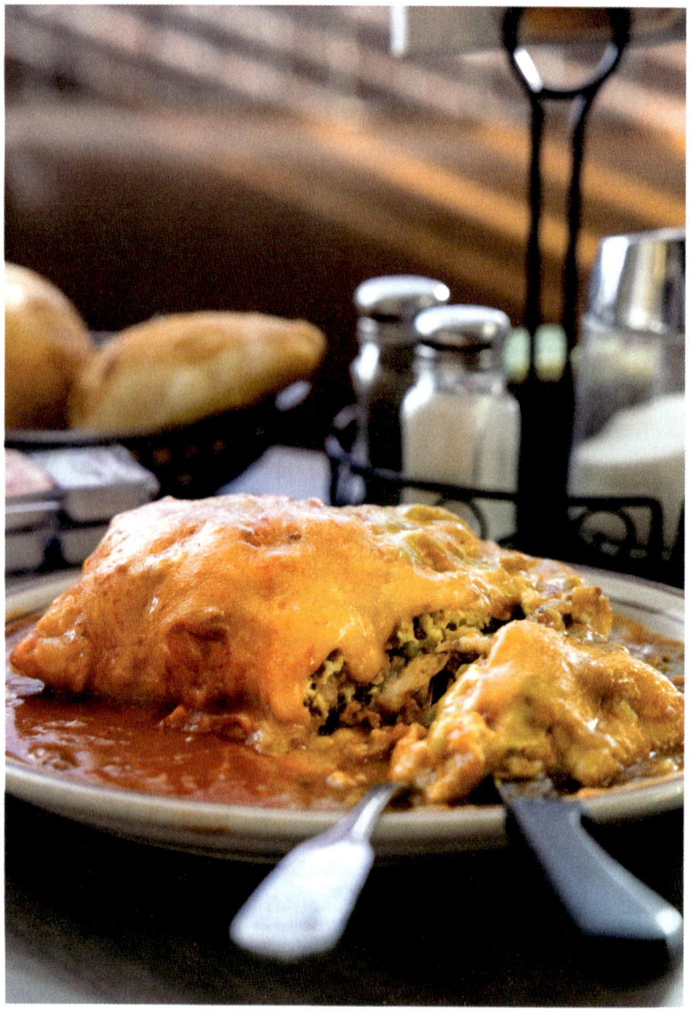

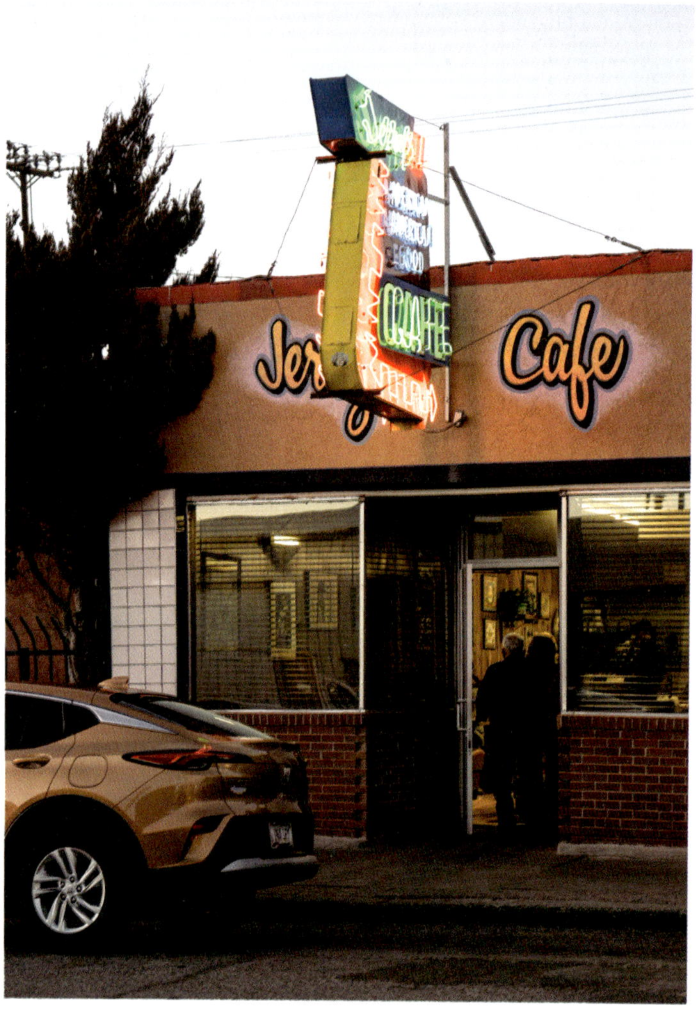

L
Follow the bright yellow arrow (right) to the legendary Jerry's Cafe in Gallup, where the breakfast burrito is a great way to start the day (left).

R
The country-fried steak with gravy lures customers to Earl's Family Restaurant in Gallup, as does the turquoise awning over the entrance.

TRADITION IN EVERY BITE

Gallup's homestyle favorites are more than what's on the menu.

Long known as the Gateway to Native America, Gallup is also famous for good eats. Since 1976, diners at Jerry's Cafe have tackled giant platefuls of chile rellenos and flat cheese enchiladas smothered in red chile, made from scratch using Hatch pods. "We pride ourselves in the quality of the food," says Jerry's owner Archie Baca. Earl's Family Restaurant, in business since 1947, is equally treasured for frybread-wrapped Navajo burgers and country-fried steak and gravy. Customers can buy handmade Native jewelry directly from artists who walk from table to table. Owner Ralph Richards says customers appreciate the chance to shop, eat, and talk with local Navajo, Santo Domingo, Zuni, and Hopi artists. "Almost everybody leaves here with some kind of souvenir," he says. ✶

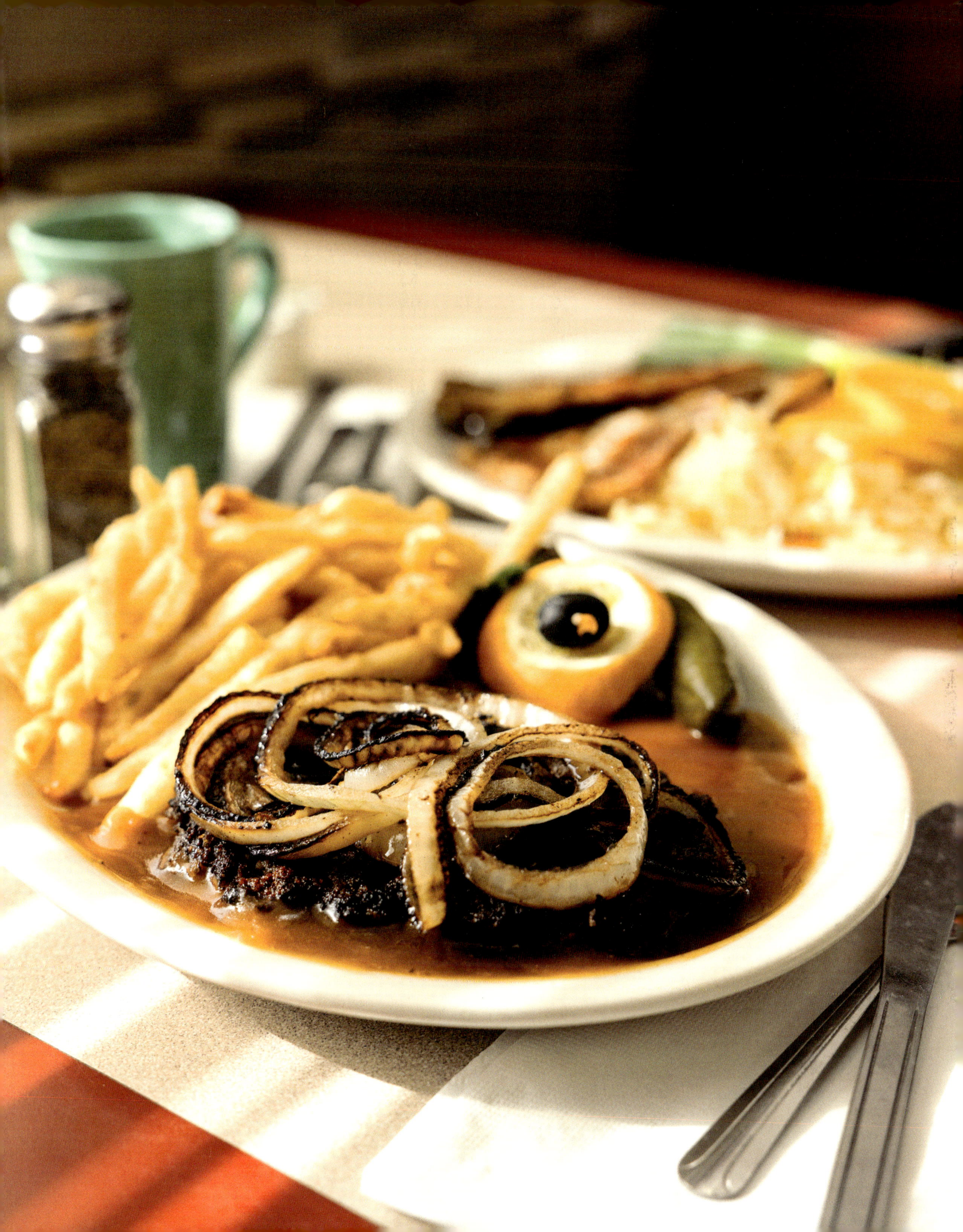

Christy and Summer Willis

The mother-and-daughter team steers the family's 66 Diner, a treasured Albuquerque throwback serving tasty burgers, handmade milkshakes, and heaps of nostalgia since 1987.

THE BRIGHT NEON GLOW of the 66 Diner tempts people to step inside and travel back to the 1950s. A jukebox, an old-fashioned soda fountain, and a riot of colorful road signs, license plates, and other memorabilia fill every available space. The restaurant is the vision of Tom and Christy Willis, who transformed what had been built as a Phillips 66 station in 1945 into a *Happy Days* revival. After Tom passed away in 2021, Christy and their daughter Summer have kept the wheels turning with plates piled high and a warm welcome to Route 66 motorists from around the world who roll in for an authentic taste of Americana.

R
The 66 Diner duo, Summer Willis, left, and her mom, Christy Willis, keeps the Route 66 spirit flourishing.

SUMMER WILLIS

The 66 Diner building was a transmission shop when my parents bought it—a big white building that got my dad's wheels spinning.

My dad was always an avid collector of road signs, license plates. He loved the music of the Route 66 era, the cars, the style. It was just his fun thing.

The Pez dispensers that he collected are all up on the ceiling.

When my parents first opened the diner, it was my dad's whole goal to stay as true as possible to that era, while obviously being in a new era.

With the decor, the style of our building, the way we make our milkshakes by hand, it's a bit of a throwback.

We're in the middle of a city that's grown up around us, and here we are with historical signs. We're kind of like a beacon.

The majority of the tourists are European and Asian— people from China, South Korea, Japan, Australia, Germany.

Our vanilla milkshake is our biggest seller. Our 66 Burger with bacon, chile, and cheese is our biggest shebang. We have a lot of liver and onion lovers, and I will never understand it.

My daughter Piper, who's 3, is with me at the diner all the time. She already takes people their milkshakes. She loves it. My dad used to make me do that as a kid. I enjoy the love of Route 66 and passing it down to future generations.

CHRISTY WILLIS

Tom was an avid Route 66 person. It was something that interested him and that he really loved.

I love our trademark Route 66 Pileup. It's a breakfast dish with eggs, bacon, green chile, and potatoes—a deconstructed burrito piled on a plate.

Our banana split has nine scoops of ice cream, two bananas, pineapple, cherries, peanuts, caramel sauce, and an entire can of whipped cream.

People come specifically for it.

Our menu says you need to share it, but they order it for one and then you should see their faces when they get it.

I'm always intrigued by how people find us.

People bring their travel books and guidebooks from their country, and they show us that we're in them. Sometimes they want to take your picture and have you sign their book. It's always really fun. ✶

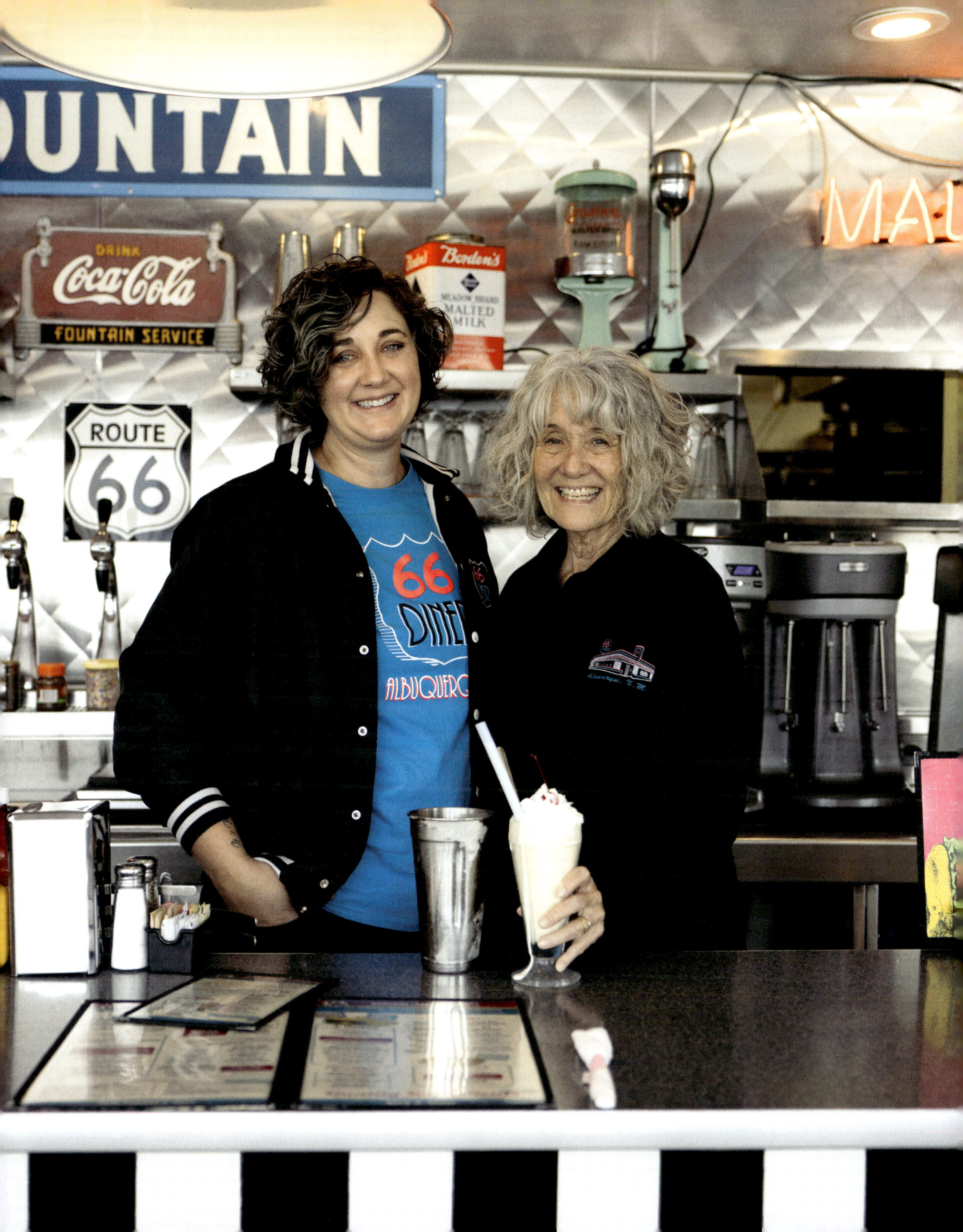
DRINK
Coca-Cola
FOUNTAIN SERVICE
Borden's
MEADOW BRAND
MALTED MILK
ROUTE
66

L
In Santa Fe, the Pink Adobe still serves some of the same dishes, including Steak Dunigan, enjoyed by road-trippers on the original 1926 alignment (top left). It has also added elevated dishes such as barramundi with spiced carrot coulis (top right). Stop for a World Famous Laguna Burger at the original Laguna Pueblo location inside the 66 Pit Stop (below).

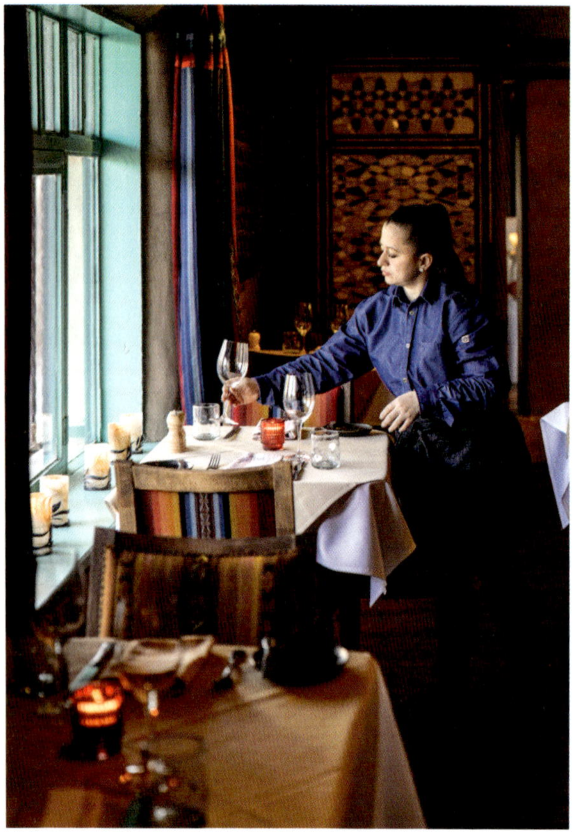

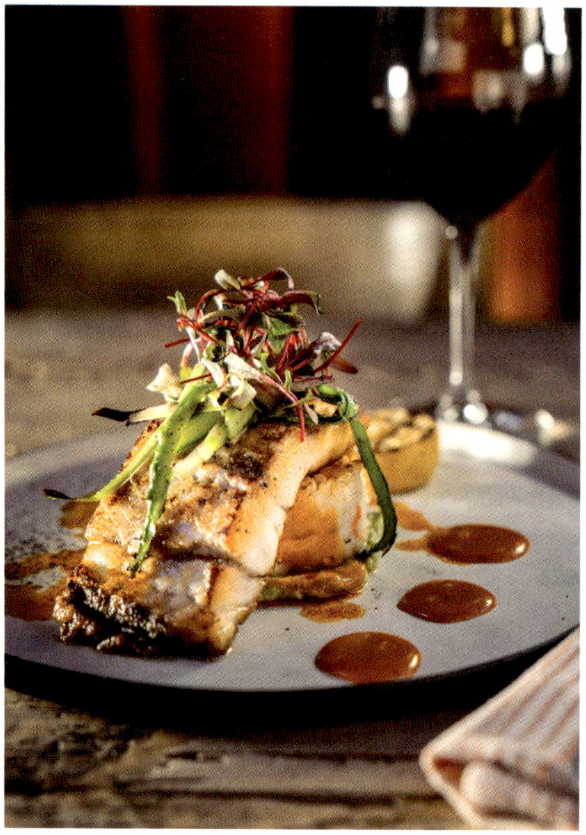

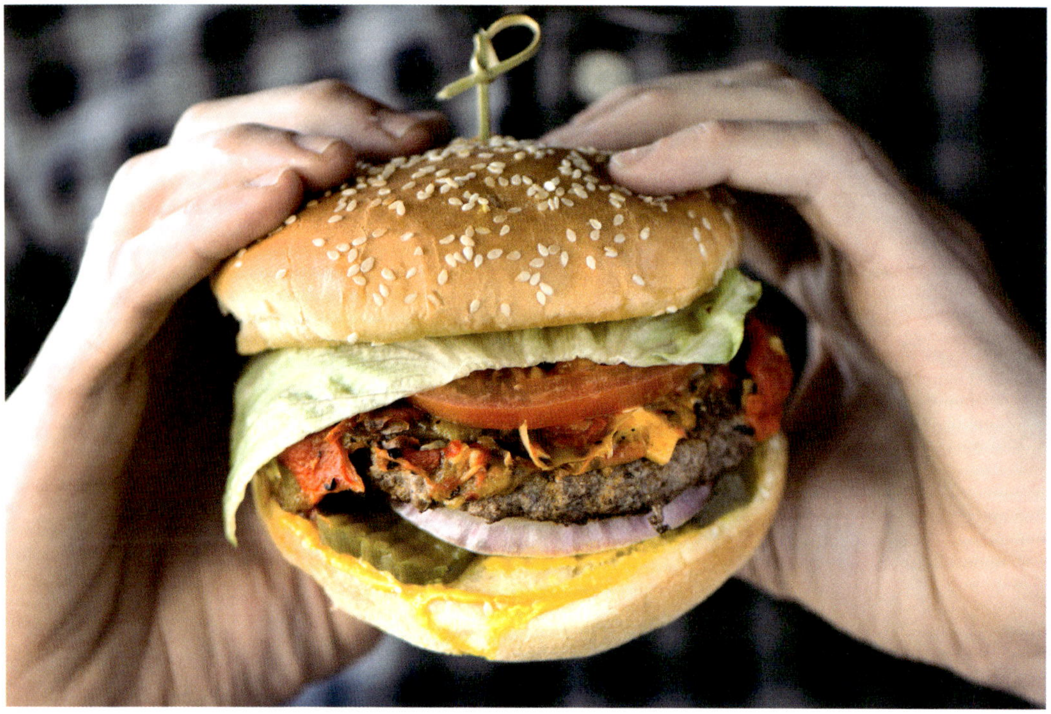

R
The 1926 alignment through Santa Fe runs past Tin-Nee-Ann Trading Co., which has specialized in Native jewelry, souvenirs, and nostalgia since 1968. "A lot of our customers are European travelers interested in Route 66," says co-owner Jo Christen, whose mother opened the shop. Christen's daughter, Emilie Boggs, is a co-owner.

LAGUNA BURGER: DOUGLAS MERRIAM

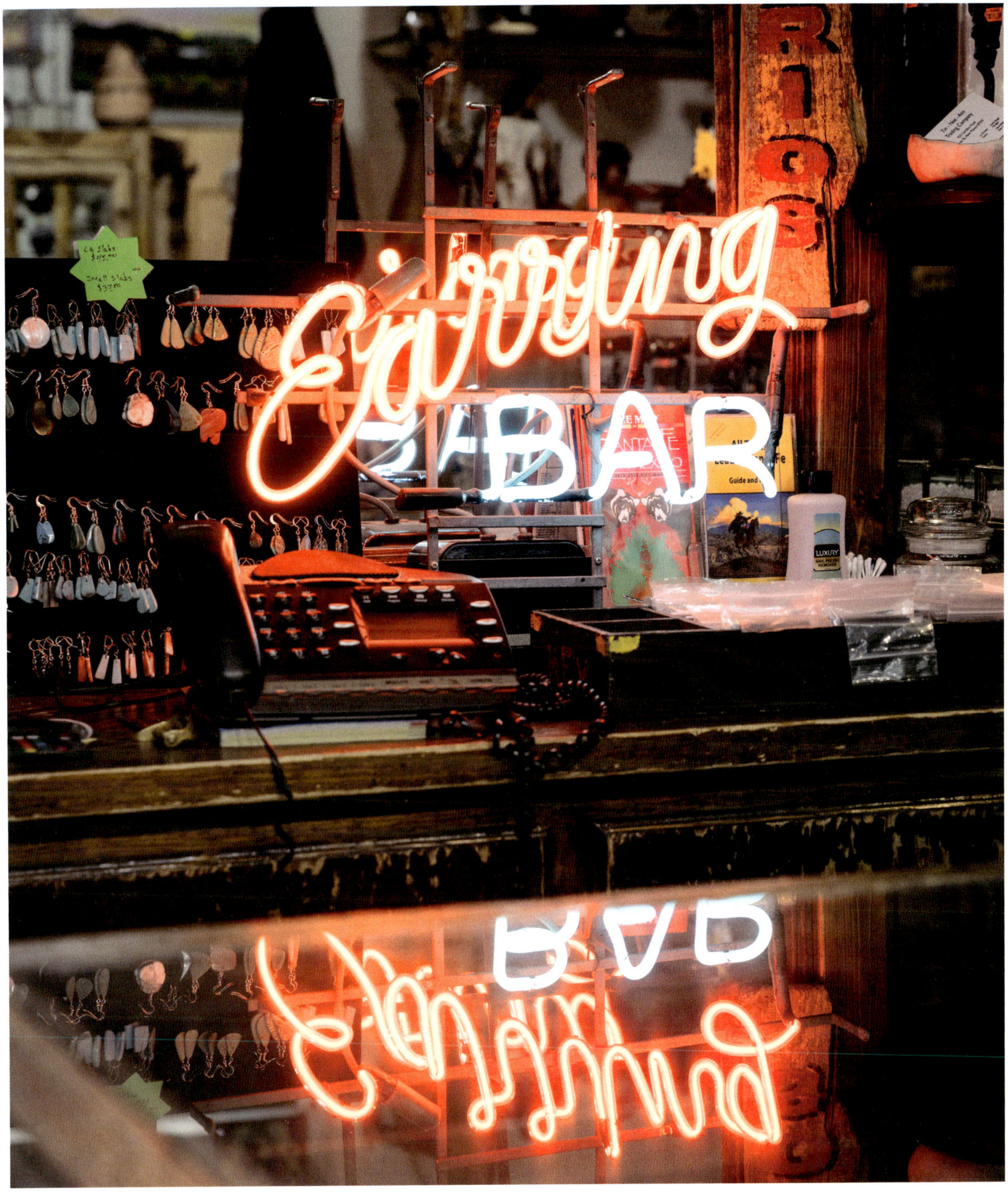
Earring
BAR
LUXURY

CHAPTER

4

HEART & SOUL

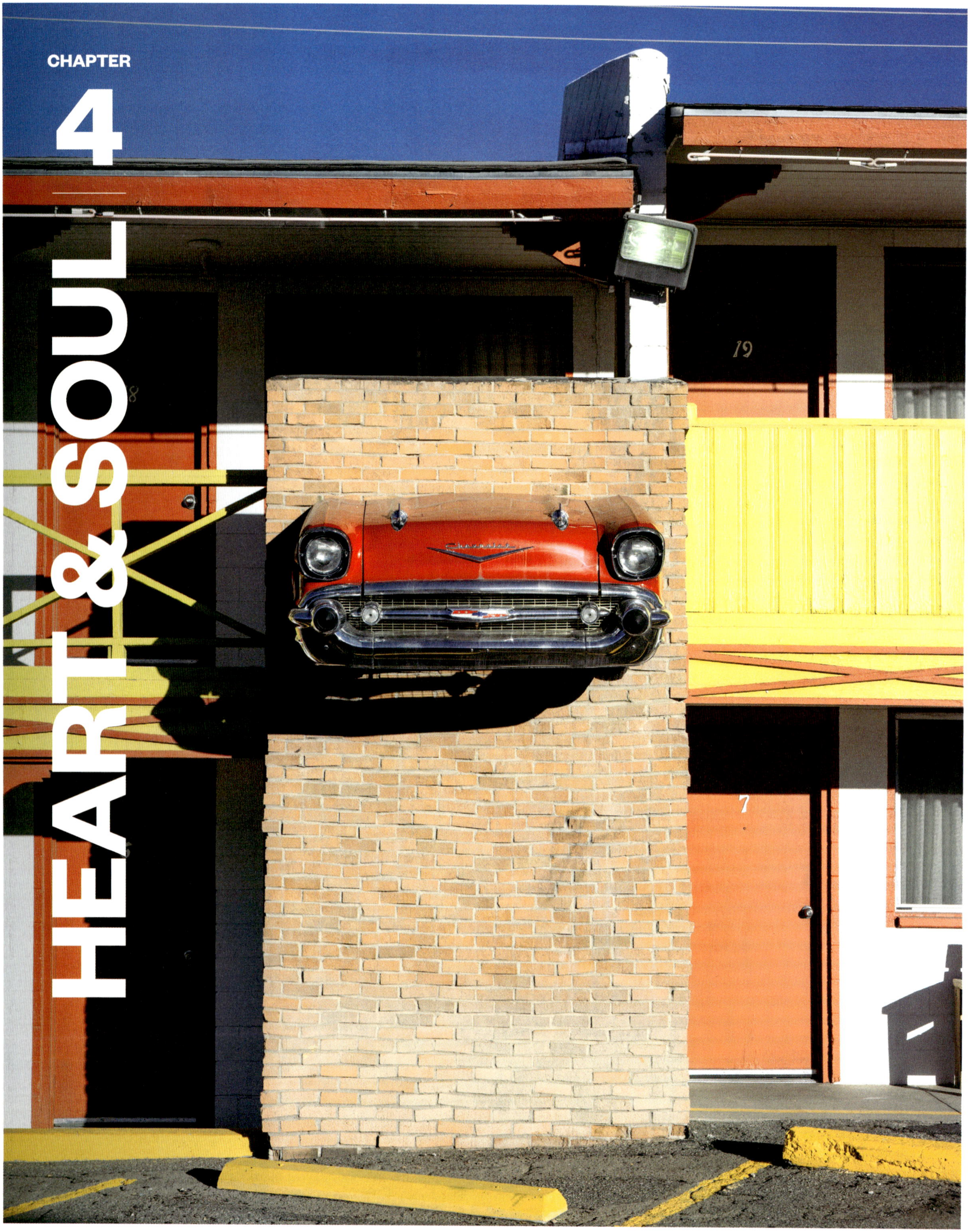

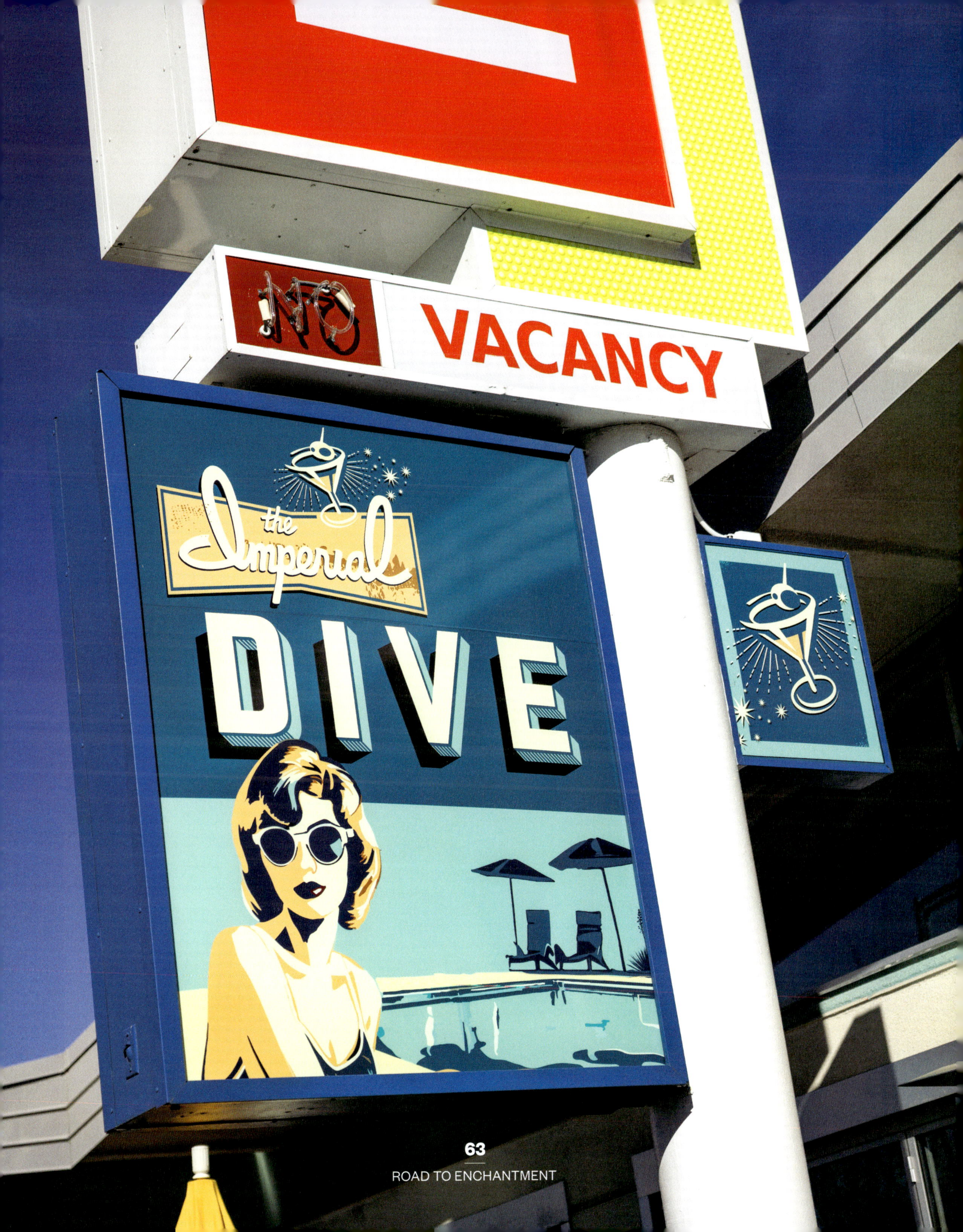
NO
VACANCY
the Imperial
DIVE

ROOM KEYS

More than a place to stay, the roadside motel serves as a connector that energizes both communities and travelers alike.

By Madison Garay

One brisk March morning, my sweetheart and I departed Tucumcari's Blue Swallow Motel before sunrise, equipped with black coffee, cameras, and a rickety hatchback. Rather than journeying west into the sunset as Route 66's legacy would suggest, we drove into the morning toward Texas for a chance to photograph the former State Line Motel in Glenrio.

As the air grew warm with the first blush of spring, the sunrise's faded pinks painted the State Line's whitewashed walls. Bare tree branches clawed over the former motel, gas station, and bar—unmarked and hollowed-out but distinguished buildings in this expanse of ghost town nothingness. Except for the birds and the hum of semis on the interstate, there was only silence. Our voices carried in the wind.

Yet the graffiti scrawled on the walls of the 1930s structure reminded me that we were far from the first or last visitors to pay our respects. Some might find the eight-room motel grim, but I found resilience in its sturdy shell. There we were, at the dawn of a new day on a great American highway, and roots were breaking through the asphalt like a new generation ready to push through.

For landscape painters, photographers, ghost town hunters, and lowrider enthusiasts alike, New Mexico's high and dry climate leaves good bones behind on Route 66. Motels, classic cars, and orphan signs trace the landscape: human blips on the geological clock. For a revival of anything, there must be a perceived death. Frank Lloyd Wright once wrote that a house is a "fussy counterfeit" to the human body, requiring "constant tinkering to stay alive." As I stood in the frame of the State Line, simultaneously inside and out, I was struck by its integrity as it became one with the earth.

Still, being here made me think: *What would a place like this give back if someone had been able to keep it going? How can Route 66 adapt to our fast-paced, always-connected world—and should it?*

Across New Mexico, Route 66 motels survive by balancing legacy with labor, history with modern comforts, heart with soul. Tucumcari's Blue Swallow Motel, opened in 1941, is a neon testament to the

R
"It's extremely important to us to always have every piece of neon glowing at the Blue Swallow Motel," says Dawn Federico, who owns the Tucumcari property with her husband, Richard.

PREVIOUS SPREAD:
Across the parking lot from El Rancho Hotel, El Rancho Motel opened in 1974 and received a Route 66 makeover with themed decor and a "hood ornament" (left). After an extensive renovation, The Imperial, in Albuquerque, reopened with its Food Hall and Dive Bar (right).

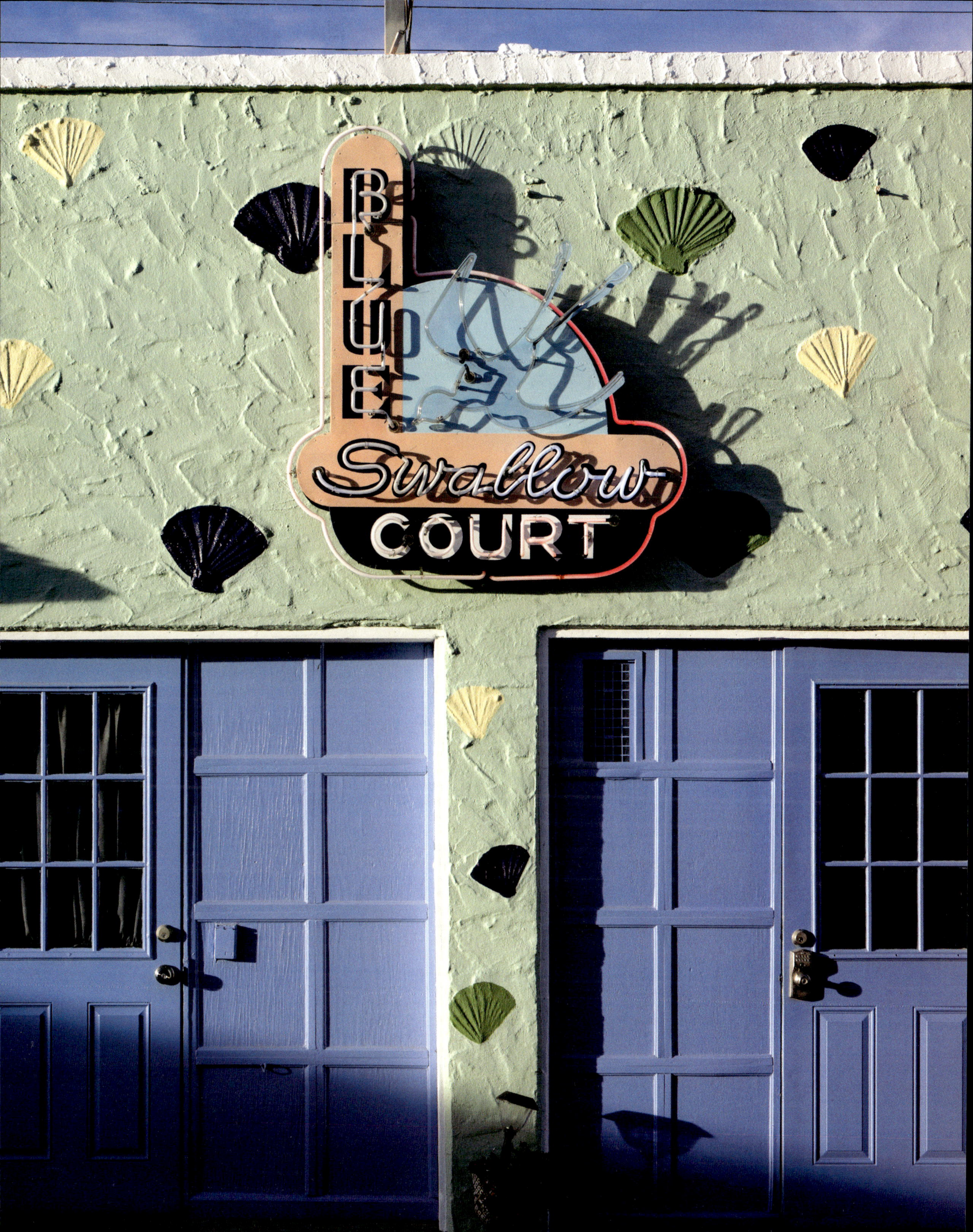
BLUE
Swallow
COURT

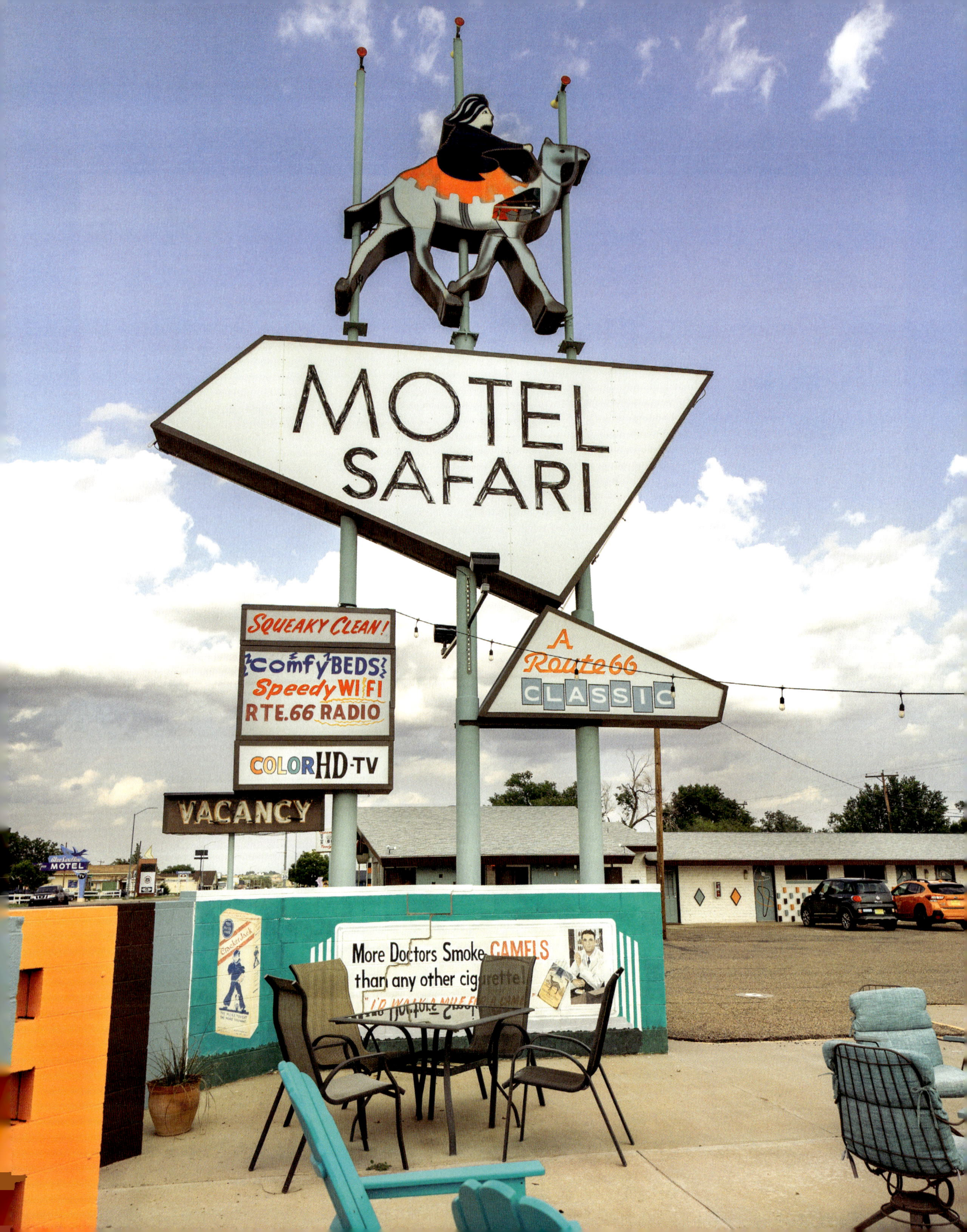
MOTEL
SAFARI
SQUEAKY CLEAN!
Comfy BEDS
Speedy WI FI
RTE.66 RADIO
COLOR HD-TV
A
Route 66
CLASSIC
VACANCY
MOTEL
More Doctors Smoke CAMELS
than any other

endurance of small-scale hosts against the pull of chain hotels and the interstate's gravity. Gallup's 1937-built El Rancho Hotel remains a grand wooden ranch-style contradiction on the border of Zuni, Hopi, and Navajo lands. It was built for Hollywood stars who filmed Westerns nearby, packaging a romanticized pioneer West for postwar motorists. Na'nízhoozhí ("the Bridge")—as Gallup is known in Diné—sits at the threshold, where the Indigenous present and Hollywood myth share a lobby.

Then there's a tale of two motels, the 1936 El Rey Court in Santa Fe and the 1937 El Vado Motel in Albuquerque, designed by the same man, Daniel Murphy, a year apart. Both exemplify the prewar trends of roadside motor courts inflected with the regional Spanish-Pueblo Revival style.

Both now boast watering holes—the upscale cocktail bar La Reina at El Rey and the cozy taproom at El Vado—that have become fixtures of their communities in the 2020s. Whether the draw is a musician putting on an intimate show at La Reina or an artisan market filling El Vado's patio with multigenerational community, these properties have become social anchors where distinctions between travelers and locals dissolve.

"In a world where everything is touchless interaction, it makes a mark on a visitor to be able to chat with a front desk agent and chat with people in the bar," says Cecilia Doria, area marketing manager of El Rey. "Those small moments get at the heart of Americana: connection."

The idea has sparked a motor court revival that brings color back to New Mexico's main streets and gathers people together around a pool or a patio. Travelers cherish what locals are proud of. When someone loves where they live, it's contagious. And life returns to a place when people have a reason to stay.

"Places are for people," says Michelle Negrette, an Albuquerque architect and a Nob Hill neighborhood resident. "The essence of placemaking is in the emotional moments that occur between place and collective memory."

Negrette's adaptive reuse projects throughout Route 66 landed her right on motelier Sharmin Dharas's radar. The duo collaborated on the ambitious transformation of a 1956 Sleepy Bear Travelodge into Hotel Zazz, a neon oasis on Central Avenue. Together, Negrette and Dharas dug into the motel's archive, excavating documents of a property that had many faces.

In the 1940s, before the motel opened, the property was a service station and soda fountain specializing in root beer. Today, a hidden speakeasy serves centennial root beer floats as a wink to its past on the Mother Road. Dharas calls this approach "newstalgia." "I don't consider myself at all a preservationist—I'm a storyteller," she says. "I pay homage to the past while embedding it into the new."

Hotel Zazz is personal for Dharas. Her parents owned the Travelodge and were among the many immigrant families stewarding hotels along Albuquerque's Route 66 after the road was decommissioned in 1985. Route 66 was Dharas's front yard. Today she dedicates Zazz to her little girl, Shayrooz.

During the remodel, Sharmin brought Shayrooz around the property often. Even before she could speak, Shayrooz would create a diamond gesture with her hands to refer to the motel, mimicking the shape of its carport breeze blocks. "That became the foundation for everything," Sharmin explains. "Diamonds became our motif on our sign and on the mural." Those breeze blocks are painted in Zazz pink, a signature accent shade as bold as its creator.

The Mother Road also has a way of welcoming strangers. Take Rich Havlik, who purchased Tucumcari's Motel Safari in 2025. After a long career in the Minnesota funeral business, he craved more out of life.

Havlik had driven parts of the Mother Road twice before the Covid-19 pandemic got him serious about motel ownership. "The idea of running a motel on Route 66 checked off all the boxes," he recalls. "I love serving families, and I haven't met someone in Tucumcari that I haven't liked yet."

Havlik can often be found transmitting oldies at Motel Safari's own radio station or happily hosting neighbors and strangers alike around the firepit. Thanks to Route 66, he's found his groove again, connecting with people face to face and heart to heart.

No doubt, the future of Route 66 depends on the people who run its businesses. It cannot survive on aesthetic nostalgia alone. Cristina Rogers, the director of Barelas MainStreet, understands that neon allures but stewardship sticks. "Back in the day, little businesses were built in front of people's homes, these multigenerational compounds," she says.

Her work reimagining Fourth Street in Albuquerque focuses on the idea that adaptation is core to New Mexico's history. "People were responding to Route 66 and the business it brought," she adds. "That agility is revealed in the architectural layers here."

In 1926, few could have predicted that a mostly dirt road would become an icon, but the resilience of its communities built a legacy. And the motel is a microcosm, where people from all walks of life are placed in close quarters, connected by the unified structure itself.

New Mexicans build "future memory" every day, with an eye on the rearview. Strong foundations allow new visions to germinate. Like the old State Line Motel, some places deserve the dignity of death. Yet with every return to the fertile earth, life can rise again, carrying the DNA of yesterday into the soul of who we are right now and inspiring what we can become. ✶

L
Tucumcari's Motel Safari sports Googie architecture and a bright palette. "Everything is midcentury modern here," says owner Rich Havlik.

GABRIELLA MARKS

MADISON GARAY is a scholar of New Mexico's Route 66 history and American art and architecture.

Mike Pogue

The co-owner of the Sunset Motel in Moriarty helped lay its foundation brick by brick.

AS OWNERS of the Sunset Motel in Moriarty, Mike and Debbie Pogue put their heart and soul into keeping the classic American midcentury property in tip-top shape. Debbie designed the iconic neon sign. Mike helped his dad build the original 18-room motor court, laying bricks with his brother in the evenings after school. Mike eventually purchased the motor inn from his mother and moved back to Moriarty to run it in 2010. The property is once again a hot spot with Route 66 travelers, with exposed block, original paneling, and midcentury modern furniture.

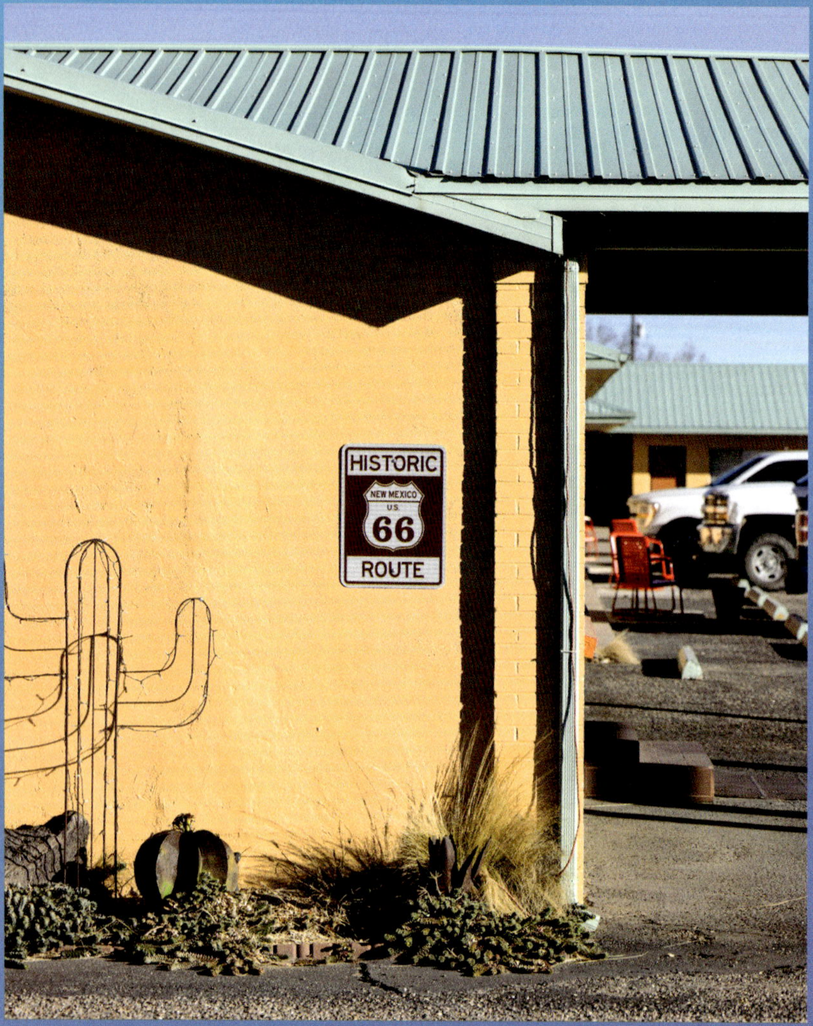

When we started building the motel in 1956, I was five and my brother was seven. My dad gave us a shovel and said, "Alright boys, we're going to start a motel."

We dug a trench and built six rooms at a time. I do have a soulful connection to that property and the guests.

People are looking for personal experiences. One guest left a review saying, "If I could bundle up this motel and take it with me everywhere I go, I would."

The first thing a guest hears when they arrive is "How are you?" We have a conversation.

We'll never sell this motel. It's too much fun. Once or twice a week, we ask people to join us for dinner, typically people I've had conversations with at the desk. We become friends.

They come back every year. We say, "Don't have dinner plans—we're going to have that same green chile stew we had last year." It's like having an extended family. ✶

L
The Sunset Motel, in Moriarty, is still owned by its original family.

R
Mike Pogue grew up in his family's Sunset Motel and has met Route 66 travelers from around the world.

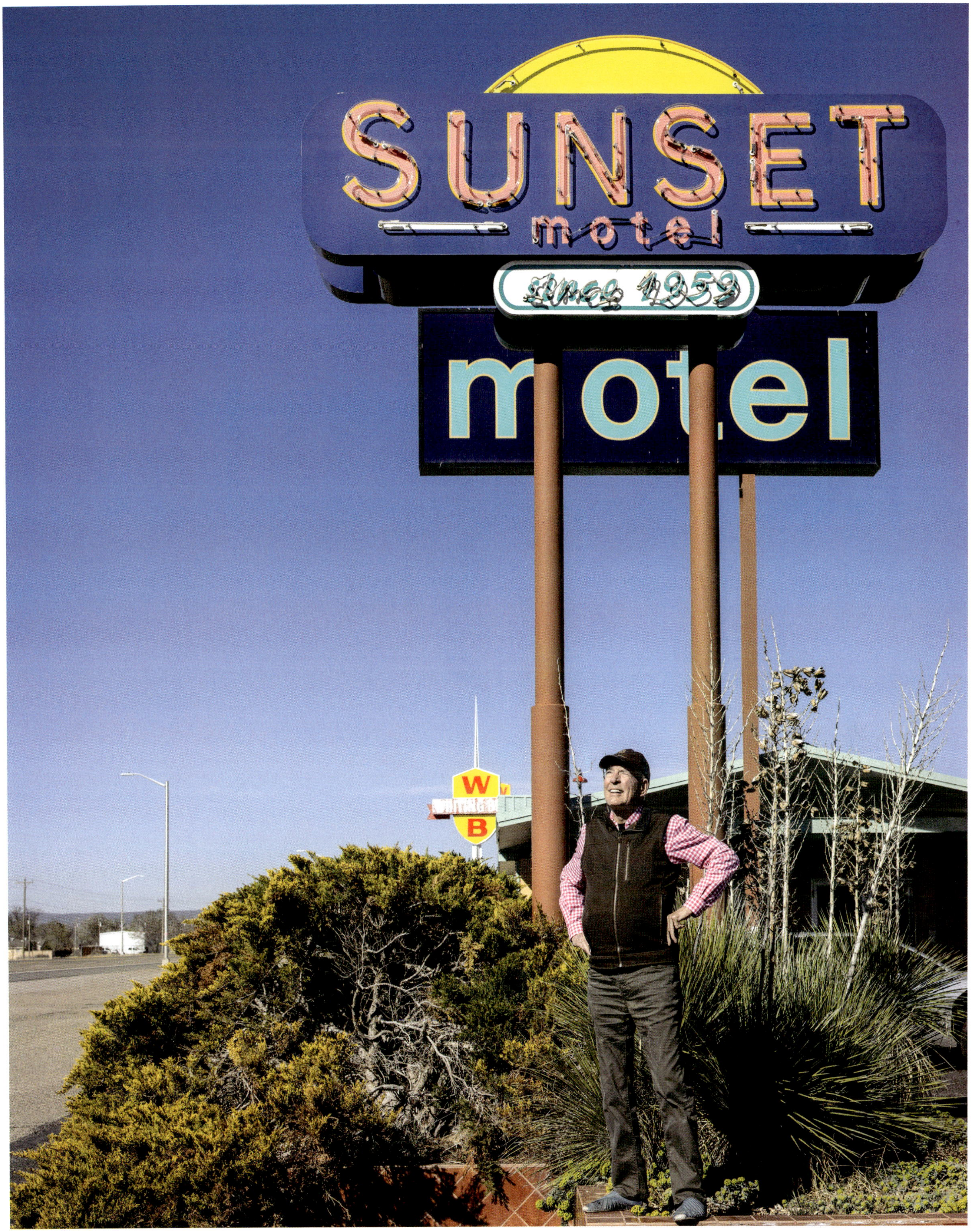
SUNSET
motel
Since 1959
motel

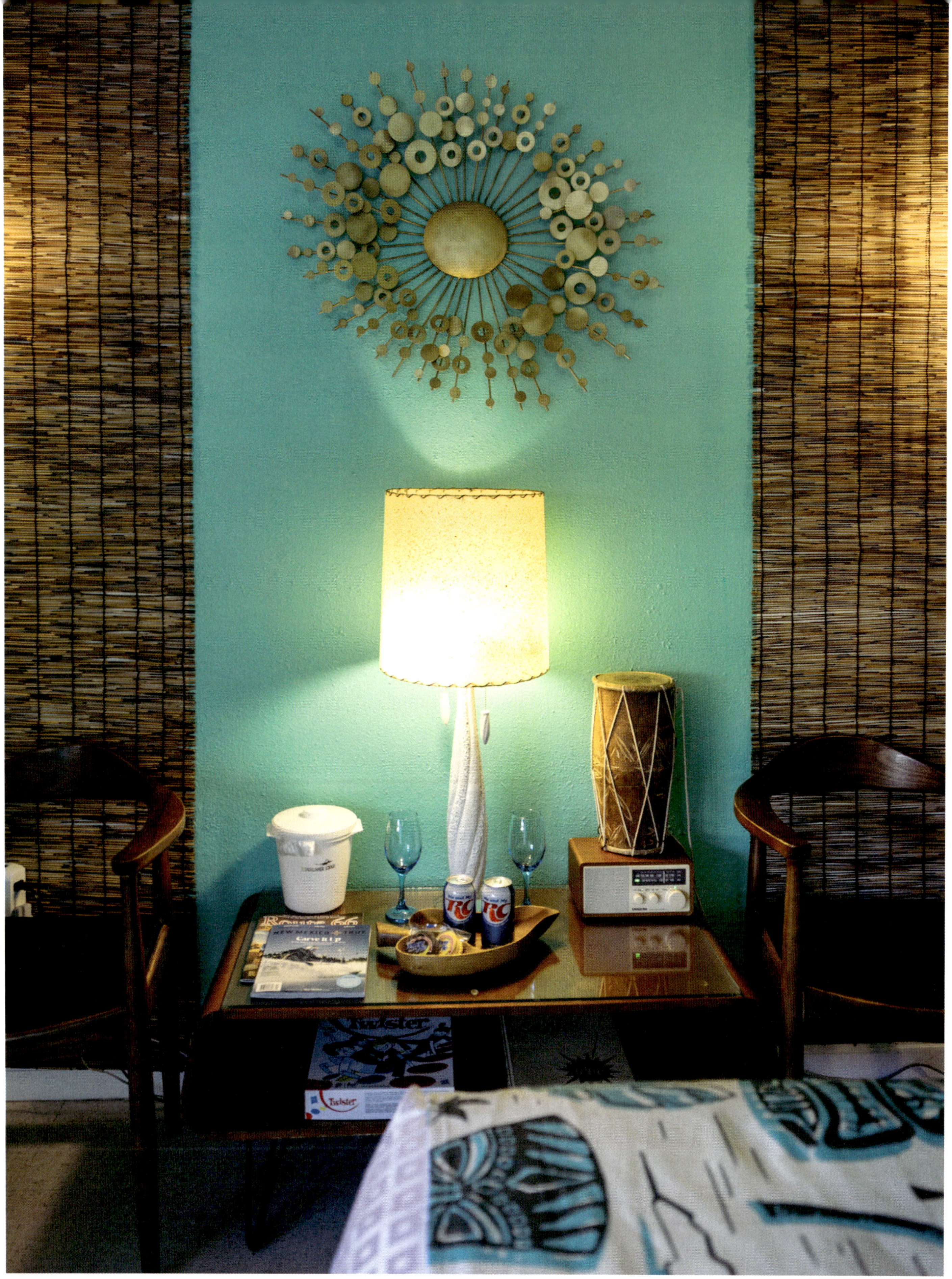
RC
RC
Twister

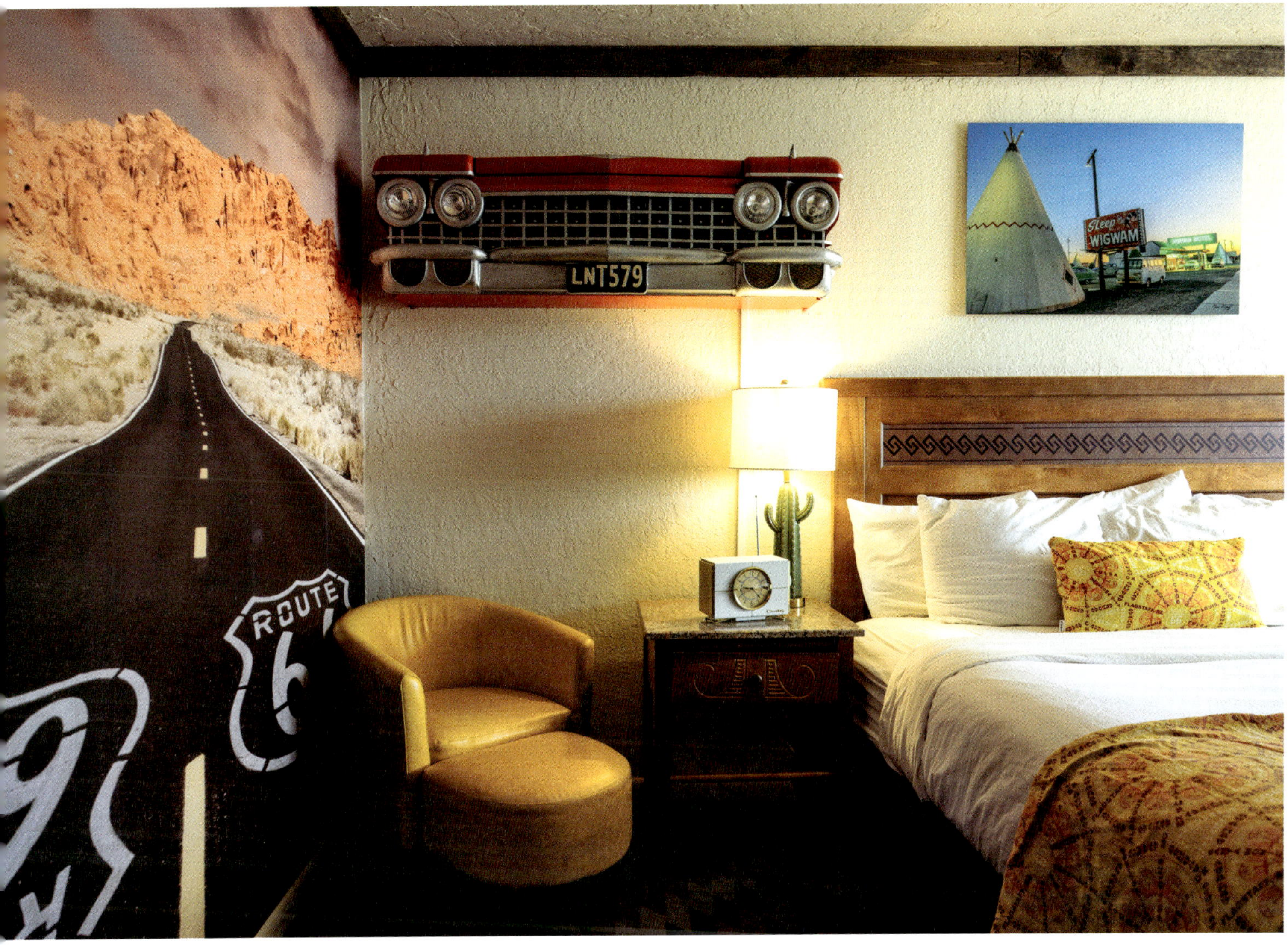

L
The vintage radios at Tucumcari's Roadrunner Lodge are tuned to sounds from the 1950s and '60s, complete with retro commercials.

R
The grill and hood of a bright red Cadillac and a massive wall mural highlight the Route 66 decor at El Rancho Motel in Gallup.

NEON DREAMS

At Mother Road motels, vintage decor still glows after all these miles.

Check in to a vintage room on Route 66 and time travel to the fabled highway's golden era. Many motor court rooms are outfitted with streamlined midcentury furniture and decor. Every room at the Blue Swallow Motel in Tucumcari has an original 1939 Bakelite Bell rotary-dial phone. Nearby, Motel Safari offers a suite done up in cowboy gear. The Mystic Santa Fe's 1950s-themed room is drenched in throwback decor, from the kitschy cowboy lamp to the old-timey bedside radio clock. "I wanted guests to appreciate the nostalgia of Route 66 in a space where they could find their layer of connection," says co-owner Rick Goldberg, "either with themselves or the people that they're with." At night, most motor courts are bathed in the glow of neon, inspiring dreams of the Mother Road. ✶

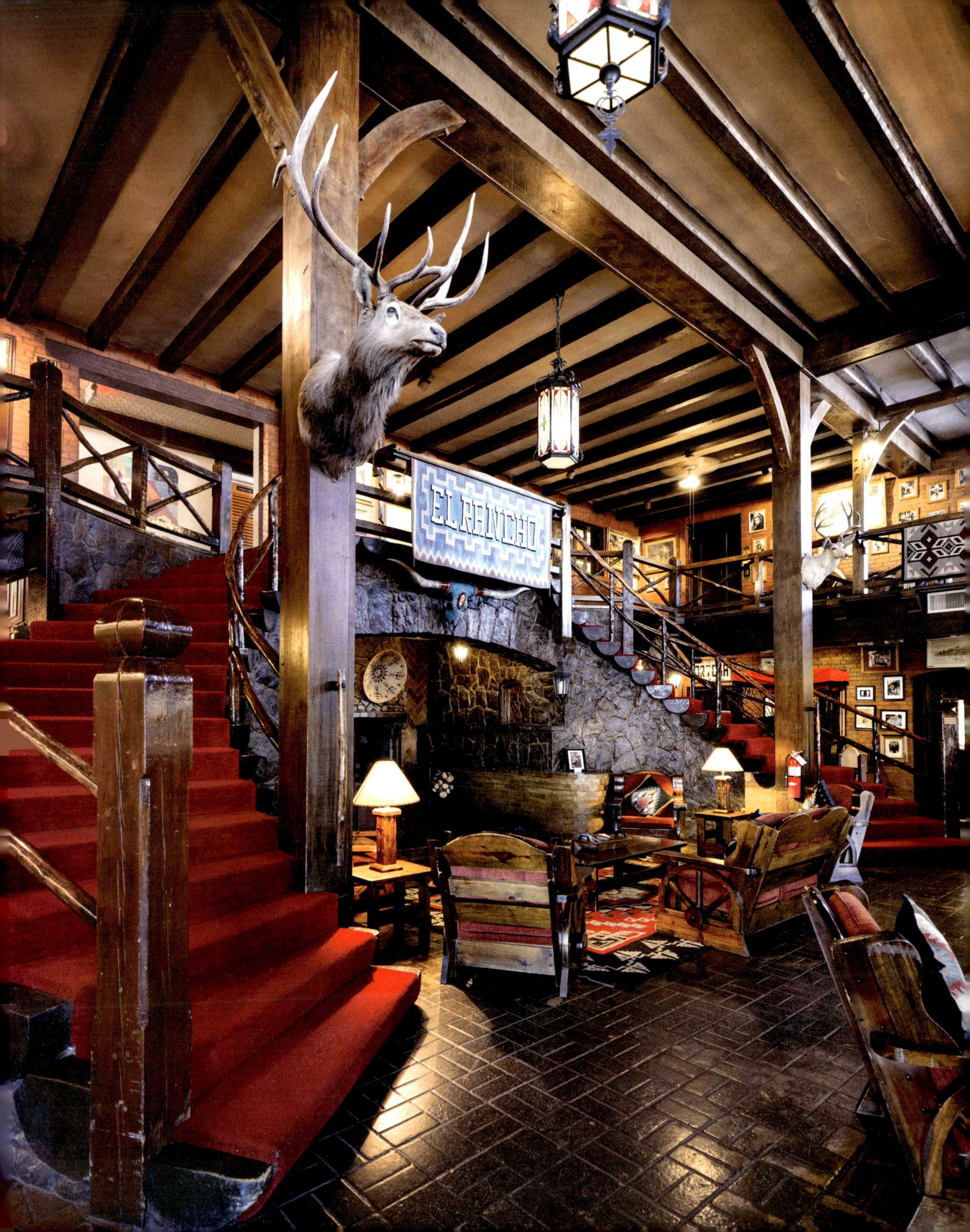
EL RANCHO

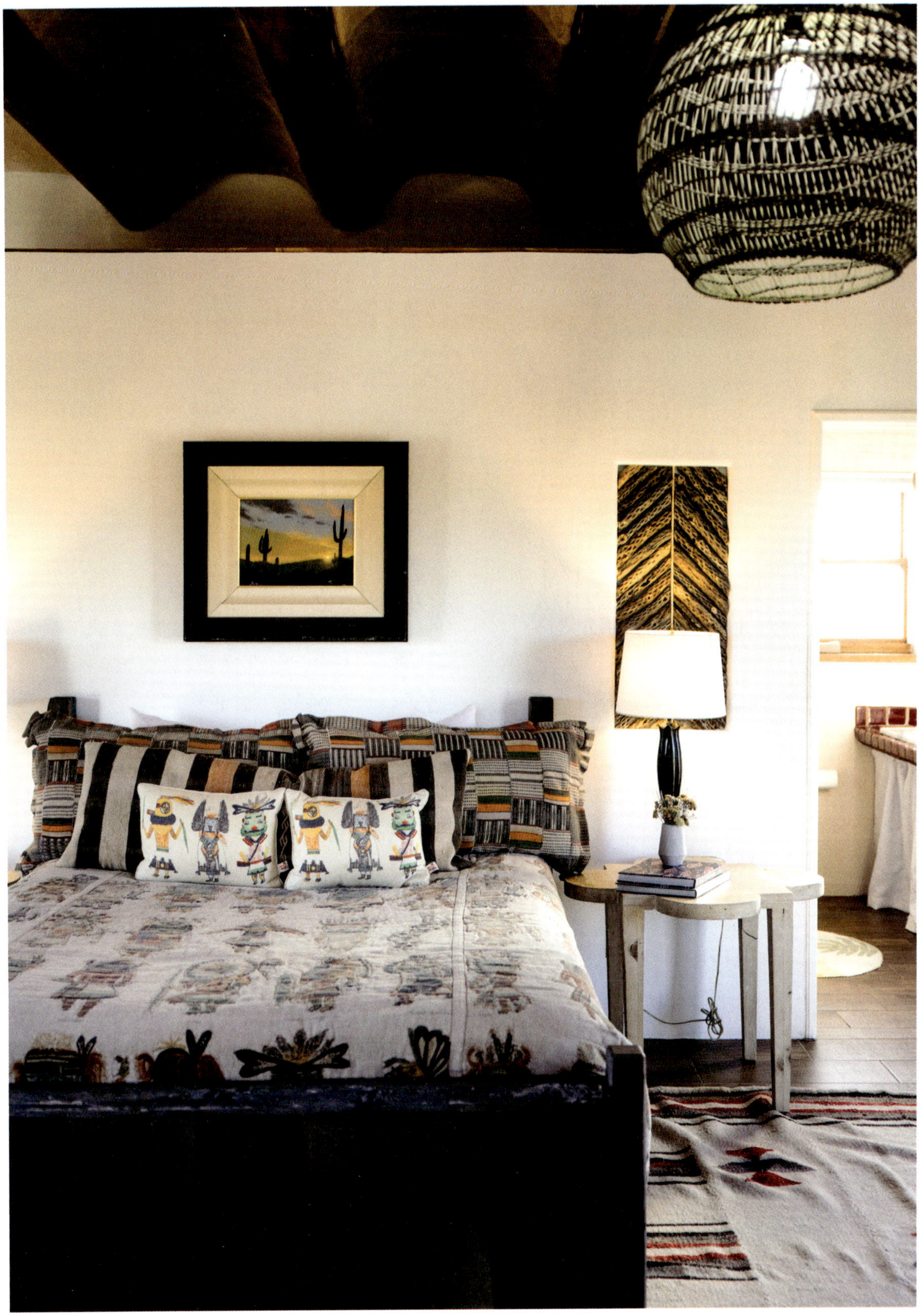

L
The lobby of El Rancho Hotel, in Gallup, features a stone fireplace, a dual red-carpeted staircase, and plenty of Hollywood memorabilia.

R
The rooms at The Mystic Santa Fe received a high desert makeover when Amanda Tucker and her husband, Rick Goldberg, transformed the former Silver Saddle Motel.

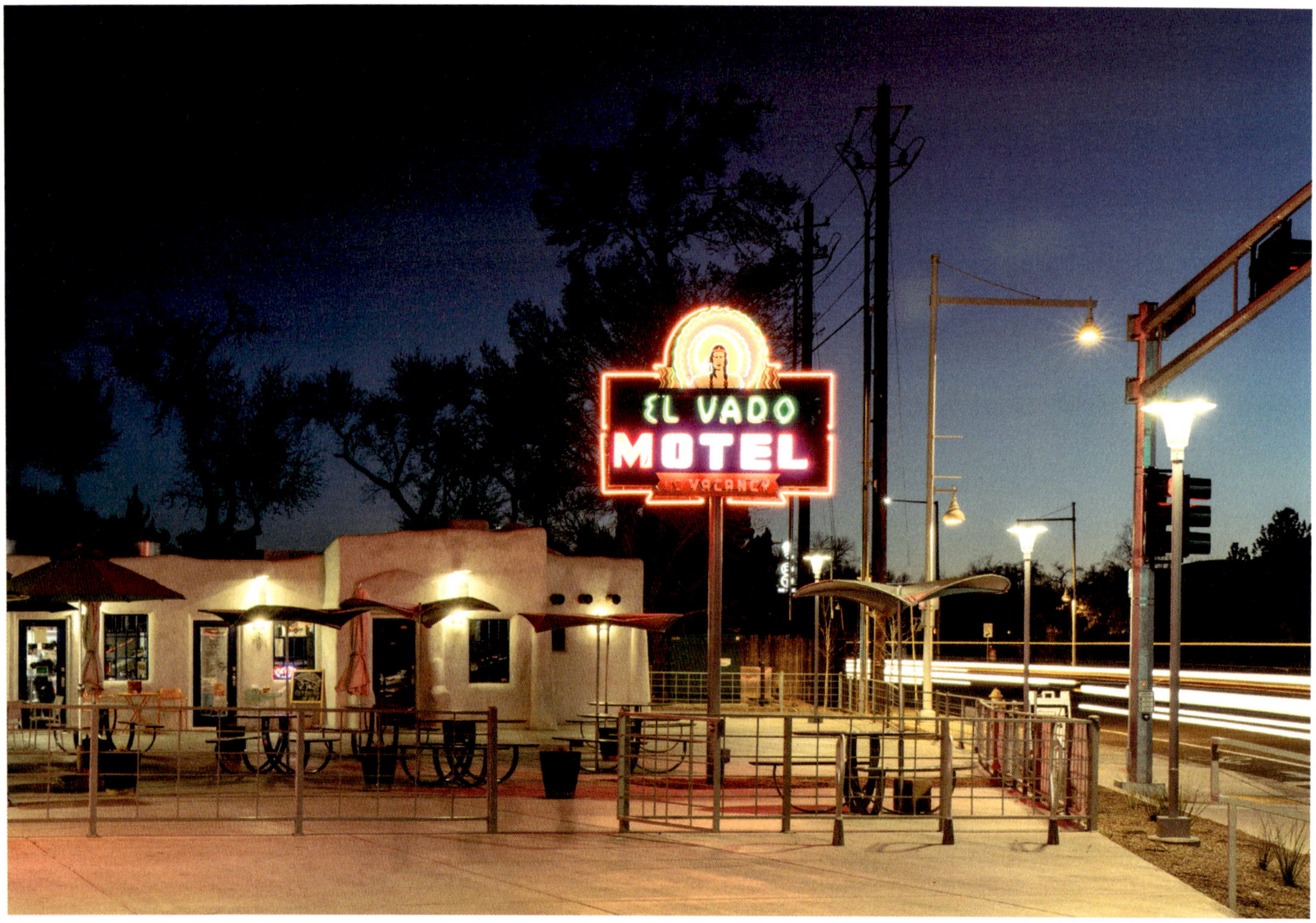

L
The El Vado Motel sign is one of historic preservationist Johnny Meier's favorites, featuring "a Native American portrait backlit with a fantastic multicolored headdress," he says.

R
Featuring a vibrant mural, The Mystic Santa Fe's High Desert Hideaway space hosts weddings, live music, and other events.

"

I love vintage and retro. I incorporate it in all my designs with modern."

— AMANDA TUCKER, WHO OWNS THE MYSTIC SANTA FE WITH HER HUSBAND, RICK GOLDBERG

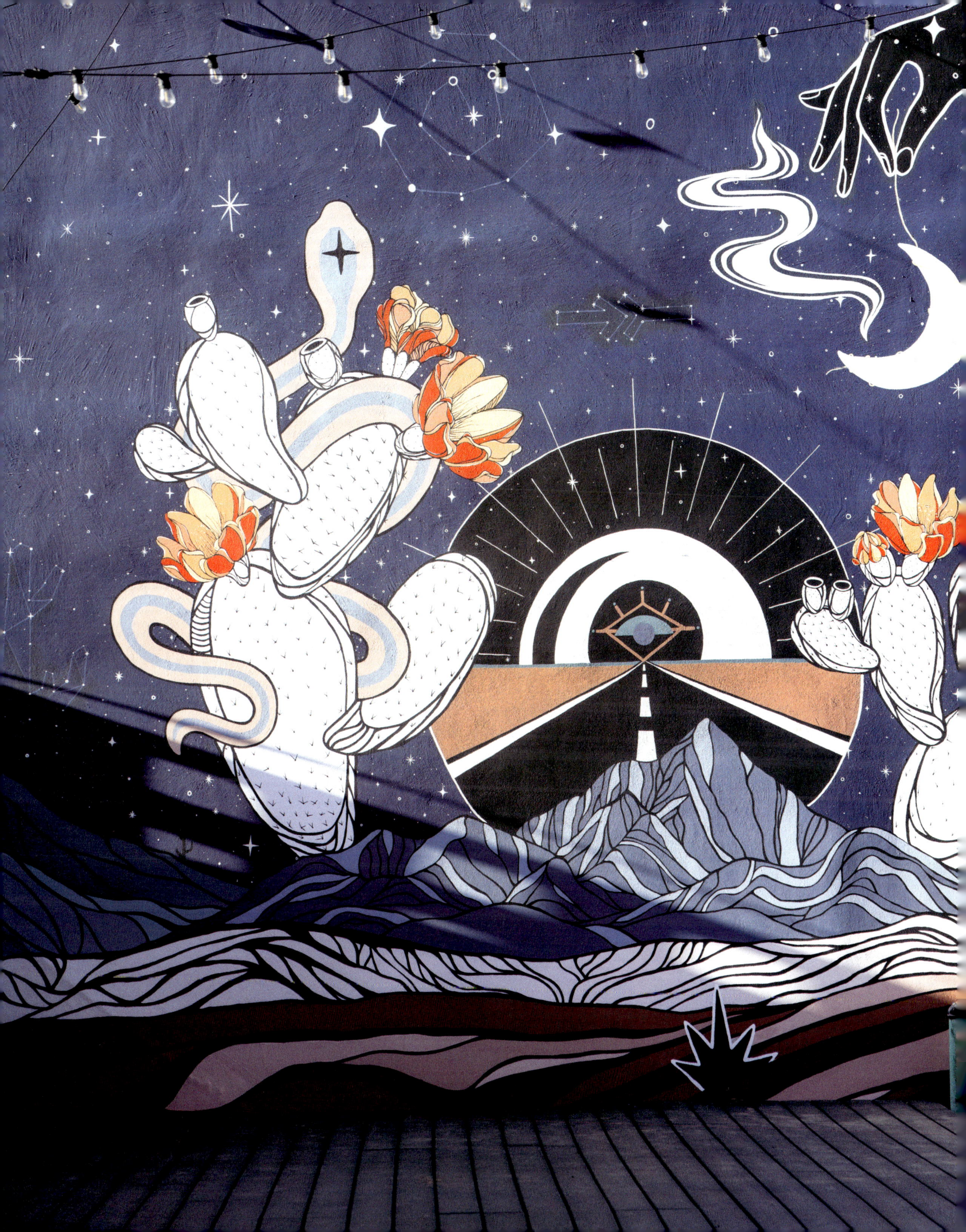

Sharmin Dharas

The Hotel Zazz owner continues her family's hospitality legacy with a happening hangout spot.

GROWING UP IN THE 1956 SLEEPY BEAR TRAVELODGE her African-born parents owned, Sharmin Dharas felt like the Albuquerque Route 66 motel was her playground. So when her parents planned to retire, Dharas couldn't bring herself to sell their midcentury motel in Nob Hill. Instead, she left her budding career as a physician to restore the motel, adding fresh paint in bright colors, local art, swanky furniture, and modern conveniences to the 48 guest rooms. She reopened the property in 2022 as Hotel Zazz, a hip boutique hotel with playful amenities such as a hidden speakeasy and a pool with a pop-up bar where guests can watch "dive-in movies." Dharas collaborated with local artists, but her chief partner-in-design was her daughter, Shayrooz, who suggested hot pink and other wild colors, a Popsicle happy hour, and the hotel's gleeful name.

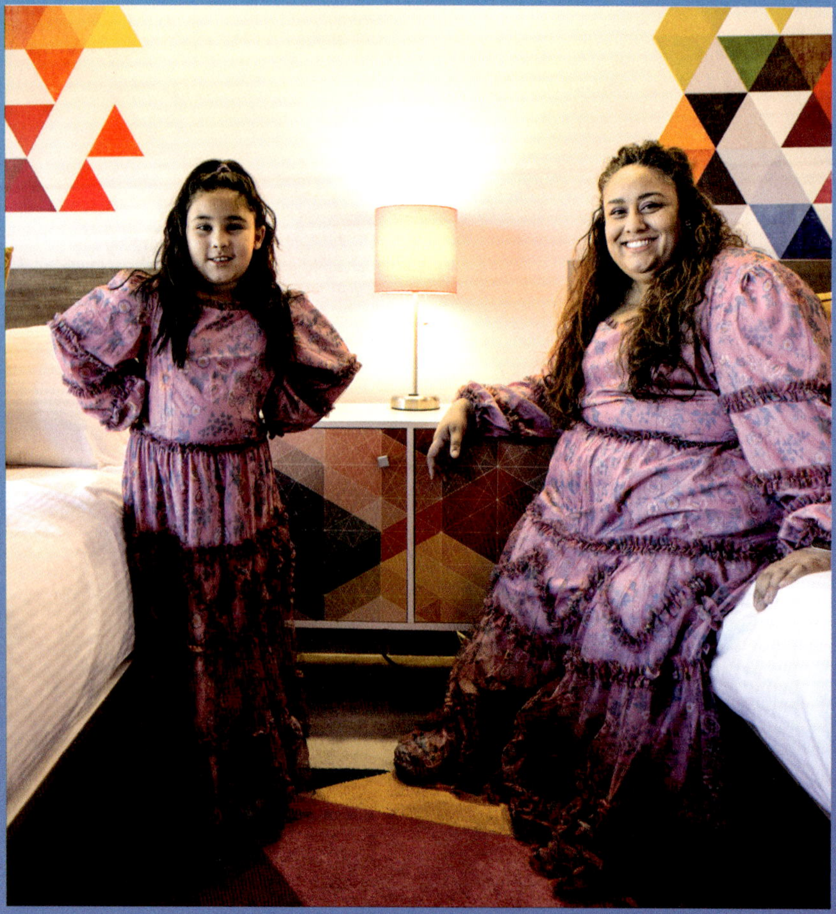

I was blessed to meet so many people who would come into town for a variety of things, including their Route 66 bucket list and an Indian trading post that used to be right next to us.

I have a whole guest book of people who still come to see us.

My dad would share his story about how he came to America, and the guests would share theirs. I was there as a little kid, and I just listened.

It's important that we're keeping this place and seeing another generation carry on this legacy instead of demolishing it. It needed a lot of love, repair, and fixing.

It's "newstalgia," in terms of bringing back memories and still creating a new passion and desire for people to want to stay on Route 66.

How many roadside motels have what we have—a speakeasy, a spa? And every summer we have "dive-in movies" at the pool.

The one thing that remains the same, all these years later, is the phone number. ✴

L
Owner Sharmin Dharas and her daughter, Shayrooz, enliven Hotel Zazz.

R
Even on neon-lit Nob Hill, the Hotel Zazz sign stands out, welcoming guests.

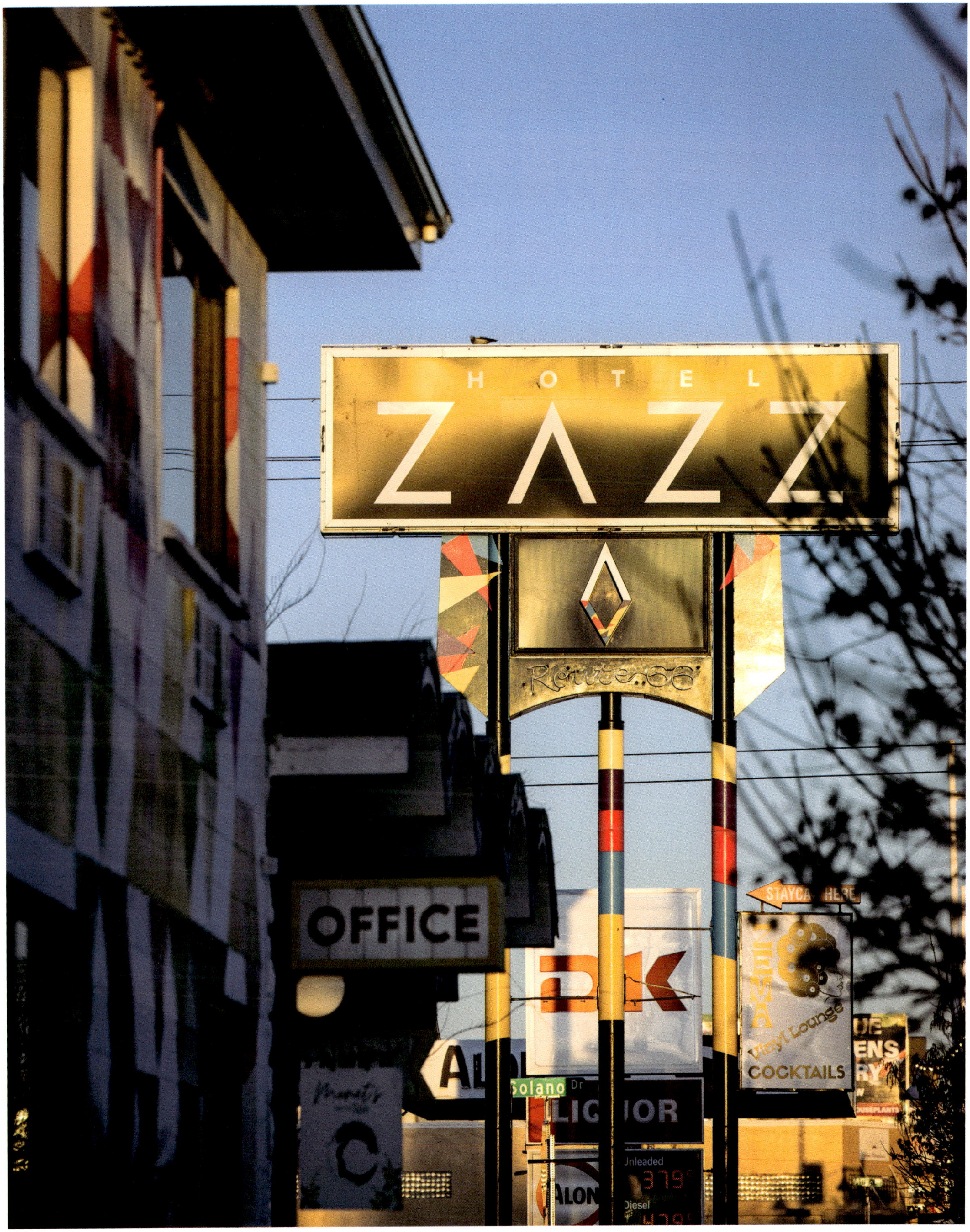
HOTEL
ZAZZ
Route 66
OFFICE
Vinyl Lounge
COCKTAILS
Solano
Unleaded
Diesel

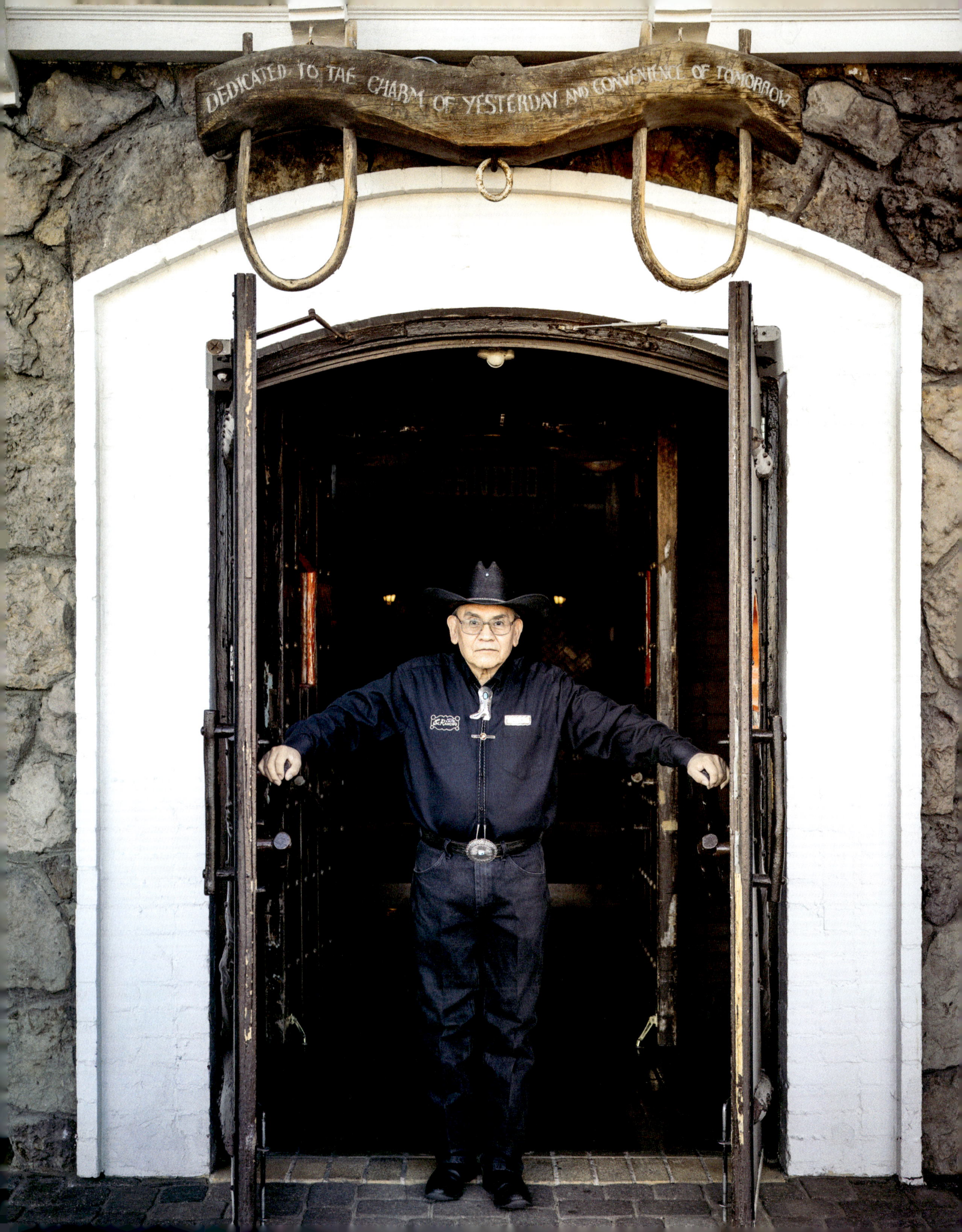
DEDICATED TO THE CHARM OF YESTERDAY AND CONVENIENCE OF TOMORROW

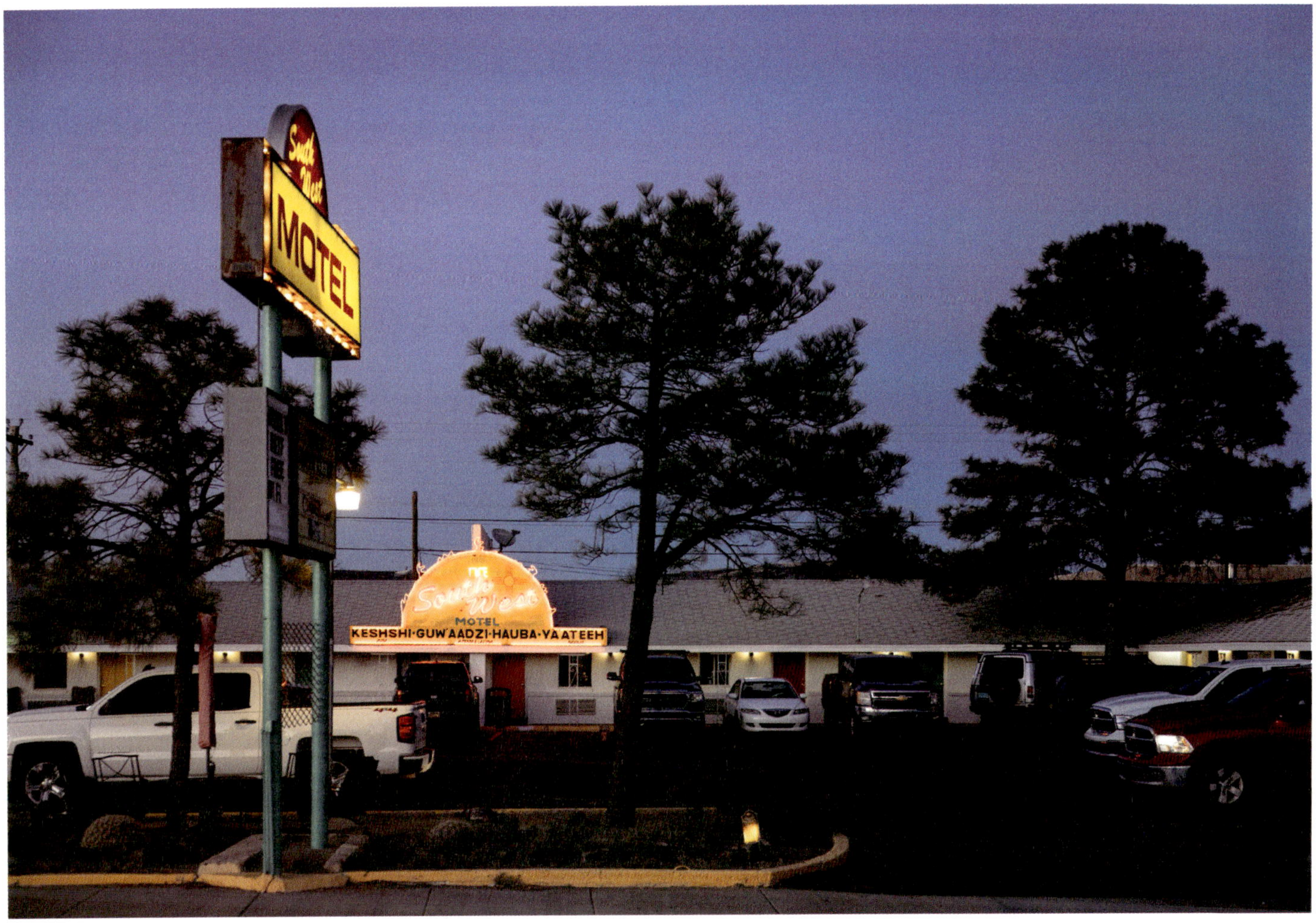

L
El Rancho Hotel historian Leroy McCray began as a desk clerk more than 30 years ago. "Every day, [visitors] come through here and say, 'We're doing Route 66,'" he says.

R
The restored South West Motel in Grants makes a great jumping-off place for nearby El Malpais National Monument, the Ice Cave and Bandera Volcano, and the Continental Divide Trail.

ROUGHING IT

Route 66 hospitality has come a long way since early travelers pitched a tent near the roadside.

Before the rise of motor courts, early Route 66 travelers camped beneath a tent they pitched on the side of the road. Then auto camps and tourist cabins sprang up, offering less primitive lodgings with individual sleeping spaces and access to water, showers, and other amenities. "In Albuquerque in 1932, the facilities were called tourist cabins, with a simple design to get out of the rain and snow," says Frank Norris, a Santa Fe–based historian. "The public wanted that for a while, but then they wanted a few more amenities than that—a lamp and maybe a radio." Amenities in today's retro motels have come a long way, but it's still nice to hear the songs of yesteryear on a bedside radio. ✴

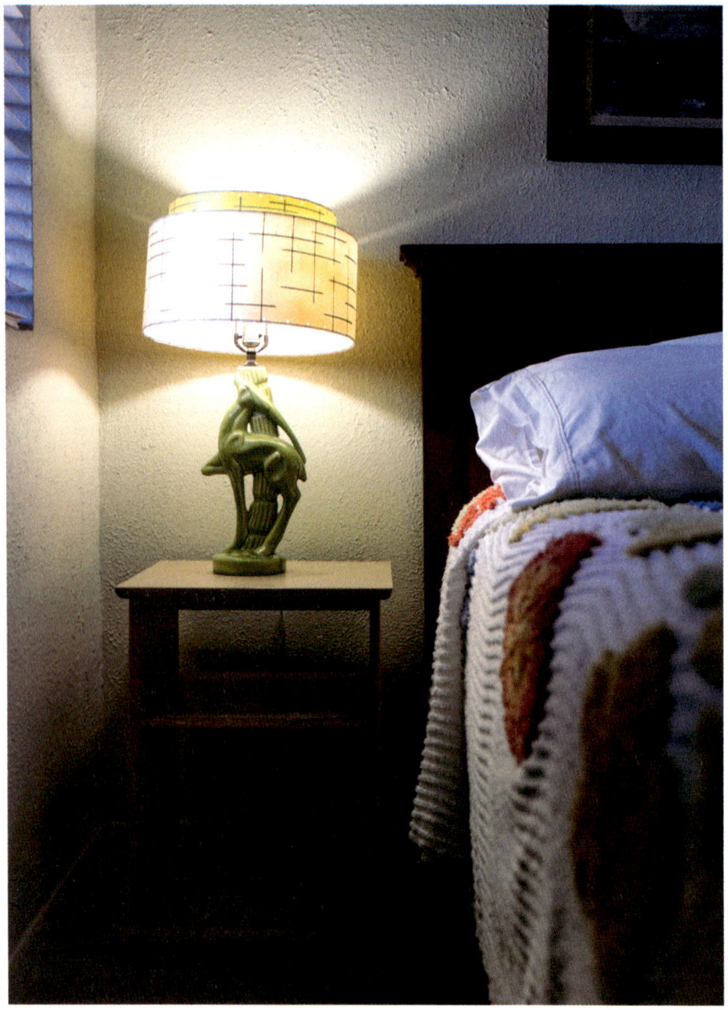

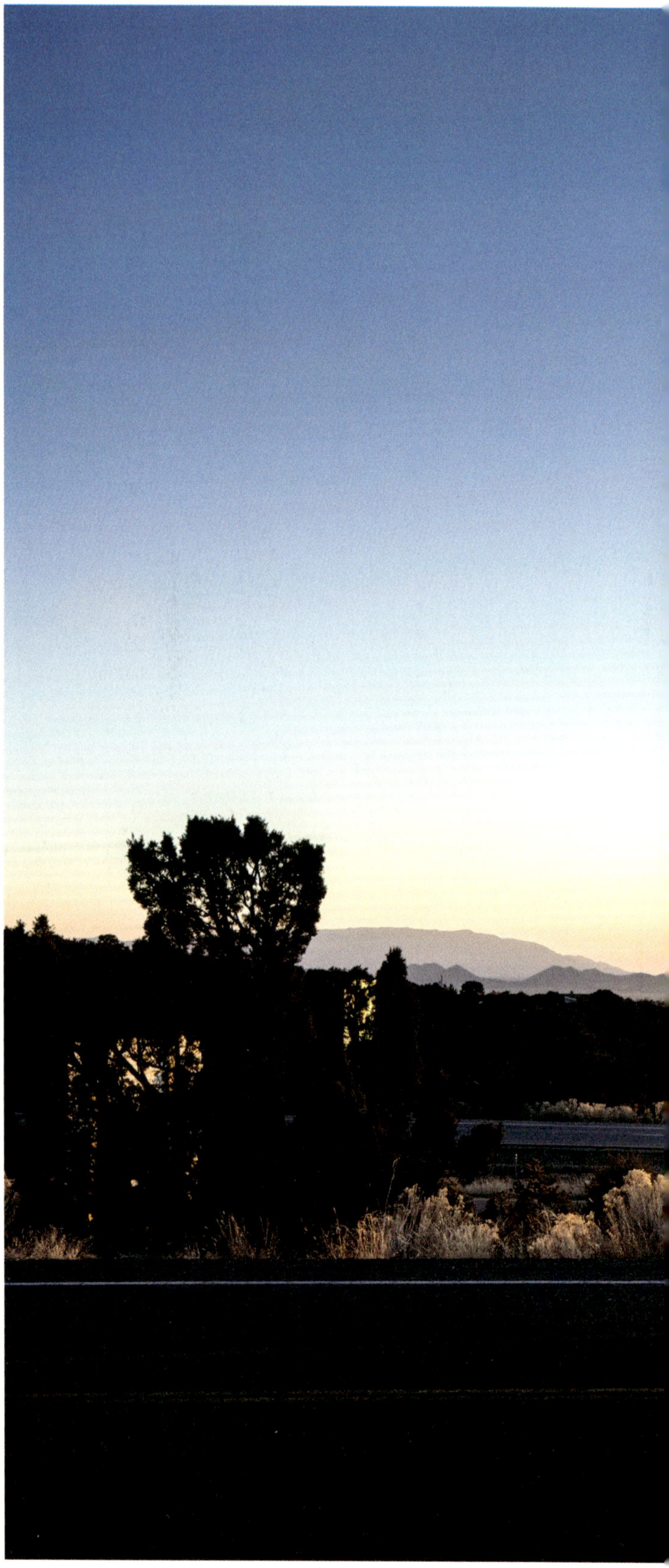

L
In Tucumcari, the Blue Swallow Motel's 12 rooms feature midcentury modern art, furniture, and fixtures.

R
At sunset, a Jeep follows the original alignment of Route 66, running from Santa Fe down to Santa Rosa.

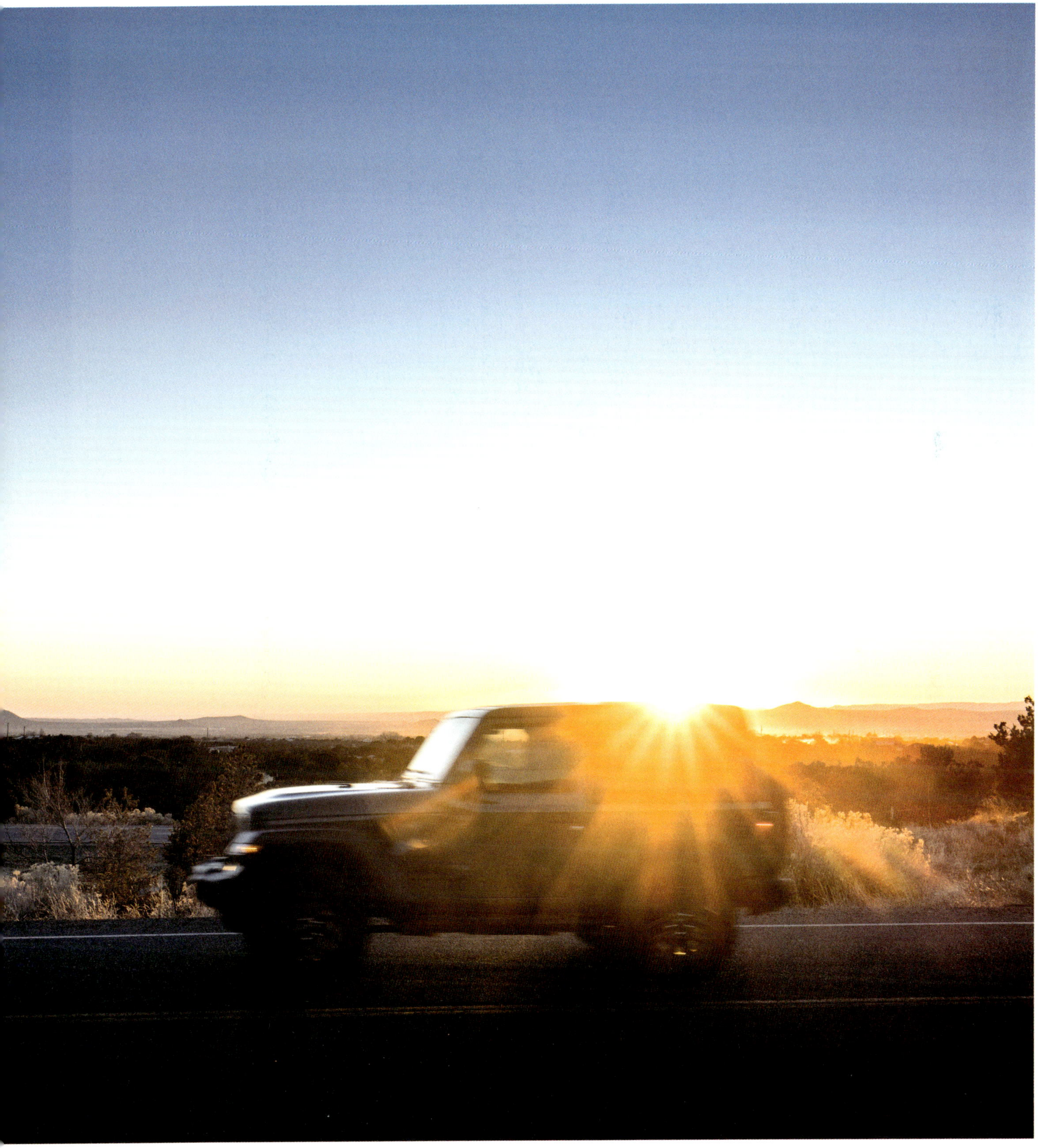

CHAPTER

5

LAND & LEGACY

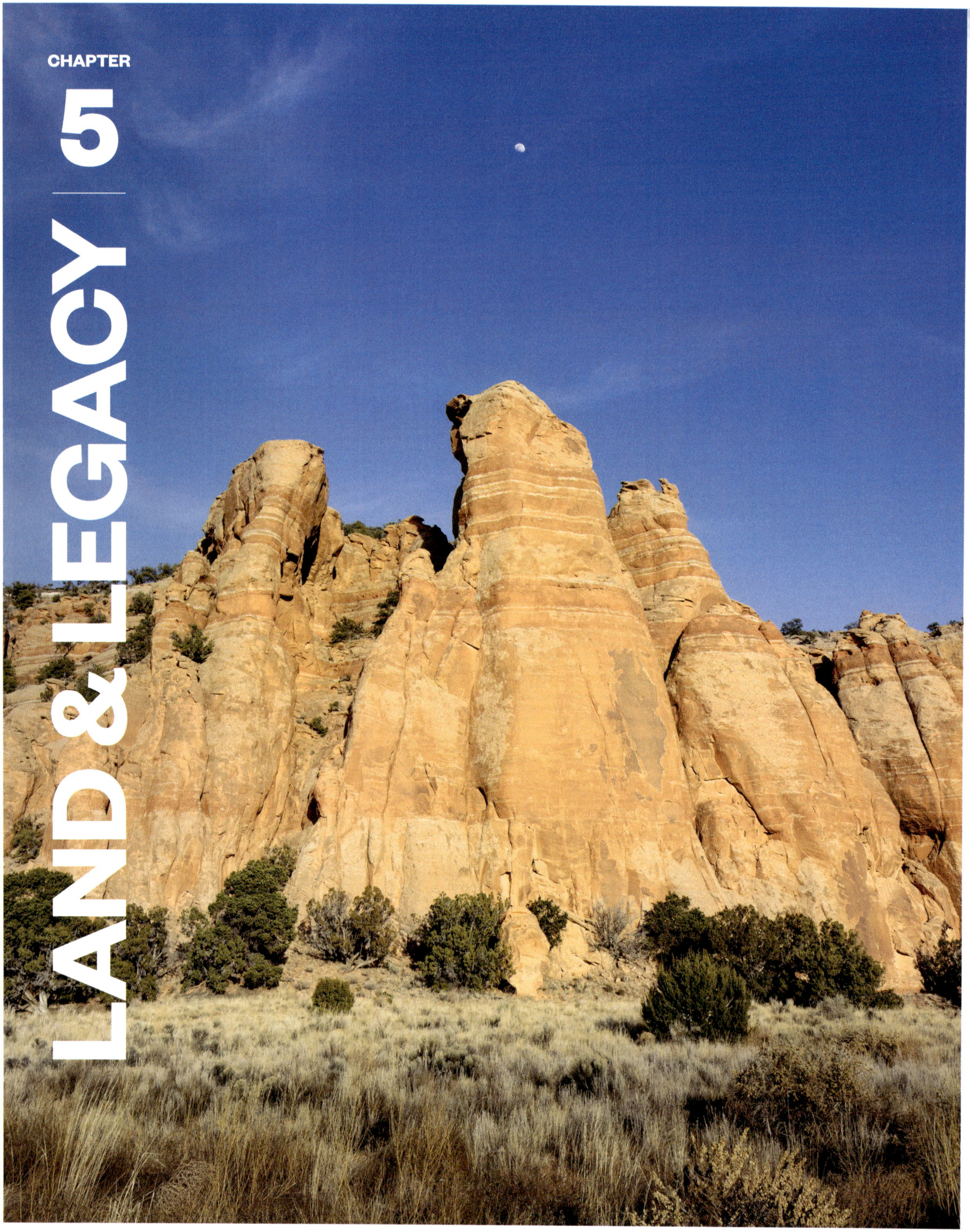

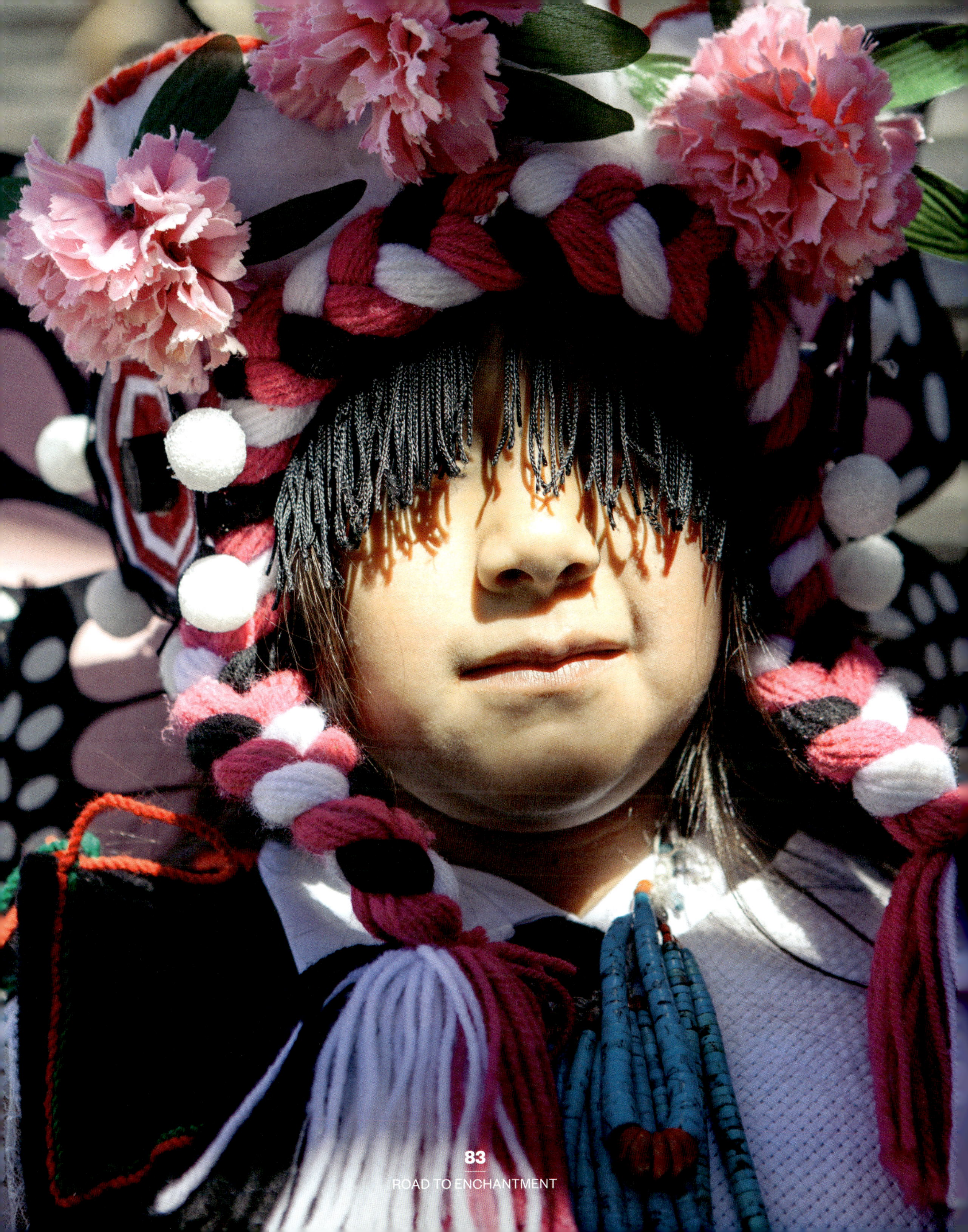

A ROAD DIVIDED

While Route 66 brought progress and change, it continued a story that had been playing out over centuries.

By Ungelbah Dávila

They called the road Mother. But mothers, I've learned, are complicated. They bring us from one world into another, they guide us, and they thrust us into the future, even when it's uncertain.

In New Mexico, the Mother Road arrived late to a landscape that knew roads long before she did—paths pressed into the earth by Indigenous feet, by Pueblo and Navajo traders, by centuries of movement that did not require pavement to be real. As New Mexico state historian Robert Martinez reminds us, Route 66 was never an origin story but "another chapter of trails and roads that have changed us and changed our cultures and our economies." Route 66 is a piece of living history. It reminds us that the United States is a country of migration for some and invasion for others.

Long before the Mother Road learned our names, Indigenous peoples had mapped the land through use and memory. Spanish, Mexican, and U.S. travelers followed those same veins, repurposing Native pathways into royal roads, trade routes, and finally highways. When Route 66 followed those corridors through Laguna Pueblo, Acoma Pueblo, and parts of the Navajo Nation, it layered 20th-century ambition onto land already thick with its own mythology. The Mother Road didn't ask permission to absorb the children of this land.

She brought opportunity with her, the way a mother might bring food home after a long day—necessary, imperfect, transformative. Cars meant commerce. Travelers meant money. Pueblo and Navajo families sold pottery, jewelry, textiles—objects already rich with story, suddenly reframed as souvenirs of the Southwest. "It changed their economies," Martinez notes, allowing Indigenous communities to commercialize parts of their culture to survive within American capitalism. During the Great Depression and beyond, that income mattered. It fed families. It carried art from kitchens and community spaces into national consciousness.

Tourist demand flattened complexity. It rewarded the expected, the stereotypical, the familiar. Visitors wanted culture they could recognize at a glance, culture that fit neatly into a glove compartment. But culture cannot be leveled, and stories cannot be squashed between a car title or registration certificate and a packet of tissues.

When you look closer, when you take the time to sift this soil through your fingers, breathe the kiss of piñon in the air, and contemplate the galaxy winking at you above a quiet campout, you will realize that the original artists of Route 66 never compromised the narratives their art forms held; they only simplified and condensed them for foreigners looking for a souvenir. In this, their art was a gift, a taste, a tiny offering to strangers. And eventually, their generosity led to deeper exploration by other newcomers.

R
The balanced pottery style of dancing performed by the Zuni Olla Maidens began in the 1920s.

PREVIOUS SPREAD:
Along Route 66 from Prewitt westward, sandstone cliffs can be seen along the route to the north (left). The Indian Pueblo Cultural Center in Albuquerque features traditional dances in the courtyard every weekend (right).

NMTD

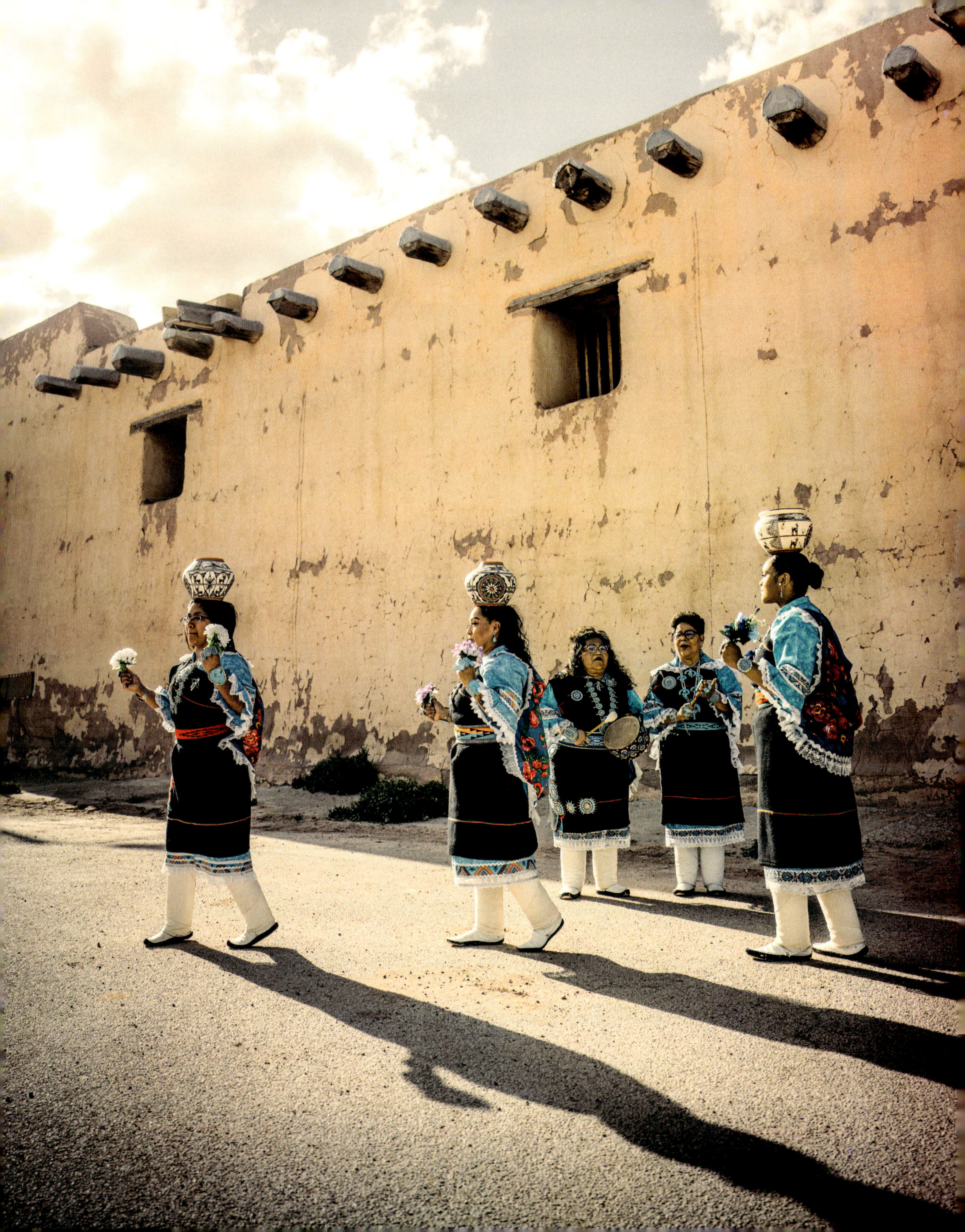

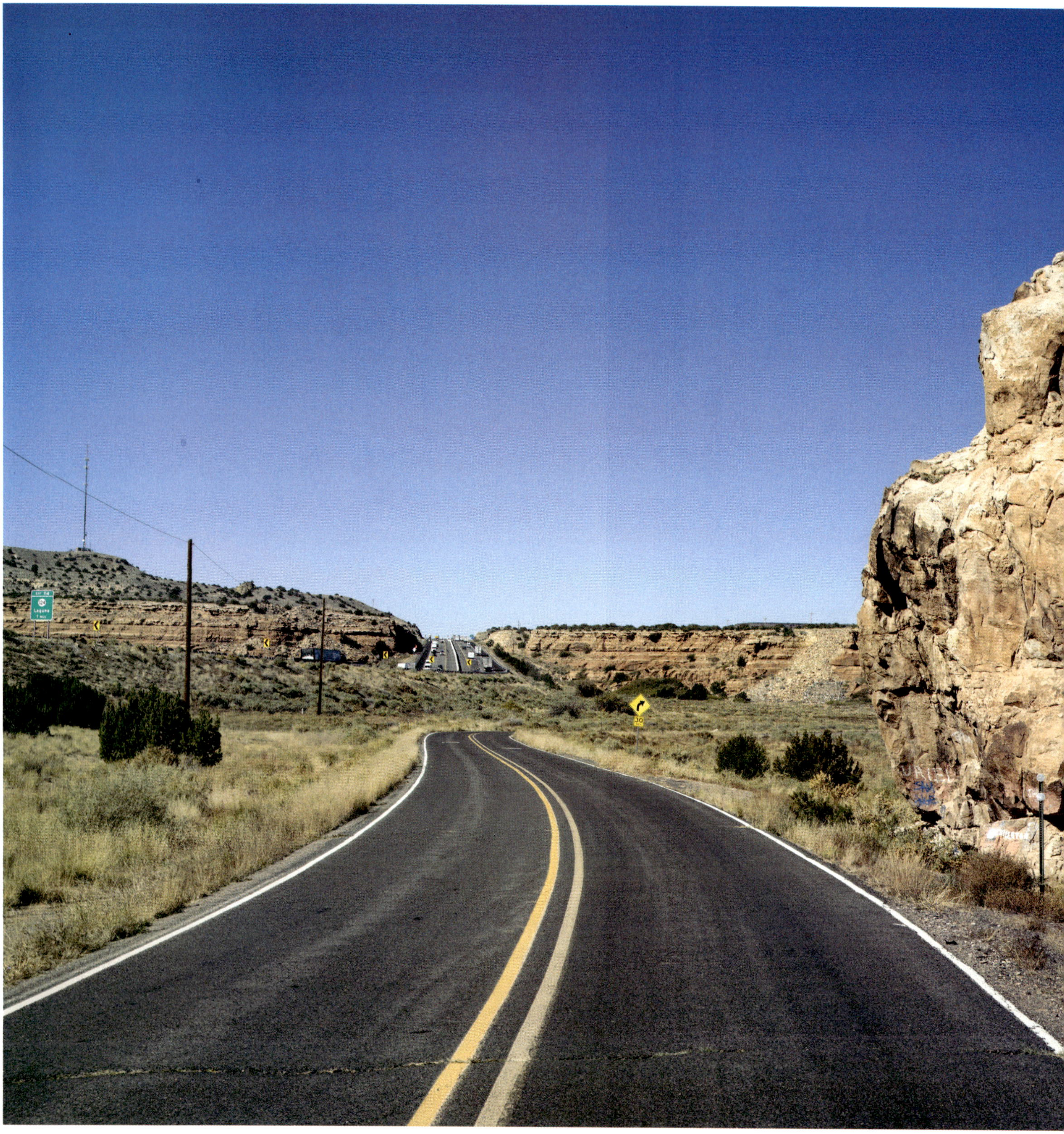

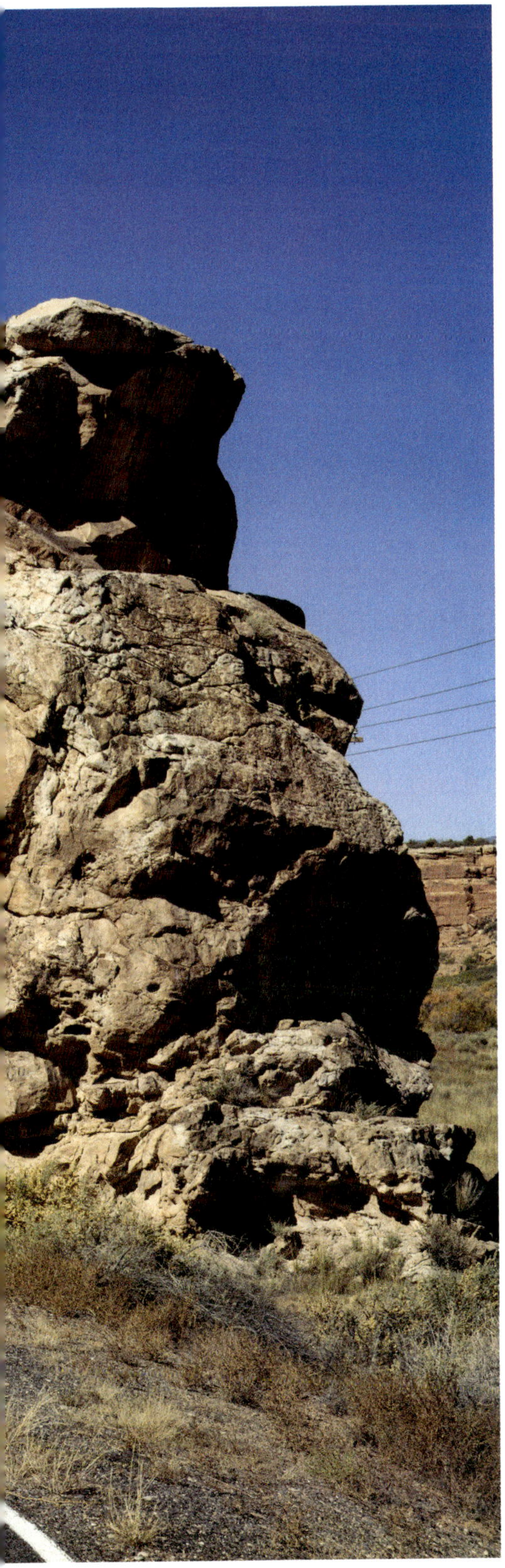

Pueblo storyteller dolls have always showcased Indigenous communities while also acknowledging foreigners coming into the area, such as circus performers and priests. Even today, depictions of such newcomers can be seen in the early work of artists Virgil Ortiz (Cochiti) and Kathleen Wall (Jemez), whose dolls tell stories from past and present dialogues. Less commonly, Navajo rug weavers incorporated pictorial designs reflecting postcards, automobiles, highways, and other new arrivals from the Anglo world.

While non-Native traders often controlled prices and access to buyers, Indigenous makers fueled and influenced the market with their imagination, artistry, and ability to meld real-life narratives into traditional art forms. One school of thought says the Mother Road's love came with conditions: What could be shared was shaped by what would sell. The Indigenous perspective is different: During a tumultuous time, the market found family matriarchs, and through skills they were raised to perfect, they fueled that market and supported their communities.

Even cultural expression felt the Mother Road's influence. Public performances—like those at the Gallup Inter-Tribal Indian Ceremonial—became sites of negotiation between survival and sanctity. "Route 66 changed us, just like the Santa Fe Trail changed us," Martinez says. "It brought different technologies and people, and it can't be stopped."

Hispanic communities along Route 66 felt her presence differently but no less deeply. In towns like Tucumcari, Santa Rosa, Albuquerque, and Gallup, the Mother Road connected families to a national bloodstream of people, ideas, and possibility. Martinez places Route 66 in context alongside the Camino Real, the Santa Fe Trail, and the Old Spanish Trail. Along these routes came foods, faiths, technologies, and institutions that reshaped daily life. "Route 66 is one of the many ways that change has arrived in New Mexico," he says.

L
In Mesita, near Laguna Pueblo, the route includes two distinctive features: Owl Rock and Dead Man's Curve, up ahead.

Hotels bloomed. Restaurants stayed open late. Service stations became gathering places. Along Central Avenue in Albuquerque and Coal Avenue in Gallup, architecture itself learned to blend—Pueblo Revival was softened by Art Deco curves at the KiMo Theatre in Albuquerque and El Morro Theatre in Gallup. These buildings were never meant to be monuments, Martinez says, but they became symbolic anyway—proof that when cultures meet under pressure, they don't disappear. They transform.

Still, the Mother Road was not gentle. Construction carved through farmland and sacred spaces with little consultation. Noise, pollution, and disruption followed. For Pueblo, Navajo, and rural Hispano communities, whose identities are bound to the land, these were not abstract losses. They were daily. Tribal lands, such as Acoma, Laguna, and Navajo, were sliced by Route 66 and later I-40. Today New Mexico's stretch of I-40 is a high-risk area for missing Indigenous women and girls; it has been given the moniker Highway of Tears.

Yet Martinez situates this within a longer truth: New Mexico's people have survived centuries of conquest and colonization by learning when to resist and when to adapt. When I-40 arrived, the Mother Road was quietly sidelined. Traffic thinned. Businesses closed. The same mother who once demanded constant attention now moved on, leaving communities to grieve and regroup. And yet, in that absence, something softened. The pressure eased. The story became ours again.

As we mark Route 66's centennial, I find myself less interested in mythology than honesty. "It's unifying," Martinez says. It connects Gallup to Chicago, Albuquerque to Los Angeles, Tucumcari to Flagstaff. But unity doesn't mean sameness. The Mother Road reminds me that change is reciprocal. "The people who conquered were also changed," Martinez notes. No one passes through New Mexico untouched.

Route 66 didn't just guide our growth. We raised her too—fed her stories, shaped her meaning, resisted her when we had to. Like any mother, she is both shelter and scar. And like all good inheritances, she leaves us with a choice: to repeat the story she told or to tell it better. ✴

UNGELBAH DÁVILA is a mother, daughter, working creative, land steward, animal friend, and enrolled member of the Navajo Nation.

Teri Frazier

The director of the Gallup Cultural Center helps highlight the region's rich history, vibrant culture, and welcoming approach.

BORN AND RAISED IN GALLUP, Teri Frazier (Laguna-Hopi/Chippewa) serves as director of the Gallup Cultural Center, organizing exhibitions devoted to Native art and culture, Navajo Code Talkers, Edward S. Curtis photographs, and Route 66. Road-trippers have long made it a point to visit Gallup, located near Navajo, Zuni, Hopi, and other tribal lands, for the Gallup Inter-Tribal Indian Ceremonial. Launched in 1922, the 10-day event brings together Native people from across the continent to showcase their culture and heritage with dances, pageants, art shows, and rodeos.

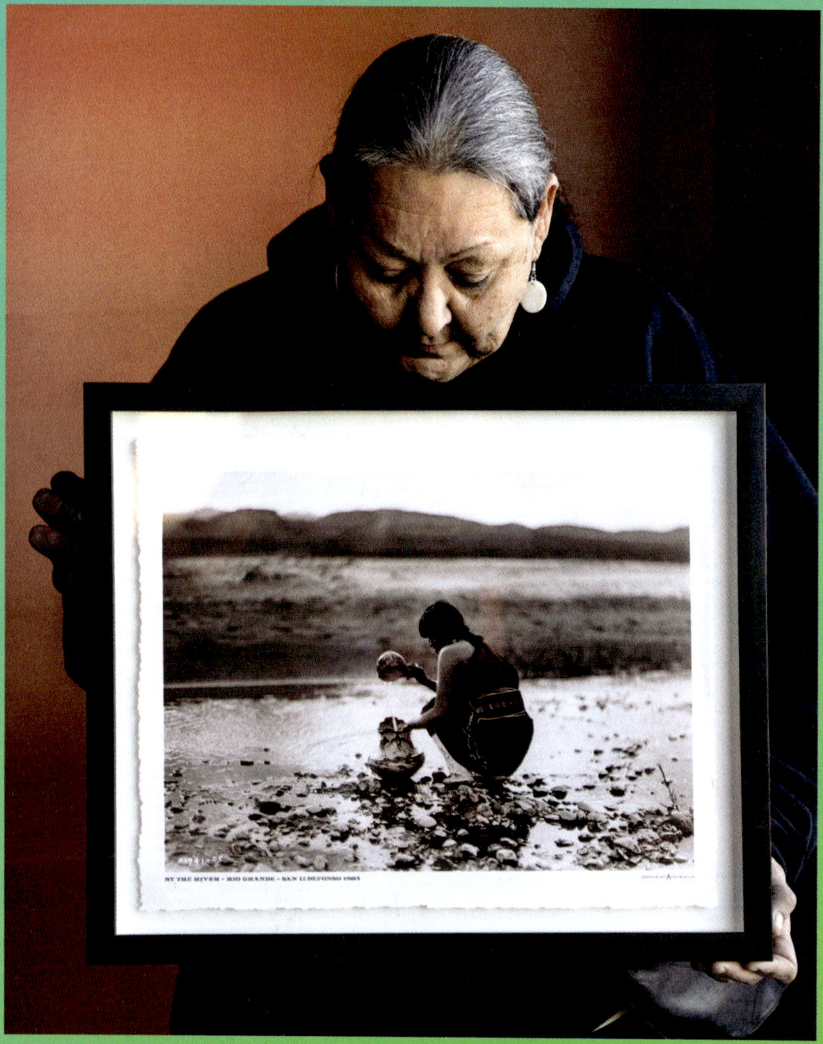

Route 66 changed the layout of Gallup. It provided for much-needed commerce and gave people access to the Native arts and crafts and railroad industries.

I've been involved with the Gallup Ceremonial since I was two years old.

My lifelong involvement encourages me to keep as much culture alive as possible. I'm all about culture.

The ceremonial is a very welcoming environment.

For early Route 66ers, the ceremonial was a major eye-opening experience. They were engaging with cultures that they may have heard about but had never really seen up close.

I've asked people about their experience with the ceremonial, and one of the things that comes up when you go to a powwow is that many tribes are represented there. They're all integrated into that one section at the ceremonial, with a banner in front of each group.

My favorite thing about Gallup is the community feeling that we have. It's a place to live and thrive. ✴

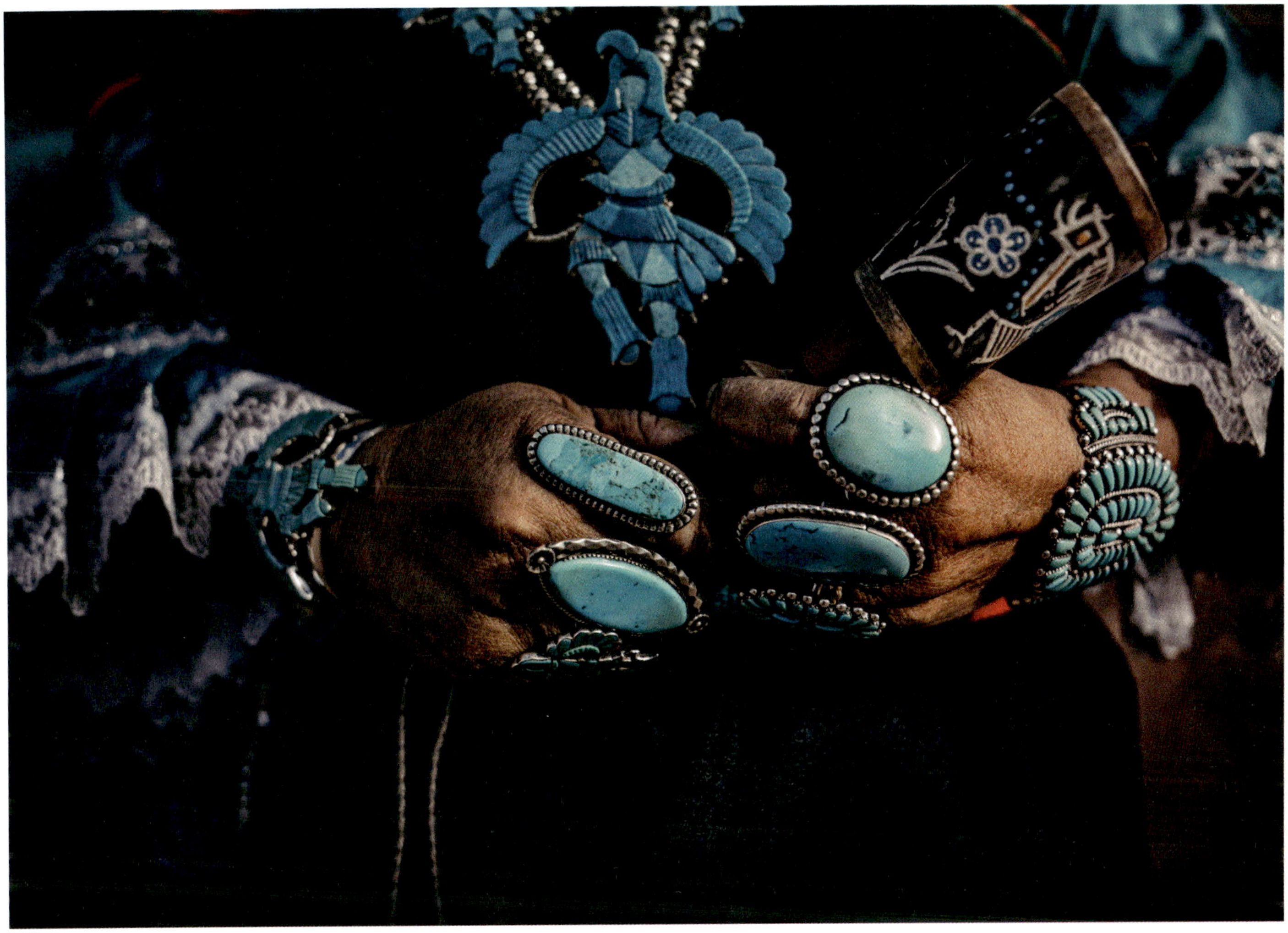

L
Teri Frazier, director of the Gallup Cultural Center and a member of the Laguna-Hopi and Chippewa tribes, holds a 1905 photograph by Edward S. Curtis, *By the River, Rio Grande, San Ildefonso.*

R
For more than 70 years, Zuni Olla Maidens have showcased Zuni pottery as well as clothing and jewelry made in the pueblo.

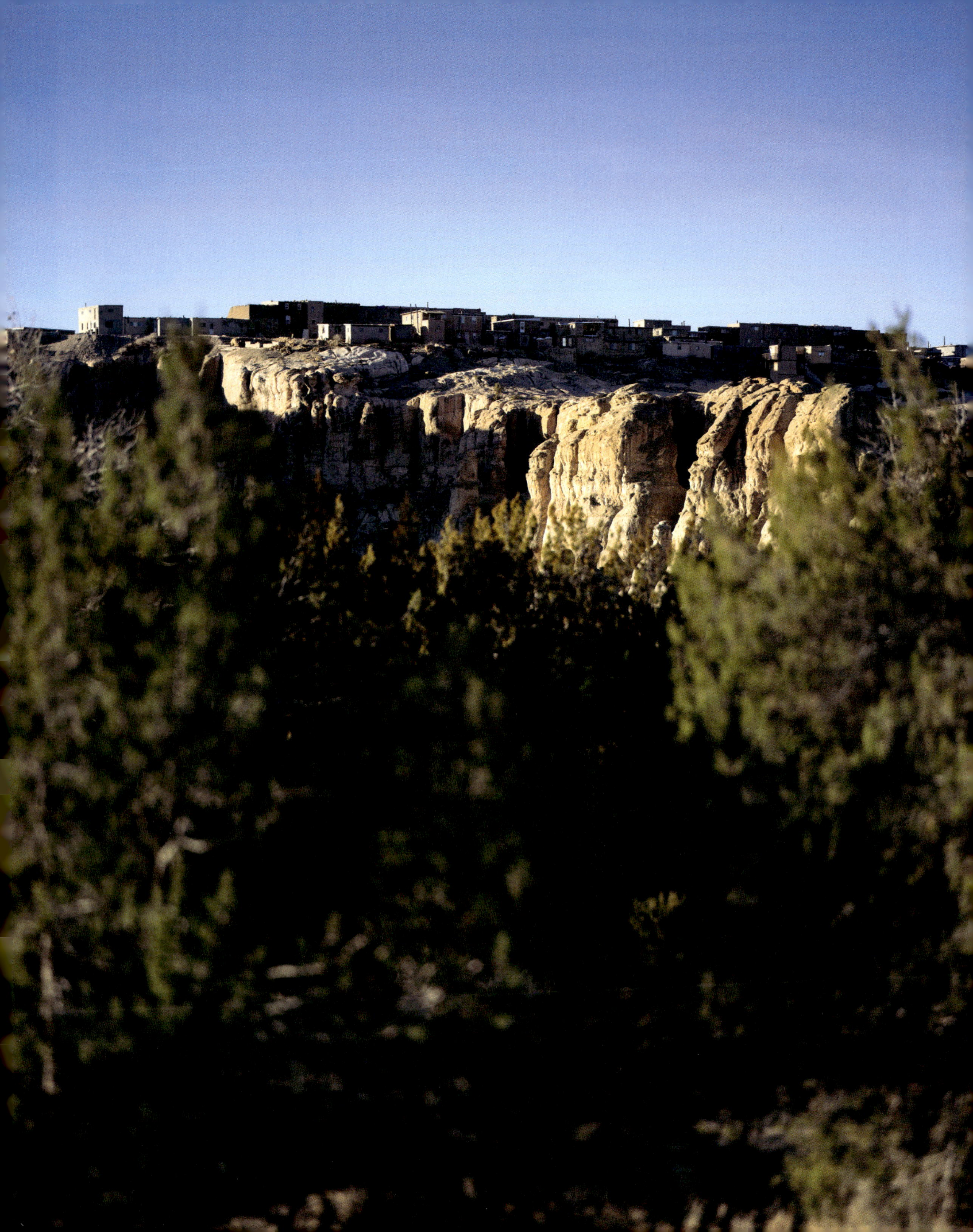

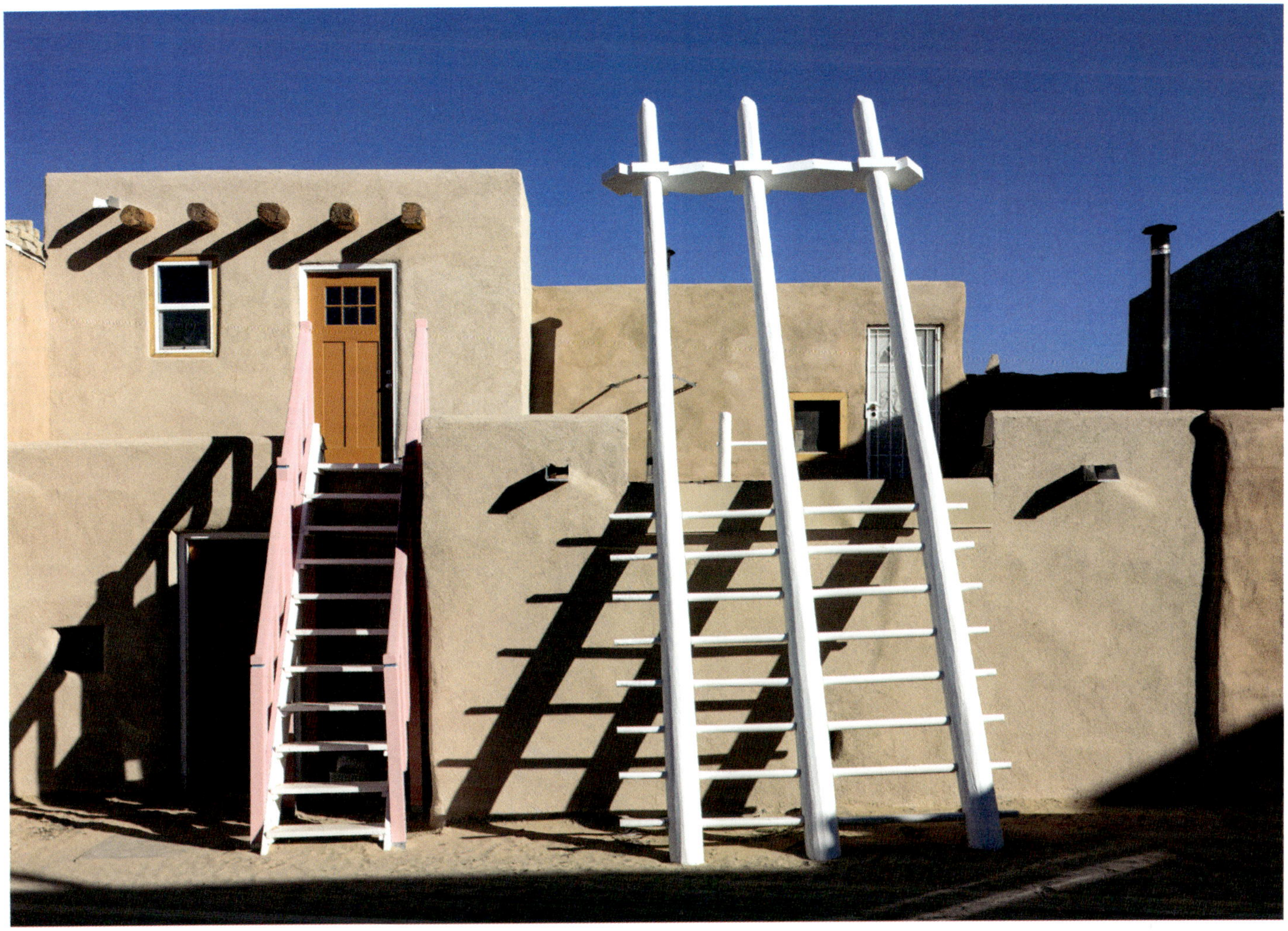

L
Acoma Pueblo's Sky City sits atop a beautiful 367-foot mesa, where about 50 tribal members, mostly elders, live today.

R
Acoma Pueblo is one of the oldest continuously inhabited settlements in North America. Visitors can take 90-minute guided tours.

"

You can go to Chaco Canyon or Aztec Ruins or any other place where a non-Native person is giving the tour. They can tell you what they researched, what they think this was. But then you come here, and that's the beauty of it: We can tell you, *That's what this is for. This is how this is. That's why we did it*. We're a part of living history."

— BRANDON "TURTLE" VALDO, ACOMA PUEBLO TOUR AMBASSADOR

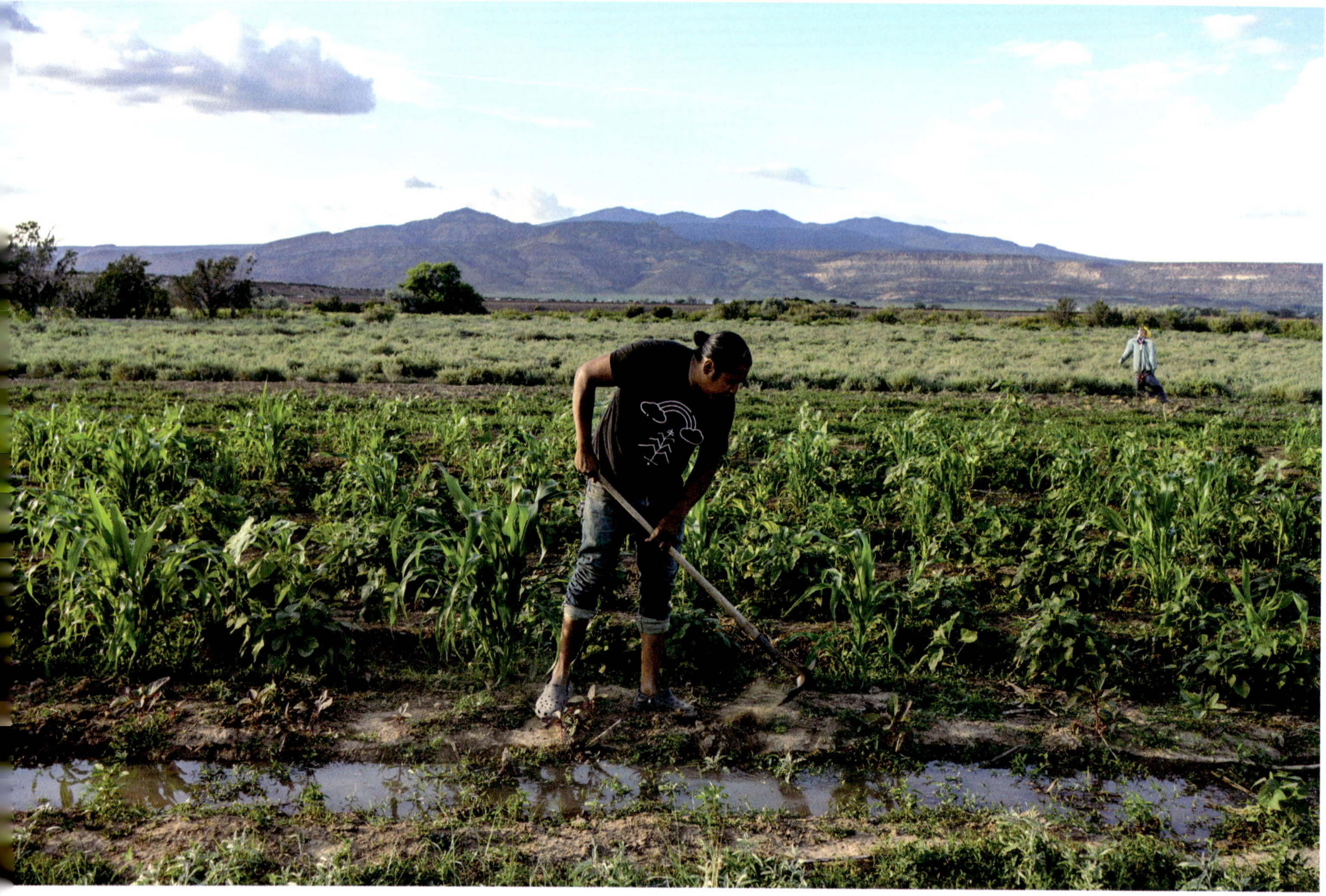

R
Aaron Lowden, formerly of the Ancestral Lands Conservation Corps, works to grow food sustainably, reviving traditional Acoma Pueblo farming practices.

L
Dancers perform in the Indian Pueblo Cultural Center courtyard.

STEVEN ST. JOHN

"Indigenous communities view these seeds as not only our biodiversity but our plant relatives. They're something we've had relationships with since time immemorial."

— AARON LOWDEN, FORMERLY OF THE ANCESTRAL LANDS CONSERVATION CORPS

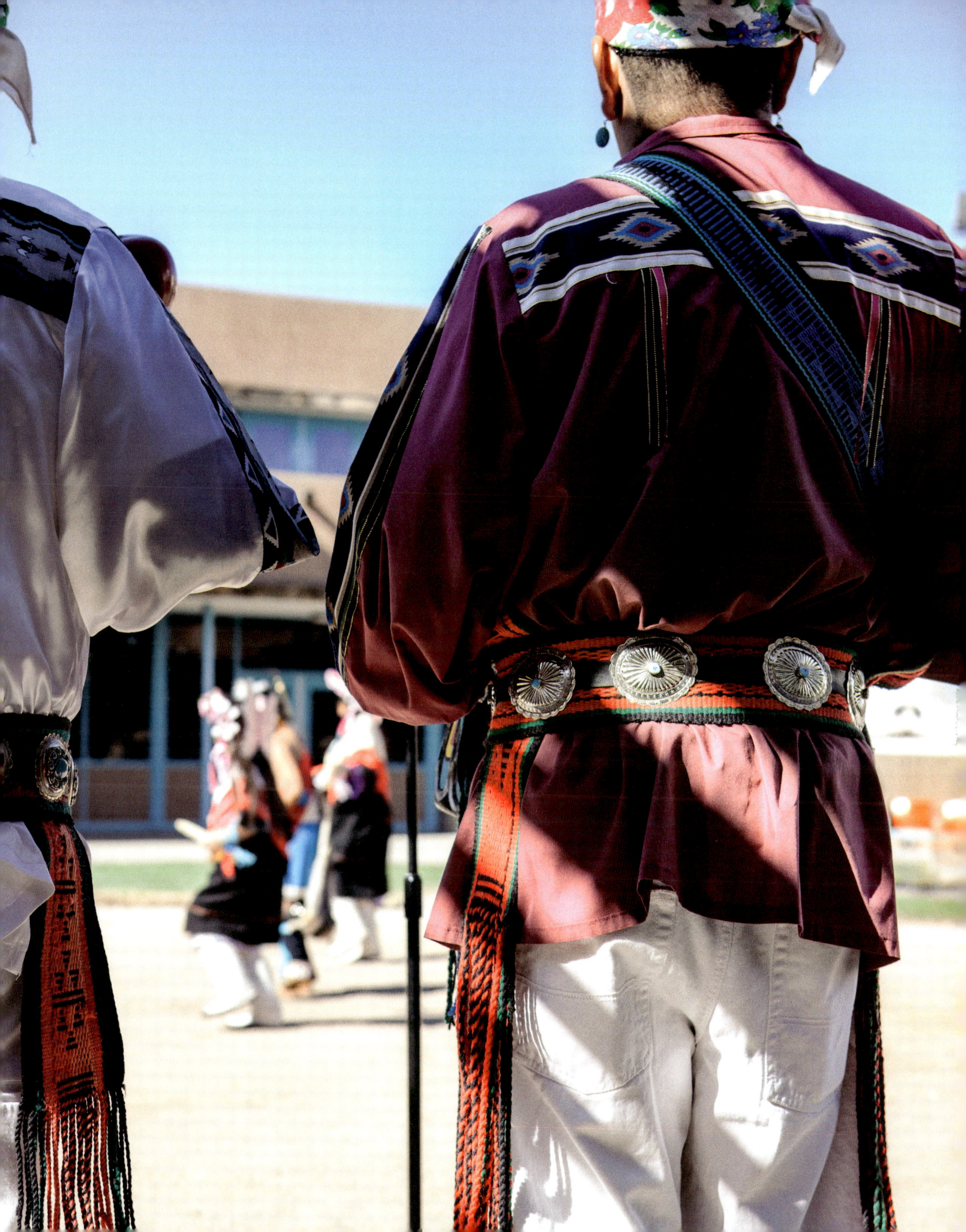

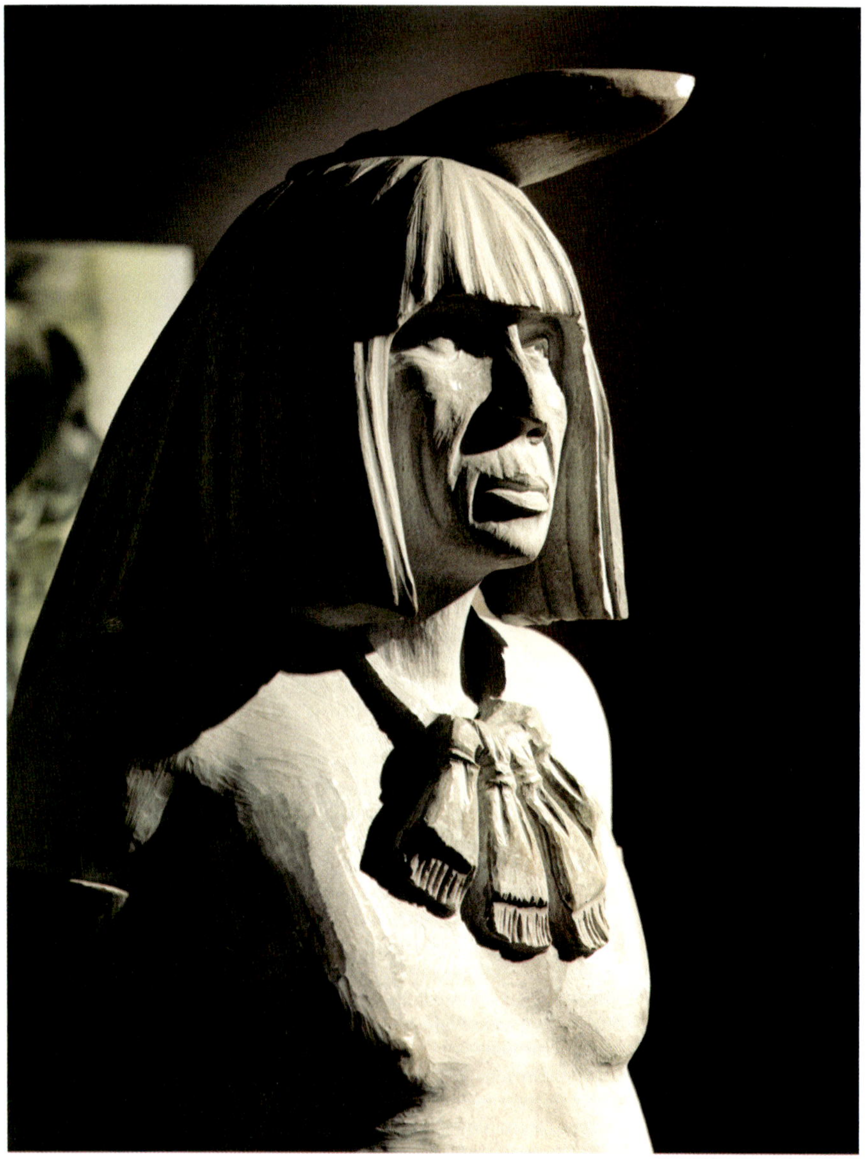

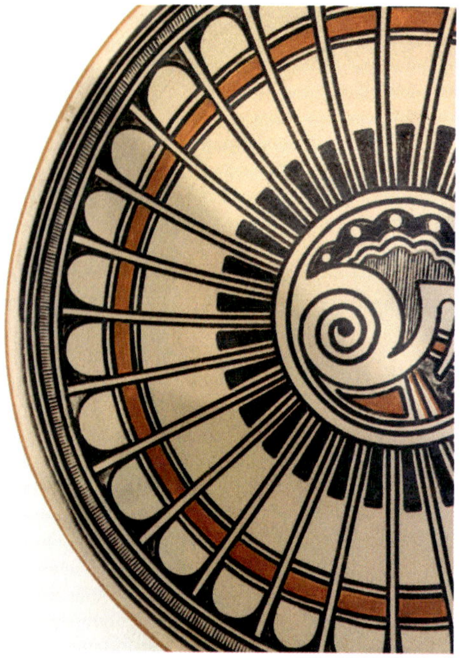

TAKE A DETOUR

The Indian Pueblo Cultural Center offers a primer on Native art, culture, and life.

"We are a gateway to the pueblos," says Monique Fragua, the Indian Pueblo Cultural Center's president and CEO and a member of Jemez Pueblo. Set on an 11-acre campus not far from Central Avenue in Albuquerque, the center serves as a convening space for New Mexico's 19 pueblos and a place where visitors can come to experience those cultures firsthand. Celebrating its 50th anniversary in 2026, the Indian Pueblo Cultural Center features a museum that includes the permanent exhibition *We Are of This Place*, galleries, a gift shop, the Indian Pueblo Kitchen restaurant, and a courtyard where traditional dances are held each weekend. "We are a contemporary center," says Michelle Lanteri, head curator for the IPCC Museum. "We are grounded in the present, and then our exhibits look both forward and backward." ✶

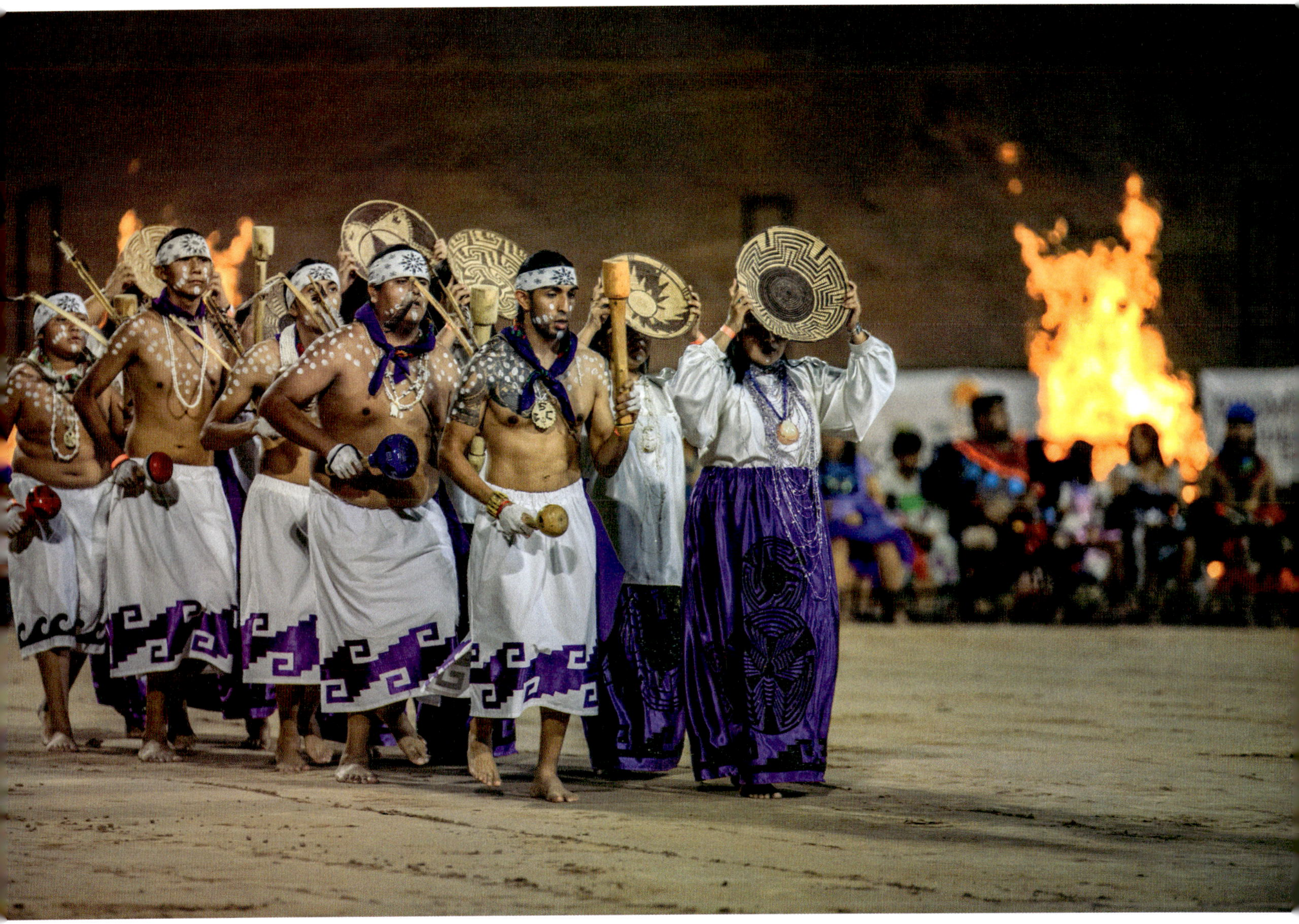

L
Find a statue of Pueblo Revolt leader Po'pay at the Indian Pueblo Cultural Center (left) as well as examples of San Ildefonso and other Pueblo pottery (right).

R
The Gallup Inter-Tribal Indian Ceremonial celebrates Native dance, art, culture, song, history, horsemanship, and food in a dazzling 10-day event that began in 1922.

VANESSA TOM

ROAD TO ENCHANTMENT

A CENTURY OF ROUTE 66 IN NEW MEXICO

EDITED BY
Lynn Cline and Steve Gleydura

ESSAYS BY
Lynn Cline, Ungelbah Dávila, Gwyneth Doland, Madison Garay, Nathaniel Tetsuro Paolinelli, and Alicia Romero

DESIGNED BY
Karin Eberhardt

PHOTOGRAPHS BY
Jen Judge

ADDITIONAL PHOTOGRAPHS BY
Gabriella Marks, Douglas Merriam, Nathaniel Tetsuro Paolinelli, Steven St. John, and Vanessa Tom

CONTRIBUTING COPY EDITOR
Peg Goldstein

New Mexico Magazine is an Enterprise Fund of the State of New Mexico and is supported by circulation, advertising, and sales revenues.

PRODUCED BY

New Mexico
MAGAZINE

Lew Wallace Building, 495 Old Santa Fe Trail
Santa Fe, NM 87501-2750